Reckless Christianity

Reckless Christianity

The Destructive New Teachings and Practices
of Bill Johnson, Bethel Church, and the Global
Movement of Apostles and Prophets

Holly Pivec *and*
R. Douglas Geivett

CASCADE *Books* · Eugene, Oregon

RECKLESS CHRISTIANITY
The Destructive New Teachings and Practices of Bill Johnson, Bethel Church, and the Global Movement of Apostles and Prophets

Cascade Books
An Imprint of Wipf and Stock Publishers
199 W. 8th Ave., Suite 3
Eugene, OR 97401

www.wipfandstock.com

PAPERBACK ISBN: 978-1-7252-7247-7
HARDCOVER ISBN: 978-1-7252-7240-8
EBOOK ISBN: 978-1-7252-7248-4

Cataloguing-in-Publication data:

Names: Pivec, Holly [author]. | Geivett, R. Douglas [author]

Title: Reckless Christianity : the destructive new teachings and practices of Bill Johnson, Bethel Church, and the global movement of apostles and prophets / Holly Pivec and R. Douglas Geivett.

Description: Eugene, OR: Cascade Books, 2023 | Includes bibliographical references and index.

Identifiers: ISBN 978-1-7252-7247-7 (paperback) | ISBN 978-1-7252-7240-8 (hardcover) | ISBN 978-1-7252-7248-4 (ebook)

Subjects: LCSH: Pentecostalism—United States. | Church—Apostolicity. | Prophecy—Christianity. | Miracles.

Classification: BR1644.5 P58 2023 (print) | BR1644.5 (ebook)

12/19/23

To my husband, Adam
I love you
—Holly

To Dorothea Weitz
—Doug

Contents

Preface

"I've never been to Bethel Church, but I want to visit." "I've heard so many exciting stories about what is happening at that church." "God is obviously doing a great work there."

We've lost track of how many times people have said such things to us. It's gotten to where it's almost predictable. Once, while lecturing at Biola University, Doug shared this observation with his students. Then, during a class break, he bumped into a teaching colleague and Bethel Church came up in their brief conversation. Before Doug excused himself to return to class, his co-worker said, "You know, I'd like to visit Bethel Church when I get a chance. I don't agree with everything they teach, but God is clearly doing a work there." Doug wasn't sure his students believed him when he recounted this exchange.

When we hear this sort of thing—and we hear it a lot—we always want to know, what is it about Bethel's teaching that they find disagreeable? And what convinces them that God is at work at Bethel Church? These are important questions. These and like questions are the focus of this book.

It's somewhat perplexing to hear someone say, on the one hand, that some Bethel teachings just can't be believed, and on the other hand, that God's supernatural activity at the church is obviously real and palpable. Many people gladly believe reports of stunning events occurring at Bethel Church, though they are hesitant to give full assent to what is taught there. Oddly, while declining to agree with everything that is taught, they often cannot say exactly what it is that they find so disagreeable. At any rate, while they may be cautious about what is believed and taught at Bethel, they express confident enthusiasm for supposed manifestations of God's presence at Bethel. What is this strange admixture of credulity and caution among those who observe Bethel Church from a distance? Do they suppose that the signs and wonders and miracles that are reported have nothing to do with what Bethel teaches?

Long-distance confidence that God is doing something amazing at Bethel rests on fantastical reports of miracles and unusual phenomena. Healings, glory clouds, and a little gold dust have secured Bethel's reputation as a center of divine activity. If such marvels are a daily occurrence, then what could be more obvious? It's a God-thing.

But is it?

How does anyone observing Bethel from a distance and hoping to visit someday know that God is doing a great work there? What justifies such confidence? Do they find secondhand or thirdhand testimonies of miracles compelling? Are they impressed by news of conferences that draw thousands of excited young adults? Is it the church's worldwide influence that convinces them? Are any of these good reasons for their assurance that God is working in a uniquely mighty way at this church?

When people speak in wonder and amazement of the doings and happenings of Bethel, we have to ask: *Do they know what Bethel leaders believe? Are they aware of the church's aberrant teachings and practices? Have they never heard what happened at Bethel with two-year-old Olive Heiligenthal? Do they know about "grave soaking" and "Prophetic Uno" and waking up "sleeping angels"?*

No doubt about it, something unusual *is* going on at Bethel. But it's not at all clear that what is going on is the work of God that so many think it is. There are compelling reasons to think it isn't that at all. Strong words? We know.

In two earlier books, *A New Apostolic Reformation?* and *God's Super-Apostles*, we documented the rise of a global movement of apostles and prophets intent on reconstructing the mission and the message of the Christian church.[1] In a more recent book, *Counterfeit Kingdom*, we explained the movement's practices, the concrete ways the New Apostolic Reformation is showing up in churches, ministries, and music. This

---

1. See Geivett and Pivec, *A New Apostolic Reformation?* (a heavily documented book) and Geivett and Pivec, *God's Super-Apostles* (a shorter book that includes anecdotes from people who formerly embraced New Apostolic Reformation beliefs).

movement is popularly known as the New Apostolic Reformation or NAR (pronounced NAHR).[2] NAR is not an organization or a denomination: it consists of churches and other Christian organizations that have developed intentional networks with one another in pursuit of a common mission that is rooted in shared beliefs and realized through distinctive practices.[3] The core belief is that present-day apostles and prophets must govern the church. These authoritative apostles and prophets purport to deliver new revelations that the church must have if it is to develop miraculous powers. Healings, resurrections, and other miracles—mightier than those worked by Moses and Jesus—are to spur an end-time global revival, positioning the church to establish God's kingdom on earth and usher in Christ's return. These recycled teachings of the post-World War II Latter Rain movement have much more traction today than they did in 1948 when a "revival" of sorts broke out in Saskatchewan, Canada. In the United States, about 3.5 million people attend NAR churches—churches

2. Many leaders in NAR do not use this label to describe their movement of apostles and prophets, though some certainly do, including the influential apostle Ché Ahn. Ahn is extremely clear that he views the "New Apostolic Reformation" as a movement through which "God is changing the expression and understanding of Christianity" and that "God is bringing about an apostolic reformation" led by apostles with "extraordinary authority." See Ahn, *Modern-Day Apostles*, introduction and chap. 5. And note the many influential apostles and prophets who endorsed Ahn's book, including Bill Johnson (who also provided the foreword), Kris Vallotton, Patricia King, Shawn Bolz, James Goll, Cindy Jacobs, and Lou Engle. Other apostles prefer to use no label (other than perhaps "charismatic" or "neo-charismatic") or another label such as "Independent Network Christianity" because of the negative connotations that have come to be associated with NAR. See, for example, Joseph Mattera (the head of the United States Coalition of Apostolic Leaders) explain his personal preference for the label "Independent Network Christianity": Mattera, Kelly, and Lipscomb, "Global Christianity Roundtable."

3. One influential network is the Revival Alliance, whose charter members include six married couples: Bill and Beni Johnson, Ché and Sue Ahn, John and Carol Arnott, Randy and DeAnne Clark, Georgian and Winnie Banov, and Heidi and Rolland Baker. NAR leaders, including Randy Clark, have responded to their critics, including ourselves, by accusing them of describing NAR in overly broad terms, thus classifying many people as NAR who really are not part of the NAR movement. (Clark makes this accusation in Lewis, Rowntree, and Clark, "The NAR Debate!" [10:00].) But we have not done this. We have made it clear that what defines NAR is the controversial belief in the present-day governing *offices* of apostle and prophet. This definition is not overly broad; it's laser-focused. And it's the one definition many NAR leaders keep skirting around. If a leader believes there should be apostles governing the church today, then he or she is NAR, whether or not the label is approved or accepted. Other teachings and practices are generally associated with NAR belief, but the *offices* are the core issue.

that are part of apostolic networks and overtly embrace the NAR vision.[4] Millions more attend churches where NAR teachings have entered through the back door, including Pentecostal and charismatic churches, as well as many non-denominational, non-charismatic churches and Protestant churches with mainstream denominational affiliations.[5] NAR influence varies. Some churches have had more or less moderate brushes with NAR. Others are under siege. Many lie somewhere between these poles of the spectrum. The trend is toward growing infiltration. Worldwide, NAR accounts for much of the explosive growth of Christianity in the Global South—Africa, Asia, and Latin America. NAR teachings and practices have reconfigured church life and altered its theological trajectory. Music, messages, and ministries have been shaped by NAR pressures. Only the most vigilant of churches can be confident that they have escaped NAR influence.

NAR leaders energetically seek to *reform* the global church, hence the label New Apostolic *Reformation*. And they intend reformation on a grand scale, as consequential as the Protestant Reformation of the sixteenth century.[6] The global effect of their efforts is indeed striking. We now hear routinely from people around the world about their NAR encounters: Germany, England, South Africa, Zambia, Ethiopia, Russia, the Netherlands, South Korea, Brazil, the Czech Republic, Mexico, Australia, China, Singapore, Israel, Malta, Ukraine, India, Norway. When we start getting email from Antarctica, it won't be shocking. These folks report chaos, confusion, and division suffered in their congregations and communities as a direct result of the NAR movement. In these reports from the front, we hear the same concerns, we get the same questions, we read testimonies that fit a similar pattern. And nearly always we are asked or

---

4. Johnson and Zurlo, *World Christian Encyclopedia*, 849–56.

5. In their *World Christian Encyclopedia*, Todd Johnson and Gina Zurlo identify "Pentecostal" Christians as church members affiliated with a classical Pentecostal denomination, such as the Assemblies of God. "Charismatic" Christians are baptized members affiliated with non-Pentecostal, mainline denominations who have had "the experience of being filled with the Holy Spirit." And "Neocharismatic" Christians are part of the Pentecostal/Charismatic Renewal but are not affiliated with any denomination. Instead, they see themselves as "Independent," "Postdenominationalist," or "Neo-Apostolic." See Johnson and Zurlo, *World Christian Encyclopedia*, 26.

6. Wagner, *Changing Church*, 10. See also Geivett and Pivec, *A New Apostolic Reformation?*, ch. 1.

told about the influence of Bethel Church in Redding, California.[7] That's quite a footprint for one church.[8]

God's Super-Apostles and *A New Apostolic Reformation?* offer a robust response to this influential movement. They address the broader sweep of NAR. This book, *Reckless Christianity*, is a natural sequel.[9] Here we tighten the focus of our lens and scrutinize what has been called the "Bethel Church movement."[10]

In chapter 1, we introduce you to the apostle Bill Johnson, senior leader of Bethel Church. Citing his own materials, we outline Johnson's vision, which lies behind the extreme teachings and practices coming out of Bethel Church. In chapter 2, we describe the church's authority structure (with top-down government from present-day apostles) and how that structure is tailored to Bethel's mission to "bring heaven to earth." We evaluate this authority structure in chapter 3. In chapters 4 and 5 we analyze Bethel teachings about prophets and the types of new revelation promulgated by them. Then, in chapters 6 through 8, we evaluate specific "new truths" propounded by these apostles and prophets—controversial new doctrines about prayer, miracles, and an alleged end-time revival.

In *Reckless Christianity*, we dive deeply into questions about miracles. This is one of the most absorbing aspects of our study. Bill Johnson, like all NAR leaders, has much to say about miracles. Much of it is surprising. Some of it is shocking. What we say in response will probably surprise some readers. We hope it will prove edifying.

Many would like to know, do miraculous gifts (such as healing and prophecy) operate in the church today? We steer clear of the vortex of forces pulling some believers toward continuationism and pushing others toward cessationism. It turns out that this long-standing debate

7. We've heard testimonies from people during our own international speaking tours.

8. Bear in mind that fewer than 100,000 people live in the relatively remote northern California town of Redding.

9. While writing the manuscript for this book, we also completed the manuscript for another book focusing on the *practices* of NAR and the concrete ways those practices are showing up in churches, ministries, and music: *Counterfeit Kingdom: The Dangers of New Revelation, New Prophets, and New Age Practices in the Church* (Nashville, TN: B&H, 2022).

10. We and others have used the term "movement" in reference to Bethel. See, e.g., Carter, "9 Things You Should Know about the Bethel Church Movement." Indeed, Bethel leaders describe their own church's reach in terms of a global movement. See, e.g., "Movement Impact."

within the church has almost no relevance for a full-throated assessment of the New Apostolic Reformation and the Bethel movement, which goes far beyond merely teaching about spiritual gifts in its promotion of the present-day offices of apostle and prophet. If you are a cessationist, you will surely object to Bethel teachings about miracles. If you're a continuationist, you should be dismayed by what Bethel teaches about the nature and use of miracles today. In due course, you will see where we part company with Bill Johnson and others.

We seek to offer a fair and balanced treatment of the Bethel Church movement. To this end, we have adopted several guidelines—which we first set forth in our book *A New Apostolic Reformation*? (2014, reissued 2018). We have followed these criteria for responsible engagement in all of our public and private interactions with leaders in the NAR movement, and in our interactions with concerned Christians.

1. We've written with the assumption that Bethel figures, and other leading New Apostolic Reformation figures, are believers and genuine disciples of Jesus, and that their intention is to do the will of God in their lives and in the world. Of course, we don't know if that's true in all cases.

2. We believe that the Bible sets forth guidelines for church governance and cultural engagement.

3. We acknowledge that the Scriptures are not specific about all details concerning church governance and cultural engagement. Thus, there is room for divergent expressions of the church's presence in the world.

4. However, we think that certain broad parameters, revealed in Scripture and practiced in the historical orthodox church, set limits on the kind of flexibility and creativity that are permissible.

5. In our judgment, the Bethel/NAR perspective crosses these boundaries, and it does so in part because of flawed theology rooted in a flawed understanding of Scripture.

6. It is natural and proper for believers to publish their respective positions and air out their disagreements.

7. Critical analysis of any theological perspective must be charitable and gracious, even if resolute and confident. As with any other activity done for the sake of Christ and his church, the work of critical

assessment should exhibit the full range of moral and intellectual virtues, insofar as this is possible for manifestly fallible believers. We do not generally insist on a particular theological perspective among several that have been historically and broadly considered viable. But our effort to resist undue advocacy does not preclude exposition of and argument for specific theological claims.

8. We acknowledge that our perspective is itself fallible, and probably mistaken at points. This is true despite our best efforts to interpret and apply the Scriptures accurately and wisely.

9. Critical assessment should resort chiefly to the Scriptures, which we believe to be the authoritative Word of God. We assume in good faith that Bethel and other NAR leaders also believe this to be true.

10. We are not psychologists or sociologists, and we do not attempt to explain Bethel or NAR beliefs and practices in terms that require special expertise in sociology, psychology, or any other disciplines outside our own. However, we do sometimes reflect on the judgments and findings of other researchers who have studied these movements.

11. This means that our analysis is informed by our own disciplines in biblical studies, theology, philosophy, and logic, by our extensive experience in ministries of preaching and discipleship, and by personal faith in Jesus.

12. We allow that Christian experience has a legitimate role in forming our theological understanding, biblical interpretation, and spiritual practice. Theological perspectives that do not much stress personal and corporate experience, as with the kind that is so pronounced within Bethel and NAR, may and should nevertheless appeal in responsible fashion to the lessons of experience.

13. We consider it an important part of any Christian leader's vocation to serve the church. A believer with the gifts of teaching and discernment is responsible for alerting the church to risky theology and practices that issue from it. But this must be done in an exemplary manner for the good of the whole body of Christ, including those with whom there is disagreement. Any assessment of another position must be even-handed and should not be needlessly sensationalist or provocative.

(good – dealing with facts... evidence)
not the people

14. We are especially cautious about passing judgment on the character or intentions of those whose work we critique.

15. We emphasize that not all people affiliated with Bethel and the New Apostolic Reformation movement adhere to all of the same beliefs. Because one leader promotes a particular teaching does not necessarily mean that all other leaders we have identified in this book also promote that particular teaching.

If we have erred in any way, we welcome corrections.

Bill Johnson champions a "reckless" Christianity. In this book, we seek to follow the decidedly un-reckless example of the Bereans who are commended in Acts 17:11—those "noble" first-century Jews who, when the apostle Paul brought them new teachings, "received the word with all eagerness, examining the Scriptures daily to see" if his teachings were true.

Acknowledgments

MANY PEOPLE ASSISTED AND encouraged us during the completion of this manuscript. Of course, that in no way implies their agreement with all we have said here. Those who supported us, in various ways, include Alan Gomes, Aaron Mapes, Rob Bowman, Jennifer Stoll, Bart McCurdy, Kevin Lewis, Steve Kozar, Brandon Kimber, Paul Carden, Richard Moore, Todd Johnson, Dianne Geivett, Adam Pivec, K. L. Marshall, Greg and Kerry Pippin, Sherina Anderson, Kara Beck, Jim and Cheryl Sackett, Mitch and Melody Flynn, and the members of Holly's church small group. We also are very grateful for our partnership with Matt Wimer, George Callihan, Chris Spinks, Robin Parry, and the rest of the team at Wipf and Stock. Working with them has been a joy.

—1—

The Man, the Ministry, and
the Movement Transforming
Churches Worldwide

God, I must have more of you at any cost!

—The apostle Bill Johnson[1]

IT WAS THE MIDDLE of the night. Bill Johnson was suddenly awakened from a dead sleep.[2] Unexplainable power began pulsating through his body, almost as if he was being electrocuted. He felt like he was plugged into a wall socket with a thousand volts of electricity flowing through him. His arms and legs shot out in silent explosions as if something was being released through them. He tried to stop what was happening. He felt embarrassed by it, even though no one else could see him. But it only got worse. It was the most overwhelming experience of his life.

Johnson soon realized what it was—the raw power of God. And he knew it was the answer to a prayer he had repeated for months: "God, I must have more of you at any cost!" That was his prayer, day and night: "I

---

1. Johnson, *When Heaven Invades Earth*, ch. 10.
2. Johnson recounts this experience in *When Heaven Invades Earth*, ch. 10.

wasn't sure of the correct way to pray, nor did I understand the doctrine behind my request. All I knew was I was hungry for God."[3]

God took him up on his offer. But the price would be high. While Johnson lay in bed, images passed through his mind. In one image, he was standing before his congregation, preaching from Scripture. Suddenly his arms and legs began to flail around as if he had a serious physical condition. Then the scene switched: he was walking down his city's main street when, again, he lost control of his arms and legs. He didn't know anyone who would believe that what was happening to him was from God. That's when Johnson realized that God was offering him an exchange—His increased presence for Johnson's dignity.

As tears flooded his pillowcase, Johnson came to a point of no return. He yielded, crying out, "More, God. More! I must have more of You at any cost! If I lose respectability and get You in the exchange, I'll gladly make that trade. Just give me more of You!" The power surges continued through the night, as he wept and prayed. They continued the following two nights, beginning moments after getting into bed.

The year was 1995. The church Johnson then pastored—an Assemblies of God church in the tiny town of Weaverville, California—was known for the manifestation of miracles, and in particular healings. In 1996, the leaders of another Assemblies of God church, Bethel Church in nearby Redding, California—formerly pastored by Bill Johnson's father, Earl Johnson—desired to see such miracles at their church.[4] So they offered him the senior pastor position. Johnson accepted, with one nonnegotiable condition: that his focus would always be the pursuit of revival, which, in his view, was inseparable from a pursuit of miracles.[5] The leaders unanimously agreed, though much of the congregation disapproved of the more extreme emphases Johnson had planned to bring to the church. Johnson recalls:

> I remember when I first started pastoring Bethel Church in Redding, California. On one of the first Sundays, I announced that my lifestyle required the liberty to experiment. . . . I then announced that if the people in the church didn't like it when

3. Johnson, *When Heaven Invades Earth*, ch. 10.

4. Johnson is a fifth-generation pastor on his father's side and fourth on his mother's. See also Christerson and Flory, *The Rise*, ch. 2.

5. Bill Johnson Ministries, "Bill." Johnson's focus is reflected in Bethel Church's mission: "Bethel's mission is revival—the personal, regional, and global expansion of God's kingdom through His manifest presence." See Bethel, "About Bethel."

things didn't work well the first time around, I would make them very uncomfortable, and that they might want to consider attending one of the many other fine churches in our city. It wasn't as rude as it sounds in print. But it was honest. I believe this is my call in life.[6]

About half of the two-thousand-member congregation did leave—a portent of controversy that was to come.[7] But those remaining granted Johnson the "liberty to experiment." And spiritual experimentation has since become a hallmark of his church. As Johnson writes: "For years, I have called Bethel 'The Great Experiment.'"[8] His goal: to discover— through trial and error—what yields miracles at Bethel and create a "model" for miraculous ministry that (in his words) can be "exported" and "duplicated" in churches throughout the world.[9]

A "Risk-Taking" and "Reckless" Church

Following the mass exodus, the church's remaining members voted to withdraw Bethel from the Assemblies of God in 2006. The official statement indicated that the church could not pursue Johnson's vision for experimentation while remaining within the denomination.[10] And today Bethel leaders boast that their church has a "risk-taking culture": You "must be willing to fail to succeed."[11] Acting "recklessly" is also valued, though outside Bethel that trait is generally viewed negatively. Johnson

---

6. Johnson, *The Way of Life*, ch. 3. (Note that this is the updated 2019 edition, not the original 2018 edition. Both are cited in this book.)

7. Johnson and Farrelly, "Episode 6" (1:20:00) and Christerson and Flory, *The Rise*, ch. 2.

8. Johnson, *The Way of Life*, introduction (updated 2019 edition).

9. Winger, "Bill Johnson's Theology" (10:00).

10. The statement explained that Bethel members had felt the church's call is "unique enough theologically and practically from the call on the Assemblies of God that this change is appropriate." See Bill Johnson and the Leadership of Bethel Church, "Bethel and the Assemblies of God." See also Johnson and Farrelly, "Episode 1" (1:00), in which Johnson explains that it would have been difficult for Bethel to "experiment" while remaining in the Assemblies of God.

11. Johnson, quoting Randy Clark, in *When Heaven Invades Earth*, ch. 10; Vallotton, *Heavy Rain*, ch. 2. See also Vallotton and Farrelly, "Bethel's Risk-Taking Culture." A risk-taking approach to the Christian lifestyle is encouraged throughout Johnson's books. (See *When Heaven Invades Earth*, chs. 1, 4, 8, 9, 12, 16, 17; *The Supernatural Power*, chs. 2, 11, 12; *God Is Good*, chs. 5, 9, 10, 11, 12.)

urges his followers to pursue God with "reckless abandon."[12] This alleged virtue even made it into the lyrics of a popular Bethel Music song, titled "Reckless Love." The song generated controversy, since God himself is described as "reckless." Critics say that God would never act without regard for the consequences.[13] The songwriter later clarified—he didn't mean to say that God is reckless; rather it is "the way He loves" us that is reckless.[14] But a single poor choice of wording is not the real trouble with the song. It raised concerns because it reflects a guiding philosophy and a methodology at Bethel that is itself deeply worrisome.

Johnson admits that his church's reckless, or risky, behavior "makes a lot of people nervous." And it sometimes causes "messes" or failures.[15] He sees failures as inevitable.[16] Bethel seeks to experience "biblical realities that are no longer the norm" in the church at large. "Someone has to get the breakthrough so the others can benefit."[17] Having to clean up "messes" is a small price to pay. Johnson contends that too much caution has held other churches back.[18]

At Bethel Church, Johnson's risk-taking approach has paid off.

---

12. Johnson, *When Heaven Invades Earth*, chs. 9, 10, 17. Johnson says that "reckless abandon is not the same as spiritual carelessness." (See chapter 10, note 10.) But he does not explain how the two differ. He says only that, as he pursues "dangerous things," he "keep[s] accountable" to other people and "work[s] to protect [his] relationships on all levels." (One might wish for greater clarity.)

13. To learn more about the controversy surrounding "Reckless Love," written by Bethel musician Cory Asbury, see Boorman, "Sorry, Bethel Music"; Coats, "My Take."

14. Hill, quoting Asbury, in "Defending God's 'Reckless Love.'"

15. Johnson and Farrelly, "Episode 2" (53:00); Johnson, *When Heaven Invades Earth*, ch. 15.

16. Johnson references Prov 14:4—"Where there's no oxen, the manger is clean, but much increase comes through the strength of the ox"—in defense of the "messes" that are created by Bethel's risk-taking culture. In other words, any time someone tries to accomplish something new, they will experience failures. (See Johnson and Farrelly, "Holy Laughter.") We note that his quotation of the verse appears to combine wording from different Bible translations. You must read the passage for yourself to see if you agree with Johnson's application of it. This is one of many cases illustrating Johnson's slack use of the Bible.

17. Johnson, *The Way of Life*, ch. 3 (updated 2019 edition).

18. Johnson writes: "Many leaders think their job is to discourage people from trying, so then they won't fail." But he clarifies: "When I speak of failing, I'm not referring to moral or ethical failure or experimenting with lifestyles that are contrary to the teaching of Scripture. I am referring to the God-given desire to learn how to represent Jesus well in purity and power." (*The Way of Life*, ch. 3 [updated 2019 edition].)

Soon after taking the helm, he saw the answer to his prayer for "more" of God. Healings at the church, including multiple cases of cancer healings, were reported.[19] In the years since, other unusual phenomena have occurred during Bethel services: the appearance of gold dust dropping like rain; a glittering "glory cloud" floating overhead; "angel feathers" falling from the ceiling; and unexplained, indoor gusts of wind.[20] Videos of the glory cloud—appearing a reported twenty-six times over a period of eighteen months, beginning in 2011—went viral.[21] Accounts of these things rocketed the church and its leaders through the clouds, from relatively unknown status on the outer fringes of the churchosphere to their current reputation as social media influencers with followings in the hundreds of thousands.[22] Interpreted as a sign of God's presence at Bethel, the glory cloud phenomenon is a major stimulus to the church's staggering growth.

Today, more than eleven thousand people call Bethel Church "home."[23] It's known as a global hub for revival—a Christian "Mecca"— where people flock to experience physical or emotional healing and to

19. Bill Johnson Ministries, "Bill." Johnson credits two individuals for having a major influence on the miracles occurring at Bethel Church today—John Wimber and the apostle Randy Clark: "When I heard John Wimber speak in 1987, I realized that a supernatural lifestyle was possible even for a normal person. . . . But I never met John. All I learned was from a distance, until I met Randy Clark. Randy has been the largest contributor to my understanding and experience of the miracle lifestyle. Before he came to Redding, we saw miracles weekly. After a few days with Randy, we saw the miracles multiply until they became daily happenings." (See Johnson and Clark, *The Essential Guide*, Dedication and Acknowledgments.) Johnson also credits the "Toronto Blessing revival," which began in 1994 at John and Carol Arnott's Toronto Airport Vineyard Church, for influencing his focus on revival. (See Johnson, "Bill Johnson's Testimony.")

20. Multiple videos of the glory cloud, which first started appearing during Friday night meetings at Bethel in 2011, were posted online. Johnson addressed the glory cloud phenomenon, and skepticism about it, in the *Rediscover Bethel* video series. (See Johnson and Farrelly, "Glory Clouds.") To hear Johnson describe the angel feathers, gold dust, and indoor gusts of wind, see Johnson, "Response to Glory Cloud."

21. Johnson said the cloud appeared twenty-six times. See Johnson and Farrelly, "Glory Clouds."

22. At the time of this writing, Bethel Church had 787,000 Instagram followers, Bill Johnson had 558,000 Facebook followers, and Kris Vallotton had 381,000 Facebook followers.

23. This number includes all Bethel Church attenders, members, BSSM students, and children, according to Bethel's 2019–20 annual report. See "Movement Impact."

receive a personal "word" from God.[24] Many of Bethel's attendees are young people, which is remarkable at a time when Millennials and Gen Zers have left churches like buildings on fire.[25] The Bethel School of Supernatural Ministry (BSSM)—a center for training miracle workers—has an annual enrollment of more than two thousand six hundred students and has deployed more than thirteen thousand alumni (hailing from more than one hundred countries) throughout the world.[26]

Some BSSM alumni are very influential abroad. Awakening Europe's director, Ben Fitzgerald, coordinates stadium events in major cities that include Vienna, Prague, Stockholm, and Nuremberg. These events feature Bethel leaders, enlarging their influence on that continent. And Bethel Music—a collective of worship leaders from Bethel and like-minded churches—dominates the Christian music industry. The record label produces songs played on radios and sung in churches across the United States.[27] Through this music, the church aims to "plant" the Bethel model into those churches, says Johnson.[28]

24. According to statistics provided in Bethel Church's 2019–20 annual report, more than 5,800 Sozo inner healing and deliverance sessions were conducted locally at Bethel or at Bethel-affiliated ministries around the world; 14,977 prophetic words were given by the church's prophetic ministry as well as 305 dream interpretation sessions, and 13,089 people received prayers for healing from Bethel's Healing Rooms ministry. See "Movement Impact."

25. According to a 2014 Barna poll, "59 percent of Millennials who grew up in the church have dropped out at some point." A 2018 poll revealed that only 1 in 5 members of Gen Z said attending church is "very important" to them. See Barna Group, "Americans Divided"; Barna Group, "Atheism." See also Deckman, "Generation Z." According to Deckman, "A truism of the American religious landscape is that Americans are becoming more religiously unaffiliated and that this tendency is especially pronounced among the Millennial generation (born between 1981 and 1996)." She shows that, so far, Gen Z Americans are following suit.

26. See "Movement Impact." BSSM was launched in 1998 with just thirty-seven students.

27. According to Bethel's 2019–20 annual report, Bethel songs were streamed more than 249 million times that fiscal year and three of their recording artists were named in the Top Fifty Christian Artists. ("Movement Impact.") Jesus Culture, another well-known Christian music group, was started at Bethel in 1999, in the church's youth group. See Jesus Culture, "About Jesus Culture."

28. Winger, "Bill Johnson's Theology." Bethel Church emphases found in Bethel Music lyrics include the notion of bringing heaven to earth, making "prayer declarations," and working miracles, including resurrections. Bill Johnson has stated, "Music bypasses all of the intellectual barriers, and when the anointing of God is on a song, people will begin to believe things they wouldn't believe through teaching" (quoted in Pivec and Geivett, *Counterfeit Kingdom*, ch. 8, titled "Toxic Worship Music").

Bethel has planted numerous churches in the United States and abroad: Bethel Atlanta, Bethel Austin, Bethel Cleveland, Bethel New Zealand, Bethel Valparaiso, and Bethel New York. Other pastors—seeking to replicate the Bethel experience in their own churches—utilize Bethel-produced music and books, invite Bethel speakers into their pulpits, and have even launched their own schools of supernatural ministry.[29] And thousands of people travel to Redding each year to attend annual conferences, such as the School of the Prophets.[30] At this event, aspiring prophets receive training to "accelerate" their "prophetic calling" for $425 a person.[31]

With conference rates like these—not to mention the tithes and offerings received by the church, music royalties, and revenue from BSSM and Bethel's other businesses—the church pulls in loads of money. In 2017/2018, leaders reported an overall income of $60.8 million.[32] Also in 2018, they launched a fundraising campaign to build a new $96 million, 171,708-square-foot campus to accommodate the growth.[33]

Extreme Teachings and Practices

Of course, with this success has come much controversy. Though Bethel describes itself as a "charismatic" church, its teachings and practices go far beyond what would be considered typical for charismatic churches, starting with its peculiar take on the Great Commission.[34] Through the

29. Many of these schools utilize a curriculum produced and sold by BSSM. In addition, BSSM has a School Planting division, which provides support to churches that launch their own BSSM affiliates. And recently Bethel launched BSSM Online.

30. Those who can't attend Bethel conferences in person can watch them on Bethel TV, which streams Bethel content online.

31. This was the price for in-person or online attendance for the 2022 conference. See Bethel, "School of the Prophets."

32. Pierce, "The Really Big Business of Bethel Church, Part 1."

33. Chandler and Benda. "Ask the Record Searchlight."

34. Bethel holds that its doctrine is "consistent with Charismatic/Evangelical churches." (See Bethel, "Bethel Statement Regarding Christalignment.") Yet, if that were the whole story—if it were a standard charismatic church whose teachings were, more or less, in line with evangelicalism—it is unlikely that it would generate the controversy it has. Most people believe that something new is going on there. Also, as we will show in this book, what Bethel leaders say about their beliefs often seems inconsistent with their practices. And, finally, we note that a few statements affirmed in the church's "statement of faith," as outlined in the church's 2017 bylaws, seem to go beyond historic charismatic beliefs. The statement reads: "The victorious redemptive work of Christ on the cross provides freedom from the power of the enemy—sin, lies,

working of miracles, Bethel seeks nothing less than to "bring heaven to earth."[35] This means eradicating all poverty, depression, disease—basically, anything that cannot be found in heaven. In line with that vision, one of its most controversial teachings is that it is *always* God's will to heal a person of a sickness or disease.[36] There are no exceptions.[37] And the goodness of God entails that he never causes or allows sickness or suffering.[38] To believe differently is to make God out to be a cosmic child abuser.[39] Johnson insists: "I refuse to create a theology that allows for sickness."[40]

---

sickness and torment. . . . The Church exists to carry on the ministry of Jesus Christ and further advance His kingdom by undoing the works of the enemy, . . . discipling the nations, baptizing and teaching them to love and obey God. [We believe] in the ever-increasing government of God and in the Blessed Hope, which is the glorious visible return of the Lord Jesus Christ to rule and reign with His overcoming bride—the church." (See Bethel Redding, "Membership Requirements.")

These statements create space for Bethel's more extreme teachings about healing (i.e., that it is *always* God's will to heal), its dominionism (i.e., the belief that the church at large is tasked with discipling "nations," not individuals within nations), and its doctrine that the church (under the leadership of present-day apostles and prophets) will progressively succeed in bringing God's physical kingdom to earth (i.e., "the ever-increasing government of God"). We explain Bethel's teachings about "bringing heaven to earth" in chapter 6.

35. We explain this Bethel teaching in depth in chapter 6.

36. That it is always God's will to heal is proven, in Scripture, by the fact that "Jesus demonstrated the Father's will in healing all the sick and demonized he encountered," according to Johnson. (See *The Way of Life*, ch. 19 [updated 2019 edition].) Since Jesus healed every sick person he encountered, we know it is the Father's will to heal, through us, every sick person we encounter because, in Johnson's words, "Jesus Christ is perfect theology." In other words, "He perfectly illustrates the Father in every way." (See *The Way of Life*, chs. 1, 4 [updated 2019 edition].) He concludes, "We should never again question what God's will is in a given situation, if in fact it involves sin, sickness, or torment. It may be challenging. But it's not complicated." (*The Way of Life*, ch. 2, updated 2019 edition.)

37. Johnson implies that there are no exceptions in his many teachings about the topic. See, e.g., Johnson and Clark, *The Essential Guide*, ch. 5, where, pointing to Jesus as our model, he notes that Jesus healed every person who came to him—with "no exceptions." Yet, with little concern for consistency, he also states that he has seen two exceptions: both times he was praying for someone and sensed God did not want him to pray for their healing. See Johnson and Farrelly, "Bill Johnson: The Theology."

38. Johnson, *God Is Good*, ch. 1.

39. Johnson, *God Is Good*, ch. 1.

40. "Bill Johnson False Teacher." Johnson defends this statement in Johnson and Farrelly, "Episode 2." He does not back down from it but explains that he did not mean to say that, if someone is sick, they necessarily have sin in their life or a lack of faith. But we note that he has frequently stated that when someone is not healed the responsibility for the lack of healing does not lie with God but with the sick person

Of course, this new understanding of God's goodness parts ways with the views of most other Christians, who also tenaciously uphold God's goodness, yet whose theology *does* allow for sickness. Those include classical Pentecostals and historic charismatics (who believe that divine healing is available to believers but also acknowledge that God does not always choose to heal).[41] Furthermore, Johnson's theology of physical suffering doesn't align with the harsh realities of lived experience. Sadly, his wife, Beni Johnson, died on July 13, 2022, after a four-year-battle with breast cancer. She died despite her claim in 2017, the year before her diagnosis, that she had received healing power (from heaven) for cancer and despite the many prayer "declarations" by Bethel leaders that Bethel is a "cancer-free zone."[42] And she died despite the fact that Bill Johnson reported that a couple of days before his father, M. Earl Johnson, died of pancreatic cancer in 2004, the influential prophet Rick Joyner had told

or the person praying for the sick person's healing. For example, he has said, "We owe them [the world] our best attempt at representing Him [the Lord] well, making sure that, when there's breakthrough, He gets the credit, not us. And when it doesn't work, I take the responsibility." (See Johnson and Farrelly, "Episode 1" [30:00].) He also has said, "For many, it's just become easier to blame God by calling it the 'mysterious will of God' than it is to accept the fact that we've not arrived yet and get alone with God." (Johnson, *God Is Good*, ch. 10.) And he has said, "How can God choose not to heal someone when He already purchased their healing? . . . There are no deficiencies on His end. . . . All lack is on our end of the equation. . . . It's a very uncomfortable realization—not everyone can handle it. . . . If someone isn't healed, realize the problem isn't God, and seek Him for direction as well as personal breakthrough (greater anointing for consistency in healing)." (See Johnson, "Is it Always.")

41. See the Assemblies of God position paper, "Divine Healing," which states, "In this period of the 'already and not yet' some are healed instantly, some gradually, and others are not healed." ("See Divine Healing.") And an article featured on the Assemblies of God website, written by former Assemblies of God General Superintendent Thomas Trask, states: "Someone might say, 'When God doesn't heal, it shakes my faith.' On the contrary, it should ground us in our trust in Him. . . . Suppose I said to the infinite God, 'God, You've got to do it my way.' God might reply, 'No, I know what's best, and I will do what is best in this situation.'" See Trask, "Defining Truths." We see in Scripture—both before and after Jesus's healing ministry—that God sometimes directly causes illness (and even death) as a form of judgment or discipline for sin (Num 12:9–10; 2 Sam 12:14–18; 2 Chr 21:16–20; 26:16–23; Acts 5:1–11; 1 Cor 5:4–5; 11:27–32; Rev 2:22). He also uses illness to display his power and mercy (Exod 4:6; John 9:1–3). Even when Satan desired to attack Job's physical health, he first had to seek God's permission (Job 2:1–7). And he doesn't always choose to heal (2 Sam 12:16–18; 2 Cor 12:7–9; 2 Tim 4:20). (Note that most New Testament scholars believe Paul's "thorn" in the flesh, which the Lord declined to heal, was a physical ailment.)

42. Blair, "Bethel Church Pastor"; Jenn Johnson, "By the Blood"; Bill Johnson, *The Way of Life*, ch. 6 (updated 2019 edition).

him that the loss "would give me access to a seven times greater anointing against this particular disease."[43] Also, Bill Johnson's son, Eric—a senior pastor at Bethel from 2011 to 2021—suffers from deafness. And Johnson himself wears glasses to correct poor vision. In short, Bethel's theology does not line up with the leaders' personal experience. But Johnson is resolute: "We can't lower the standard of scripture to our level of experience. . . . If someone isn't healed, realize the problem isn't God, and seek Him for direction as well as personal breakthrough (greater anointing for consistency in healing)."[44] Johnson's teaching about the goodness of God is so critical at Bethel that he calls it the "cornerstone" of the church's theology.[45] Similarly, the church at large must undergo a radical shift in its view of God if it is going to represent him accurately, according to Johnson.[46] After all, Christians won't seek to heal every sick person they encounter if they do not believe it is *always* God's will to heal.

Another provocative teaching is that Jesus emptied himself of his divine powers when he came to earth. He could not heal the sick or raise the dead. He couldn't cast out demons. According to Johnson, "He had NO supernatural capabilities whatsoever!"[47] While he was still fully God, he worked all his miracles as a man fully dependent on the Father and empowered by the Holy Spirit. One reason Jesus did this, according to Johnson, was to show that *every* believer can learn to work miracles, including prophesying and healing sickness.

To help their followers learn to work miracles, Bethel Church has popularized a number of practices that, according to Bethel's critics, have no biblical support. These practices may even be spiritually harmful. What are they? They include running through "fire tunnels,"[48] "Treasure

43. Johnson, *God Is Good*, ch. 11.

44. Johnson, "Is It Always."

45. Johnson, *The Way of Life*, ch. 4 (updated 2019 edition).

46. Johnson, *God Is Good*, ch. 1.

47. Johnson, *When Heaven Invades Earth*, ch. 2.

48. Near the conclusion of many Bethel meetings, leaders form two lines, facing each other, and encourage the churchgoers to walk through the "fire tunnel." They place their hands on the churchgoers as they walk through the tunnel to "impart" to individuals a miraculous healing or some other type of work of the Holy Spirit. The fire tunnels allow Bethel leaders to accelerate the "laying on of hands" on many people—a practice that is common in the New Apostolic Reformation and more extreme charismatic churches. (For the definition of "impartation" and "the laying on of hands," see chapter 5.) To view a fire tunnel that took place at Bethel Church in 2010, see "Kundalini at Bethel Church."

Hunting,"[49] and taking part in so-called "prophetic activation exercises," such as "Telephone Prophecy," "Tattoo Interpretation," and playing "Prophetic Uno."[50] Prophetic activation exercises are such a critical component of Bethel practice that they are taught during Bethel's adult Sunday School class called "Firestarters," a twelve-week course designed to create "modern-day revivalists" (also known in NAR as "Firestarters"). Controversial BSSM prophesying practices also include setting up tents at psychic fairs and offering visitors "dream interpretations, healings, and spirit readings."[51] The similarities to the practices of psychics and fortune tellers have not been lost on Bethel's critics.[52] Some will be surprised to

49. Treasure Hunting is a form of "prophetic evangelism," also known as "supernatural evangelism." BSSM students go into their local communities and divide into teams of three or four people. They ask God to give them specific "words of knowledge"—also called "clues"—about individuals they will encounter in grocery stores and other public places. These clues may include a person's name, details about their physical appearance, or any physical conditions they may have. Students then mark these clues on a "Treasure Map," which they use to guide them to a person ("treasure") who matches their clues. When they find a person, they ask if they can pray for their healing or give them a prophetic word. For more information about this practice, see Dedmon, *The Ultimate Treasure Hunt*. We note that local Redding residents have complained about being hounded by the Bethel Treasure Hunters as they attempt to shop or otherwise go about their daily lives. They do not appreciate that BSSM students target people in wheelchairs and others who look like they need "healing." (See Hensley-Clancy, "Meet the 'Young Saints.'")

50. In a new spin on an old card game, Uno cards from a standard deck are used as prompts to teach BSSM students to prophesy on the spot. Groups of six to eight players are instructed to "Grab some Uno cards (a few of each color) and place them in the middle of the group." They take turns turning over cards. If a red card is turned over, "you give a prophetic word to the person on your left about their financial situation." If a yellow card is turned over, "you choose who to give a prophetic word to in the group about their career/employment/job." In other words, divine guidance is facilitated with the use of Uno cards. (A screen capture of a BSSM School Planting Facebook post promoting this practice was preserved by Bethel Church and Christianity, "They'll stop at nothing.") For descriptions of other prophetic activations, including "Telephone Prophecy" and "Tattoo Interpretation," see BSSM School Planting, "10 Ways."

51. See BSSM School Planting, "Are You More Religious." In addition to setting up tents at physic fairs, some BSSM alumni have also taken part in giving "Destiny Card" readings at psychic fairs with a Christian organization called Christalignment, which is led by Ken and Jenny Hodge, the parents of a Bethel pastor and BSSM alumnus, Ben Fitzgerald. Critics, including one of the authors of this book, likened the Destiny Cards to a Christianized version of tarot cards. See Pivec, "The 'Christian' Tarot Card Controversy." See also Bethel's statement saying they had no formal affiliation with Christalignment, though they do "have a value for what they [the Hodges] are seeking to accomplish": Bethel, "Bethel Statement Regarding Christalignment."

52. Former New Agers who have become Christians, including Doreen Virtue and Melissa Dougherty, strenuously warn people about Bethel's practices.

learn that Bethel leaders openly acknowledge the likenesses and claim that New Agers stole these practices from Christians and that they must be reclaimed for the global church.[53] Little wonder, then that BSSM students fondly refer to their school as the "Christian Hogwarts."[54]

Another controversial practice is the effort to raise the dead. The Dead Raising Team was founded in 2006 by a BSSM graduate.[55] It has been publicly praised by Johnson.[56] This team makes the rounds to churches and has trained sixty other teams worldwide to go to the scenes of accidents, hospitals, and morgues and to pray for resurrections. They claim to have seen fifteen resurrections to date.[57] Even children at Bethel are taught to raise the "dead." In their classes at the church, leaders wrap children in toilet paper, like mummies, and urge the other children to pray for a resurrection.[58] The children are just pretending, but the message for them is meant to be very real.

But their most controversial practice is "grave soaking." During this practice—also known as "grave sucking" and "mantle grabbing"—BSSM students and alumni lay on (or lean against) the graves of well-known miracle-workers, such as the British faith healer Smith Wigglesworth and the American healing evangelist Kathryn Kuhlman.[59] The purpose is to

53. A book sold in the Bethel bookstore titled *The Physics of Heaven*—featuring chapters written by Bill and Beni Johnson and a foreword written by Kris Vallotton (the senior associate leader at Bethel)—promotes a plethora of New Age-type practices, including meditation, trances, reading auras, clairvoyance, and clairaudience. A major premise of the book is that these practices were stolen from Christians and repackaged by New Agers, and that they must now be redeemed and reclaimed by the church. (See Franklin and Davis, *The Physics of Heaven*; Vallotton, *Heavy Rain*, ch. 14.) Randy Clark does, however, note a key difference between the Christian view of healing and that of pantheistic religions, including the New Age movement—namely, healing is not worked through the power of an impersonal force but through the Holy Spirit. See Johnson and Clark, *The Essential Guide*, ch. 11.

54. Hensley-Clancy, "Meet the 'Young Saints.'"

55. Tyler Johnson (no relation to Bill Johnson) founded the Dead Raising Team, based in Shelton, Washington.

56. Johnson, "Eat Meat."

57. See Dead Raising Team, "Our Director."

58. Flinchbaugh, "Ignite the Fire."

59. We do not know how the term "grave soaking" originated. But Bethel leaders claim that the term "grave sucking" was created by their critics. (See Johnson and Farrelly, "Does Bethel Church Teach.") However, prior to critical analysis, the term "suck" had been used to describe the practice by John Crowder, whom Bill Johnson, reportedly, has called a "friend." (See Bethel Church and Christianity, "A few people have asked Bill Johnson.") In one video, Crowder crouches at the grave of John Alexander

"soak" up, or "suck" up, or "grab" a past miracle-worker's "anointing."[60] In support of this practice, they point to a Bible verse, 2 Kings 13:21, which records an incident when a dead man's body came into contact with Elisha's bones and the man came to life.

In response to the outcry about grave soaking from other Christians, Bethel leaders acknowledge that BSSM students engaged in this practice.[61] Indeed, multiple photos found online testify to the fact—college-age kids sprawled out on their stomachs, or curled up in fetal positions, on top of grave markers. However, Johnson and other Bethel leaders deny that they have ever taught or encouraged the practice.[62] Apparently, this simply was one of those times the students did something to "embarrass" their teachers—another harmless "mess" the church must clean up.[63] Oddly, Bethel leaders say that this misguided practice is actually a "good problem" for their church to have: "every pastor in America would want" their people to display such a "beautiful hunger" for God's presence.[64] A throng of pastors worldwide would shrink in horror from this description.

Bethel's critics claim that various videos and photos posted online provide ample evidence that Bethel Church leaders have also taken part in the practice. These include a YouTube video of Bethel pastor and BSSM graduate Ben Fitzgerald, who appears to be leading a team of students in this practice.[65] There are photos showing Beni Johnson (Bill Johnson's

Dowie, places a hand on the grave and says, "We just suck it [Dowie's 'anointing'] right off his dead bones in Jesus's name." (See Crowder, "The term 'grave sucking.'") The idea that deceased miracle-workers' anointings linger at their tombs has been taught by Word of Faith leaders with connections to Bill Johnson, including Benny Hinn. (See Churchwatcher, "Documenting Benny Hinn's Necromancy.")

60. For a definition of "anointing," see chapter 2.

61. Justice and Berglund, "Banning Liebscher: Why Bill Johnson Didn't"; Johnson and Farrelly, "Does Bethel Church Teach."

62. Johnson made these denials during a radio interview with Christian radio host Michael Brown on his show *Line of Fire*. (See Brown and Johnson, "Dr. Brown Interviews.") Johnson again denied that Bethel leaders promoted grave soaking during the *Rediscover Bethel* video series. (See Johnson and Farrelly, "Does Bethel Church Teach.") In this series, however, Dann Farrelly does say that the practice among students started after a BSSM leader had a "profound encounter" with God at the grave of a deceased church leader that inspired the BSSM students.

63. Vallotton and Farrelly, "Episode 5" (1:34:00).

64. Johnson and Farrelly, "Does Bethel Church Teach."

65. See Fitzgerald, "Bethel Church Soaking." We do not know if the students were Bethel students. According to an article written by Murray Campbell, in a private meeting with some of his critics Fitzgerald admitted he had acted unwisely but denied

wife and herself a senior pastor at the church) embracing and lying on tombstones.[66] In response to the photos, Bill Johnson said his wife was not grave soaking; she was merely being "responsive" to the promptings of the Holy Spirit in the moment.[67] We are not sure quite what this means or how it explains what she is doing in the pictures. But we understand why Johnson's defense of his wife has not satisfied Bethel's critics. In a private Facebook message she had previously sent to one of those critics, she referenced 2 Kings 13:21 (the verse about Elisha and the dead man's bones) as an explanation of her actions.[68] Is this not tacit acknowledgment that Beni Johnson did take part in the practice, albeit with the disclaimer that she would not call what she did at the gravesites "sucking"? Her Facebook followers concluded that she was doing something very much like that.[69] Also, former BSSM students claim that Beni Johnson did promote

that the purpose of his visits to cemeteries was "to draw out the spiritual powers of dead saints." Instead, he said, he visited the tombs for inspiration and prayer (to God). See Campbell, "Update." But Fitzgerald's statement is strikingly at odds with his actual words and actions in the video. They certainly appear to show him engaged in grave soaking, though Bethel leaders may prefer not to use this term to describe what he is doing. While standing before the grave of Smith Wigglesworth in Bradford, England, Fitzgerald says that he and the students could feel the supernatural power that was present, including "the raising of the dead power." He also says that some students who were leaning on the gravestone could feel "a grace and a faith just rest on them." (See chapter 2 for the New Apostolic Reformation definition of a "grace.") Fitzgerald references Elisha's bones and says, "When you come into a place where the Holy Spirit was on a person, He still exists there." He then instructs viewers of the video, "Just open up your hands right now, and get ready to receive in the spiritual because there's no distance in the Spirit, and God can release this same impartation unto you." Extending his palms toward the camera, he says: "We just release over the camera right now . . . we just release the anointing of God that is in this place. . . . Just take it now in Jesus's name. . . . Take a great faith to do miracles, to work miracles. . . . We just thank you, Father, that what was on Smith Wigglesworth's life, let it come on us, let it come on them [the viewers]."

66. Bethel Church and Christianity, "Beni Johnson (right) modeling grave sucking"; Bethel Church and Christianity, "Senior Pastor Beni Johnson."

67. Johnson and Farrelly, "Does Bethel Church Teach."

68. On May 19, 2015, the Bethel Church and Christianity Facebook page published a screen capture of a private written exchange between Beni Johnson and the site's founder, Bart McCurdy. In the exchange, which took place on Facebook Messenger in 2013, Beni Johnson admitted to lying on a grave and she referenced 2 Kings 13:21 in support of her practice. She also wrote that she wouldn't call what she did "sucking." But one might reasonably wonder if there is any substantial difference between Beni Johnson's practice and the practice others refer to as "grave sucking," regardless of what she prefers to call it. (See Bethel Church and Christianity, "Here's a conversation.")

69. Pictures posted to Facebook show Beni Johnson hugging Charles Finney's grave

the practice.[70] Given the evidence of Facebook posts, photos, and videos, along with student testimony, it seems both tactless and slanderous for Bethel leaders to accuse their critics of "purposely misunderstand[ing]" and "perpetuat[ing] lies."[71] From an outsider's perspective, Bethel responses to the allegations look like a cover-up.

These practices—grave soaking, spiritual reading tents, and "Prophetic Uno"—are just a few examples showing that Bethel has wandered far beyond the bounds of Scripture and brought its followers into a dangerously speculative and experience-driven faith. To be sure, controversial practices such as these will result in failure now and then—a point that Bethel leaders themselves recognized when they agreed to embrace Johnson's "experimentation" in pursuit of a "reckless" Christianity.

Failed Experiments

Some of Bethel's failures are biggies. Especially noteworthy is a heartbreaking story that made national news in December 2019.[72] Two-year-old Olive Heiligenthal, the daughter of a Bethel worship leader, died when she suddenly stopped breathing. Rather than planning a funeral, Bethel leaders urged their followers worldwide to join them in "declaring" that the little girl be raised from the dead.[73] Their call went viral. Popular worship leaders from other churches responded. Kari Jobe told her one million Instagram followers, "We're still standing in faith for Olive to wake up."[74] Sadly, after six days and much fanfare—jumping, shouting, and

---

and lying on the grave of C. S. Lewis. The comments on the pictures indicate that at least some of those who saw the pictures were supporters of Beni Johnson and it was their belief that she was engaged in grave soaking (also known as mantle grabbing). Two different commentators wrote, "Grab some for me" and "Grab some for me, too . . . wow!" See those pictures and comments preserved by *Pulpit and Pen*: "Bethel Pastor Contradicts."

70. Wiget, "Interview with Jesse." In private correspondence with us, Jesse Westwood confirmed that he observed Bethel senior leaders, including Beni Johnson, promoting grave soaking.

71. Johnson and Farrelly, "What Does Bethel Church Teach."

72. Chapman, "'Olive Hasn't Been Raised'"; Chen and McNeal, "The Evangelical Parents"; Associated Press, "'Come Out of That Grave.'"

73. See our explanation of Bethel teachings about "declarations" in ch. 6. To see that Bethel leaders viewed their "prayers" for Olive's resurrection as "declarations," see Pivec, "What's Being Missed."

74. Jobe, "We're still standing."

commanding Olive to "come out of that grave, in Jesus's name"—Bethel leaders were compelled to admit defeat and hold a memorial service.[75]

This is hardly the only time "declarations" made by Bethel leaders have failed to produce a miracle. In the early months of the 2020 CO-VID-19 pandemic, they led churchgoers in declaring that "Everywhere I go becomes a perfect-health zone."[76] But later that year, the church and BSSM reported more than three hundred cases of the virus, the largest cluster of cases in the county. This drew the ire of local Redding residents, who disapproved of Bethel leaders' public statements questioning the effectiveness of face masks.[77]

Their declarations also fell flat when the 2018 Carr Fire ravished two counties—including their own Shasta County in Northern California. They issued a "command [for] the wind to calm down over the Redding skies."[78] The winds did not comply. Rather, the fire grew so large that within six days it created its own weather pattern. A "giant fire whirl" produced wind damage similar to a very strong EF3 tornado. Fire whirls this large are rarely documented.[79] More than a thousand homes were destroyed (including at least forty belonging to Bethel staff and church members). Tragically, eight people died in the fire.[80] Once it was obvious their declarations against the fire had failed, Bethel Church resorted to a very non-miraculous response: they partnered with the Salvation Army

75. See the press release: Bethel, "Bethel Statement on Olive." Notice that the press release states that what their churchgoers had done was "ask" God to resurrect her. In actuality, they were making prayer "declarations"—which is very different from petitionary prayer (see chapter 6). Equivocating on terms (such as "prayer") in this way is common among leaders in the New Apostolic Reformation, especially when damage control is necessitated by dramatic failures. Following Olive Heiligenthal's burial, Bethel Music released a song titled "Come Out of That Grave (Resurrection Power)," which some critics thought was an exploitation of her death because the song's bridge is similar to the words people at Bethel chanted when they were attempting to resurrect her. See Titkemeyer, "Did Bethel and Bill Johnson Exploit."

76. Pivec, "The NAR Antidote." They also took part in Communion, which, according to Johnson, releases miraculous power for healing. (See Beni and Bill Johnson, *The Power of Communion.* Their teaching about communion incorporates a novel understanding of a historic and essential Christian practice instituted by Jesus to commemorate his atoning death.)

77. Branson-Potts and Chabria, "God, Masks and Trump."

78. Bethel Church, Redding, "Father we thank you." See also the declarations made by Theresa Dedmon, who is on pastoral staff at Bethel (Dedmon, "Beauty for Ashes").

79. Erdman, "The Giant Fire Whirl."

80. Mann, "California's 7th Worst Wildfire"; Sells, "More Than 40 Bethel Members."

to open a distribution center, providing meals, supplies, and emotional support for evacuees.[81] Their declarations had almost literally gone up in smoke. Charitable efforts, though commendable, are no substitute for repentance for having promoted a naive practice and a flawed theology.

We cannot forget the sad story of Nabeel Qureshi, a Muslim-turned-Christian apologist and author of the *New York Times* bestseller *Seeking Allah, Finding Jesus*. Many people outside of Bethel knew Qureshi. Numerous people followed his series of vlogs on YouTube, poignantly chronicling his battle with stomach cancer. In one vlog, he shared that he had traveled to Bethel in December 2016, seeking healing.[82] He had gone at the urging of friends who assured him miracles were happening at the church. But many others advised him not to go, warning him of aberrant teachings and practices. Understandably, he wanted to see about the church for himself. During his visit, about 1,700 people declared his healing during a meeting.[83] Sadly, less than a year later, the thirty-four-year-old husband and father died.

Harmful Teachings and Damaged Lives

When Bethel's "experiments" fail, they do not only embarrass the church. Real people are injured.

Consider the thousands who travel to Bethel Church every year seeking physical healing. They go because they've heard Bethel leaders' claims that hundreds of healings (along with other miracles, salvations, and divine interventions) happen in the "Bethel movement" each month.[84] They've watched the "testimonies" of healing that Bethel's media department has turned into polished marketing videos and posted to YouTube.[85] These powerfully emotional videos leave countless viewers

---

81. Patterson, "Salvation Army, Bethel Church."

82. Qureshi, "Nabeel's Vlog."

83. Qureshi estimated that at least 1,700 people "prophesied" his healing when he visited Bethel Church in December 2016. (See Qureshi, "Nabeel's Vlog.") A video on Facebook shows that, during his visit, many BSSM students made declarations for his healing during a meeting. This may be the incident Qureshi was referring to. (See "BSSM: Nabeel Qureshi Testimony.")

84. See Vallotton, *Heavy Rain*, ch. 16. Also Johnson states, "We have seen thousands of people healed of all sorts of problems, including many with cancers." (*God Is Good*, ch. 11.)

85. One of the videos shows a young boy named Adrian who was bound to a

thinking, *if I need a miracle, I must go to Bethel*. But what of the many people who, like Qureshi, made the trek and returned home unchanged, their illnesses progressing and the prospects of a cure no more promising?

And what about heartbroken parents who claim they've "lost" their adult children to Bethel? A pair of distressed parents told radio host Jan Markell that their twenty-three-year-old daughter broke off contact with her entire family in 2011.[86] Another married couple who attended Bethel persuaded the young woman to move to Redding and enroll in BSSM. This couple told her she had a special musical ability that was needed at Bethel. (This tactic of affirming would-be acolytes, often used by cult-like groups, is known as "love bombing.") They also prophesied this threat: if she would not go to BSSM, a past sickness—a serious illness that she believed had been healed by God—would return. In addition, bad things would happen to her family if she didn't obey God. Under the influence of this couple and Bethel Church, she underwent a complete change in personality. Somehow, she even came to believe that her parents had abused her. Her parents suspect she "recovered" false memories while taking part in "Sozo" sessions at Bethel.[87] (Critics have described Sozo as "recovered memory therapy," a controversial and widely discredited form of psychotherapy.)[88]

---

wheelchair because of a progressive muscle disease. He also couldn't eat any food due to intestinal absorption problems and had to be fed intravenously. Expecting Adrian to die soon, his family decided to make some last special memories by taking him to a conference at Bethel. While there, he was miraculously healed and immediately began eating regular food. Soon he was walking. His mother claims that his medical providers confirmed that his absorption problems had been resolved and that new muscle tissue had grown. It's a touching and remarkable story, but it would be more compelling if the medical assessment could be independently corroborated. See Bethel, "It's a Different Life."

86. Markell, "Wolves Not Sparing."

87. Sozo is described by Bethel Church as a "unique inner healing and deliverance ministry." See Bethel Sozo, "What Is Sozo?" The aims and practices of Sozo sessions are detailed in Law, "Sozo Prayer Spreading Worldwide."

88. McClure, "Sozo Prayer"; "Victims of Johnson's Sozo"; and SwordoftheSpirit528, "Sozo Inner Healing Deception." Studies have shown that false memories can be produced during practices associated with recovered memory therapy and, for that reason, prominent professional organizations (including the American Medical Association, the American Psychological Association, the Australian Psychological Society, and the British Royal College of Psychiatrists) "have issued strong warnings against [such] practices" (Loftus and Davis, "Recovered Memories," 493). According to an entry in the Wikipedia article titled "Inner Healing Movement," the founders of Sozo ministry at Bethel denounce the use of memory recovery therapy. But the sources

One couple we've talked with says they've been contacted by dozens of parents with the same heartache. They all claim that their children cut them off after arriving at Bethel.[89]

Former BSSM students speak of the hurt inflicted by their involvement with the school. Though some might be tempted to question the credibility of these students or wonder if they have personal vendettas against Bethel and seek unjustly to harm the reputation of its school, their stories share common themes that make them more difficult to simply dismiss. In a tell-all interview with the podcast *Cultish*, Lindsay Davis describes her initial visit to BSSM.[90] During a service, while the musicians led worship from the stage, she observed the students around her exhibiting unusual manifestations. One young woman rocked back and forth like she was riding a horse. Someone else shook violently on the floor. Others laughed uncontrollably (a phenomenon known as "holy laughter"). Confused by behavior she had never seen before, Davis asked around about what she was witnessing. She was told that she just needed to "let go" and fully surrender to God. One woman asked Davis if she might be under the influence of a "religious spirit." In Bethel teaching, a religious spirit is a demonic spirit who opposes the work of the Holy Spirit. Concerned that this woman might be right, Davis went to the home of some BSSM students. The students told her they could facilitate contact with her "angels," an experience that would include visual perception of them. After some two hours of failing to see her angels, she found herself on the couch, bawling. Concluding that these students had something special that she was lacking, Davis enrolled at the school.

While at BSSM, Davis says, she witnessed disturbing practices. One noteworthy event was a school-wide "deliverance" session during which the speaker claimed to be exorcising demons from every student in the

---

for those statements are not cited, and we could not find evidence for this alleged denunciation. If it exists, it isn't to be found where you would most expect it, on the Sozo ministry website. Our research strongly suggests that Sozo does rely on recovered memory methodology. A former Sozo practitioner who received formal Sozo training from Bethel describes how memories are recalled during Sozo sessions and reports that, in many cases, false memories were produced. See Virtue and Whatmore, "Why Sozo Is Dangerous."

89. We also receive correspondence from parents with stories of severely strained relationships with their children following their involvement with Bethel.

90. We recount this story as told by Lindsay Davis. See Davis, Durbin, and Roberts, "Exclusive: Defecting from Bethel"; Davis, Durbin, and Roberts, "Defecting from Bethel (Part 2)."

school. Of this event Davis says, "It was like something from a horror movie. . . . Everyone's screaming, people are violently shaking. And I had never seen anything like it before in my life." During other meetings, students could be seen thrusting their heads into a "honey barrel" (a standard cask designed to look like a honey barrel), and then falling over as if they were "drunk" with the Holy Spirit. Davis thought these people must be having genuine experiences with God and she desperately wanted to have the same experiences. At one "evangelism" meeting, a group of students broke out in holy laughter. Desiring to encounter God in the same way, Davis joined the group and sat in the middle of them for nearly an hour. The students were cackling and pointing at her, in a mocking way. "It was very strange," she says.

Eventually, she began to think she could "hear God's voice," following the guidelines taught in her BSSM classes. She wrote a prophecy and shared it on Facebook. Her post quickly went viral, receiving more than one hundred thousand shares within just a few days. Many people asked her how they might learn to "hear God" as she did. This, says Davis, made her feel very powerful and proud.

One woman, however, rebuked Davis after she posted her prophecy and sent her a private message urging her to watch the documentary film *American Gospel*.[91] While watching the film, Davis experienced such remorse for her involvement with BSSM that she repented. She resolved to "unlearn" everything and to learn to understand Scripture correctly. When she began challenging the school's teachings publicly on social media—and wouldn't back down after meeting with the school's leaders—she was expelled.

In retrospect, Lindsay Davis said she believed the Bethel School of Supernatural Ministry has cultic characteristics. Fawning over its leaders is excessive. Students are expected to stand and applaud for the instructors every day before classes. A "false bond" is formed with authority figures as students are prompted to call Bill Johnson and Kris Vallotton "Papa Bill" and "Papa Kris."[92] Davis publicly criticized Bethel with details of her ex-

---

91. The American Gospel film series documents distortions of the historic gospel of Jesus. The first film, *American Gospel: Christ Alone* (2018), includes an exposé of several Bethel teachings. The third film, *American Gospel: Spirit & Fire* (with a 2023 anticipated release), burrows more deeply into problems with the Bethel Church movement.

92. In the next chapter we show that Bill Johnson is regarded as the head "apostle" at Bethel Church, and Kris Vallotton is regarded as the chief "prophet."

perience. And Bethel's critics believe that Bethel leaders wished to silence her. She was scheduled to speak in March 2020 about Bethel beliefs at a conference to be held at Simpson University in Redding, California. When Bethel leaders learned of her participation, they leveraged their influence with university officials, who withdrew their verbal agreement to host.[93]

Since speaking out repeatedly and strongly about Bethel, Davis (now Davis-Knotts) has changed her posture toward the church and has "repented" for the charges she made against Bethel leaders. In a public comment posted to her personal Facebook page on December 26, 2022, she wrote that, while she still has "strong disagreements" with Bethel "on points of secondary theology and practices," she no longer views the leaders as "wolves, heretics, or false teachers." Meanwhile, other former BSSM students continue to speak out against Bethel, including Jesse Westwood (who, unlike Davis-Knotts) attended BSSM's entire three-year program and was "knighted" by Bethel prophet Kris Vallotton during a graduation ceremony. Westwood's YouTube series *Breaking Bethel*, which shares his firsthand accounts of the harmful teachings and practices promoted by the school, has received thousands of views. Other former BSSM students say they observed spiritual manipulation at the school. One man, identified as "Stefan" in his interview with a reporter, attended Bethel School of Supernatural Ministry for three years (the full program). Initially, he believed he was an eyewitness to genuine prophecy and miracles of

---

93. Bart McCurdy (founder of the Bethel Church and Christianity Facebook page) was a lead organizer for the 2020 conference on Clouds without Water that was planned for Redding for March 20, 2020. Simpson University verbally agreed to the use of their facilities for the conference and issued a contract to the conference organizers on August 15, 2019. But they rescinded the contract before the event organizers signed it. In mid-December 2019, McCurdy learned that Simpson had rescinded its verbal agreement with the conference organizers. In personal correspondence with us, McCurdy reports that he spoke directly with Bethel leaders who confirmed that they had asked Simpson officials to cancel use of their facilities for the conference. Bethel leaders also confirmed that a major reason for the request was Davis's participation. It happens that Simpson University and Bethel Church have an official arrangement whereby Simpson provides housing for BSSM students. (See Simpson University, "BSSM Student Housing.") Simpson also offers a special "Bethel Revivalist Scholarship" for BSSM graduates and Bethel Church members. (See Simpson University, "Scholarship Program.") Plans were made by conference organizers to hold the event at another location, but the COVID-19 pandemic broke out and that event also was canceled. (We contacted Simpson University to see if officials could confirm the accuracy of McCurdy's account. We received the following response from the school's chief operating officer, R. Walter Quirk: "Unfortunately, it is not our policy to advertise who is contracting to utilize our conference services.")

healing there. Looking back now he "sees an array of 'psychological mind games'—healing via placebo, prophecy through confirmation bias."[94] He believes the "miracles" he witnessed were more akin to magic tricks.

Robert Vujasinovic, another BSSM alum, recalls events involving a fellow student, a paraplegic. He recalls that students prayed continuously for her, over many months, and convinced her that she would be healed. She believed them and tried repeatedly to rise from her wheelchair. But she was never able to take even a single step. According to a news reporter, "Vujasinovic found himself growing increasingly disturbed that Bethel's leadership refused to intervene and end what he perceived as an obvious cruelty. Yet he felt helpless to respond due to the 'culture of honor' cultivated at Bethel that prohibited students from criticizing the leadership and even fellow students who made fantastical claims of healing and other supernatural wonders."[95] At one point, Vujasinovic told Bethel officials that another BSSM student had made up a phony healing story. This did not deter them from sharing the fictitious story during a Sunday church service. It bothered him that "testimonies" of healing were "never researched."

Since attending BSSM, both Stefan and Vujasinovic have grown disenchanted with the Christian faith. Robert says he's still a Christian, but "barely."[96]

These men are not alone. Disillusionment with Christianity is common among BSSM graduates. A research study of BSSM alumni found that, although they enjoyed their time at BSSM, many struggled with unmet expectations after graduating. One alum, who was now "very unsure about their faith," told the researchers, "BSSM is a big fantasy bubble similar to

94. Hensley-Clancy, "Meet the Young Saints."

95. Scheide, "Losing His Religion." Bethel leaders speak frequently of Bethel as having a "culture of honor." A book written by a Bethel senior leader, Danny Silk, even bears the name *Culture of Honor*. Silk writes, "The Principle of Honor states that: accurately acknowledging who people are will position us to give them what they deserve and to receive the gift of who they are in our lives" (*Culture of Honor*, introduction). Silk stresses the importance of showing proper honor to apostles and prophets, as a condition for receiving miraculous giftings and empowerment from the apostles and prophets. Critics accuse Bethel leaders of using this principle to persuade their followers to submit to them and to avoid criticizing them. (See, e.g., "Culture of Honor.") A former Bethel elder, Mark Mack, who has spoken out publicly and critically about what he saw firsthand at Bethel, says he understood the "culture of honor" teaching as meaning "you cannot criticize your leaders" (Mack and Kozar, "Behind the Scenes," 49:00).

96. Scheide, "Losing His Religion."

Disneyland, that bursts the moment a lot of people leave and the real world hits them harder than they could have expected as they come to terms with the reality of their real environment. A lot go into a deep depression." Another said that the inability to work miracles after leaving BSSM felt like "failure." "I wasn't doing or seeing any of the stuff I saw whilst at school. It has really made me question what I believe and that sucks."[97]

Post-BSSM disillusionment is not the whole of it. The survey also found that, compared to national statistics, a "quite high" number of BSSM alumni reported "frequent levels" of depression and anxiety.[98] These statistics are reinforced by the organization of "recovery groups" on Facebook—support groups for people who have left Bethel and other New Apostolic Reformation (NAR) churches that share Bethel's distinctive theology.[99] Many report feeling theologically disoriented, ill-prepared to study Scripture for themselves, and are suspicious toward all churches. Compounding their pain is rejection by friends from their former churches and difficulty finding a new community of Christians who can relate to their experiences.[100]

97. Verbi and Winkley, "The Story of BSSM Alumni," 26. Eido Research has conducted research for large Christian organizations, including Compassion, Africa Inland Mission, Hope International, Alpha, and the UK-based Evangelical Alliance.

98. The researchers found that "overall, 12% of BSSM graduates said they were experiencing depression or anxiety, with a further 20% selecting that they 'partially' experience depression or anxiety." They add, "This is quite high when compared to the national statistics in 2015 where 6.9% of adult Americans experienced a 'major depressive episode' and while the two numbers cannot directly be compared, it is clear that BSSM graduates are struggling in this way." The study's authors have proposed an explanation for what they discovered: "However, it should be noted that BSSM is likely to attract people who are more in tune with their emotions and that spiritual 'feelers' are likely to be more affected by this than the general population. Also as BSSM teaches emotional awareness very openly, it is possible that graduates over-report their mental health because they are more aware of what a healthy emotional person should look like." (See Verbi and Winkley, "The Story of BSSM Alumni," 28.) We find it curious that the researchers offer an explanation for the worrisome aspect of their findings. We do not know what professional credentials they have for their psychological evaluations, which go beyond mere reporting of objective facts. And in any case, if their explanation is correct, it would say something about the profile of a person attracted to BSSM and raise questions about the health of a program that depends so heavily on a socio-psychological tendency of the kind described.

99. Later in this chapter (as well as in the preface) we explain that Bethel's beliefs align with the theology of the broader New Apostolic Reformation movement.

100. Many former participants in NAR churches have shared their experiences with us and asked for support and guidance. It's moving to hear them, finally free of their affiliation with NAR churches like Bethel, describe a new passion for deep

So far we've spoken of individuals who have been harmed by Bethel teachings and practices. But whole churches have experienced the fallout of Bethel mania. Church members describe attempted coups by Bethel-influenced "apostles."[101] Even more conventional churches are not exempt from NAR's tentacles. We regularly receive messages like this one from a concerned member of a Presbyterian church on the West Coast who has been seeking to turn back the tide before it is too late. "I just left a meeting at our church over this issue. They are bringing in this guy, part of NAR, to teach at our conservative Presbyterian church! And there is a church plant in our city under an influential NAR apostle that people in our church are getting involved with. And our church is partnering with another NAR leader and his organization. I'm exhausted over this, totally drained. These are my closest friends. It's hard."[102] Missionaries, too, note harmful effects on ministries throughout the world. They bemoan the mopping-up challenge of correcting the teachings and practices of departing Bethel-trained cohorts.[103] NAR evangelists and missionar-

---

knowledge of Scripture and for Bible-based fellowship and teaching. But they universally acknowledge that the adjustment is difficult.

101. For example, see Pivec, "Is It Too Late?"

102. We do not share the name of the individual who sent us this message, to protect their anonymity, and we've removed the names of the specific NAR leaders and organizations they referenced.

103. Missionaries have described for us the damage they've seen from Bethel-influenced missionaries and missionaries from other NAR churches. Those include Richard Moore (author of a book about NAR titled *Divergent Theology*), who told us, "Having been a missionary in Germany for eight years, I have witnessed the substantial and burgeoning influence of Bethel and the greater NAR here and throughout Europe. Churches in our area have been overrun with aberrant theology and practices, as well as unbiblical teaching from Bethel that shipwrecks the faith of some. Churches have split; faithful Christians have been mocked as unspiritual and repeatedly bullied into submission." And here is a Facebook comment responding to a post by Remnant Radio about one of our books about the New Apostolic Reformation: "I served with many missionaries overseas who self-identified as 'NAR.' Some from America, some from South Africa. Some from Australia. These people were a detriment to the mission field and honestly should have been sent home because of the destruction they wrought with their theology. Useless missionaries who spent 90 percent of their time looking for demons behind every rock and 'prayer walking' instead of actually engaging the indigenous population (in this case, Muslims) with the Gospel." "Prayer walking" is a NAR spiritual warfare practice that we describe in our book *A New Apostolic Reformation?*, ch. 15. Leaders of several missions agencies and various other Christian organizations have sought our assistance as they confront the infiltration of harmful teachings and practices coming through their own missionaries and volunteers who have been influenced by Bethel and like-minded churches.

ies—ever attuned to signs, wonders, and miracles, and generally on the lookout for evil spirits to exorcise—sometimes forget the simplicity of the gospel message and neglect to proclaim that message without distracting fanfare. This tendency is confirmed by someone who would know. A former BSSM teacher says that students at the BSSM affiliate where he taught in England were specifically instructed *not* to say the name of Jesus or to share the gospel during their outreaches to pubs.[104] He says that he's heard from students at other BSSM schools that they, too, were instructed not to mention Jesus. Looking back, he finds it "weird" that they viewed what they were doing as "evangelism."[105]

Bad Press and Damage Control

In addition to testimonies by parents and former BSSM students speaking out about the church, Bethel has been the subject of other bad press.

There have been allegations, reported by the media, that Bethel churchgoers have delayed calling 911 during medical emergencies that resulted in life-altering injuries and even loss of life. According to one of those allegations, BSSM students tried "faith-healing" a man who fell off a two-hundred-foot cliff rather than call the police. The man, who reportedly lay bleeding and unconscious for six hours, is now a paraplegic. In another case, a fifteen-year-old boy who had an asthma attack in the streets of Redding suffered irreversible brain damage and died. The Bethel churchgoers involved in these incidents deny the allegations, and a lawsuit against one of the students who was at the cliff found her "not guilty." But shadows from the allegations still hang over the church.[106]

104. Virtue and Whatmore, "Former Bethel Prophecy Teacher" (7:00). The BSSM students believed they were practicing the spiritual gift of prophecy described in 1 Corinthians 12:10. They called their prophetic practices "spiritual readings" in order to attract non-Christian people to their tables. When a person stopped at their tables, these prophet-evangelists would speak whatever came to mind as a prophetic word for that person. The messages were always of the positive love-bombing type—for example, telling people that they were "great leaders" and would "have influence in their careers."

105. Virtue and Whatmore, "Former Bethel Prophecy Teacher" (8:00). Bill Johnson acknowledges that a past weakness of Bethel Church was that its people—though strong in performing miracles—were weak in following through with the gospel message after a miracle had occurred. But, Johnson says, this weakness was eventually addressed by leaders so that it no longer seems to be a problem. (See Johnson and Farrelly, "Episode 2" [1:00:00].)

106. For more information about these allegations, see Hensley-Clancy, "Meet the 'Young Saints.'"

Numerous media outlets have reported, with alarm, about its promotion of the "Seven Mountain Mandate"—a "strategy" God is supposed to have given Christians to "infiltrate" society and "take over the world."[107] Those words are straight from a book co-authored by Bill Johnson. One article warns: "The Seven Mountain Mandate is a manifesto for conquering all aspects of American life."[108] Reporters alert to this NAR agenda were alarmed when Donald Trump moved into the White House in 2016. It seemed that Bethel leaders, and miscellaneous other personalities with NAR credentials, had a new and powerful ally to help enact their agenda of world domination.[109] Concerns were further elevated when a Bethel worship leader announced his run for Congress in the state of California.[110] Meanwhile, back in Redding—where Bethel Church attenders make up 10 percent of the population—some citizens spewed outrage at Bethel's plan to make their city ground zero for the establishment of "God's kingdom."[111]

To quell reporters' fears, Bethel leaders backed off their militant language and shed their strident tone. They didn't really want to "control"

---

107. Wallnau and Johnson, *Invading Babylon*, chs. 2, 3, 5. We discuss the Seven Mountain Mandate further in chapter 3 and in our concluding chapter.

108. See Hardy, "The 'Modern Apostles.'"

109. See Hardy, "The 'Modern Apostles'"; Swan, "Trump, Evangelicals." During Trump's term in office, NAR leaders, including many from Bethel Church, gained unprecedented access to the White House. This was certainly due in part to their ministry connections with Trump's spiritual advisor, Paula White. White, a well-connected televangelist and prosperity gospel preacher, is known as an apostle who concurs with much Bethel Church and NAR theology. White announced in 2019 that she would pass direct leadership of her church, City of Destiny in Apopka, Florida (formerly New Destiny Christian Center), to her son, Brad Knight. She would then function as a governing apostle over the church. However, she said, she would not adopt the title "apostle" since a title like that may be misunderstood. She favored, instead, the designation "oversight pastor." Moments after her announcement, her son told her publicly, "You truly are an apostle. And the quicker that people realize that God has granted you favor and authority, and unique favor and authority, the better off that they'll be." In response, Paula White was seen nodding in apparent agreement. (See White and Knight, "We are streaming live!" [30:00].) So, although White does not speak of herself as an apostle, she apparently does view herself as one, as does her church leadership.

110. Parke, "Worship Leader Runs."

111. Vallotton, *Heavy Rain*, ch. 10; Hensley-Clancy, "Meet the 'Young Saints'"; Sandhu, "Bethel Comes Out Against LGBT." Redding citizens have expressed misgivings about Bethel's donations to the local police department, Bethel's buyout of local buildings, and Bethel's opposition to three bills (AB 2943, AB 2119, and AB 1779), all restricting so-called "conversion therapy" in California.

the world, but merely "influence" it.[112] They definitely didn't intend to "conquer" Redding.[113] But the media will likely remain wary, especially so long as words like these from Kris Vallotton, remain in print: "The Kingdom of God is not a democracy; it is a theocracy."[114] Any line between church and state in Bethel's envisioned "kingdom" is invisible, as far as secular journalists are concerned.[115] Who can disagree?

Some reporters insinuate that false prophecies pronounced by NAR prophets, including Bethel's Kris Vallotton, fueled the US Capitol riot on January 6, 2021.[116] One Christian scholar surmises that NAR prophecies supplied "a spiritual justification for the movement to overturn the election which resulted in the storming of the [US] Capitol."[117] Why think that? Answer: even after Joe Biden was sworn in as president, many people clung to prophetic pronouncements that Donald Trump would be elected to a second term.[118] Kris Vallotton did eventually acknowledge that his prophecy was mistaken. He posted a public apology on January

---

112. In their video statement, Bethel leaders explain that kingdom leaders will "rule" with the hearts of servants and that the coming kingdom will be so attractive that coercion will not be needed to get people on board. (See Johnson and Farrelly, "Episode 6" [41:00]. See also Wallnau and Johnson, *Invading Babylon*, ch. 1.) But saying they simply made a poor choice in their word usage is not enough to diminish concerns about this mandate, given that it fits into a larger dominionist theological framework, which we explain further in chapter 6.

113. Vallotton and Farrelly, "Episode 4" (1:07:00).

114. Vallotton, *Heavy Rain*, ch. 10.

115. Badash, "'How Theocracies Are Born.'"

116. Boorstein, "For Some Christians."

117. See Christerson, "How Self-Proclaimed 'Prophets.'" Brad Christerson is a Christian professor of sociology at Biola University in La Mirada, California.

118. While many know that Vallotton predicted Trump's win, not as many realize that—in the days after the election and prior to congressional certification of the results—Bill Johnson publicly shared his own "prayer directive" (which he says is the same as a "prophecy") that God would "rise up" in defense of those who prophesied Trump's reelection, thereby hinting that God would overturn the official election results. Johnson also "decreed" a second term for Donald Trump and said, "Some situations are simply one decree short of being changed"—as if to say that the probability of a second Trump term correlates with the number of believers who decree that it will happen. (A "decree" is similar to a declaration, and the terms are often used interchangeably. See chapter 6 for an explanation of "declarations.") We know not how Bill Johnson explains the failure of his own decree. (See Johnson, Wallnau, and Sheets, "The Victory Channel" [20:00].)

8, 2021—the day following congressional certification of the election results.[119] But Vallotton's apology came two days *after* the Capitol riot.

These various criticisms—from both the religious and the non-
religious—seem to have touched a nerve.[120] Recently, and uncharacteris-
tically, Bethel leaders have yielded to the need for some serious damage
control. This marks a major shift for a church whose self-described posture has been to "ignore" its critics.[121]

Over the years, Johnson has been quite clear that he has "no time
for critics," especially critics of revivals he approves.[122] He most certainly believes that their criticisms are the price he has to pay for his
answered prayer to have "more" of God. He teaches his followers that
they, too, must be willing to be seen as part of a fringe element. And
they must bear reproach for pursuing Bethel's vision to work miracles
and bring heaven to earth.[123]

Johnson has advised his flock not to read books by authors who do
not work miracles themselves.[124] And he has frequently vilified Bethel's
critics and theologians who do not share the church's exotic beliefs. He
tags them with negative labels: they are "fear-oriented theologians";[125]
"soul-driven" and "carnal" Christians who are under the influence of an
"antichrist" demonic spirit;[126] and "self-appointed watchdogs who poison the Church with their own fears."[127] Vallotton assails his critics with

119. Vallotton, "My Apology." Vallotton had previously posted an apology on November 7, 2020, suggesting that he had resigned himself to prophetic defeat in this
case. But the post with Vallotton's first *mea culpa* was soon removed. Perhaps he had
been wrong about being wrong. See chapter 4.

120. In addition to the critics we have cited in this chapter, a growing number
of Christian social media influencers, authors, and influential pastors have critiqued
Bethel and NAR leaders, including Mike Winger, Greg Koukl, Alisa Childers, Albert
Mohler, Melissa Dougherty, Doreen Virtue, Steven Bancarz, Marcia Montenegro, Steven Kozar, Justin Peters, Chris Rosebrough, Costi Hinn, and Andy Wood. See Hinn
and Wood, *Defining Deception*.

121. Vallotton and Farrelly, "Episode 4" (starting from the beginning of this
episode).

122. Johnson, *When Heaven Invades Earth*, ch. 10.

123. Johnson, *When Heaven Invades Earth*, ch. 15; Johnson, "Response to Glory
Cloud."

124. Johnson, *When Heaven Invades Earth*, ch. 10.

125. Johnson, *When Heaven Invades Earth*, ch. 7.

126. Johnson, *When Heaven Invades Earth*, chs. 4, 7.

127. Johnson, *When Heaven Invades Earth*, ch. 7. We note that Johnson also has
prayed that God would "prosper" his critics (those who speak against him in books

equally tough talk. He speaks of Christians who "don't walk in power," and deploys Paul's warning against them: "avoid such men as these."[128] All of this defamatory censure and name-calling has had one surprisingly salutary result. Their devotees have thereby been inoculated against criticism of the church and desensitized against legitimate concerns about Bethel teachings and practices.

It is remarkable, then, that—after a long habit of dismissing, demeaning, and demonizing their critics—Bethel leaders have lately admitted that refusal to engage "is actually probably costing us a little bit."[129] They haven't been very specific about what cavalier dismissal of critics has cost them.[130] But in June 2021, they did release a six-part series of videos on YouTube, called *Rediscover Bethel*. In these video discussions, Johnson and Vallotton respond to a wide range of criticisms.[131] In the comments sections for these discussions, many people express their appreciation to Bethel for producing the videos and some say the discussions have cleared up their concerns. But many other viewers sense that the moderator (Bethel lead pastor Dann Farrelly) throws softballs to Johnson and Vallotton, who in turn evade the substance of the criticisms.[132]

---

and on radio), meaning that they would experience the "blessing of the Lord" in every area of their lives. See Johnson, "Power of Confession" (34:00).

128. Vallotton references 2 Tim 3:1, 5. (See Vallotton, "The Gospel without Power.")

129. Vallotton and Farrelly, "Episode 4" (00:00). Curiously, in the *Rediscover Bethel* series, Dann Farrelly and Bill Johnson portray Bethel leaders as gracious and accepting toward Christians who disagree with them theologically. They profess to treat their critics with "honor." (See Johnson and Farrelly, "Episode 6" [104:00–1:18:00].) But the picture they paint here seems very much at odds with the rough language they use elsewhere when denouncing, without engaging, their challengers. See our further discussion in chapter 7.

130. Persistent and incisive criticism of the Bethel movement has eroded the power of shrieks and shrugs to maintain the upper hand. We might well wonder whether recent hints of sobriety in the face of criticism bespeak a measure of alarm within the ranks. Perhaps recruitment is down, or retention is fading.

131. For example, one discussion addresses the church's practice of "drunkenness in the Spirit." (See Johnson and Farrelly, "Holy Laughter.") Another responds to the widely circulated allegation that Bethel Church operates under the influence of a demonic "Kundalini spirit" that mimics the Holy Spirit. (See Johnson and Farrelly, Episode 3 [37:00]) And another defends Johnson's use and endorsement of the controversial Passion Translation of the Bible, something we address in chapter 8. (See Johnson and Farrelly, "Is the Passion Translation Heresy?")

132. In response to the video titled "Does Bethel Church Belong to the New Apostolic Reformation?," "Aaron Garza" writes: "I've watched three of these videos now. Man, I'm really trying, but it just doesn't seem like they're dealing with the substance

For example, one video, dated July 13, 2021, addresses the charge that Bethel is part of the global, growing, and controversial movement known as the "New Apostolic Reformation."[133] Johnson denies involvement with the movement, saying that he "didn't know what it was" until recently, and "we don't belong to anything of that nature."[134] But Johnson shows little interest in what it means to be NAR-like. So it's not clear what he's denying, or even what he thinks he's denying.[135] To make things more confusing—in another video from the same damage-control series—Vallotton, Johnson's right-hand man, seems more open to the idea that Bethel promotes a NAR theology.[136]

---

of the accusations against them." (See Vallotton and Farrelly, "Does Bethel Church Belong.") This sentiment is expressed in a meme shared by an influential Facebook page that is critical of the church. The meme shows a picture of American actor Robert Downey Jr. rolling his eyes. It reads, very Babylon Bee-like: "When Bethel asks Bethel some 'hard questions' about Bethel." (See Bethel Church and Christianity, "Bethel leaders made a video.") This is sensible satire. The friendly-fire format of *Rediscover Bethel* is not especially conducive to penetrating discussion. The presentations would be far more enlightening if actual critics, rather than a Bethel staff member, were invited to pose questions for Bethel leaders. Alternatively, the Bethel host might work a little harder at playing devil's advocate, pressing his interlocutors for precision and comprehensiveness. Or better yet, Johnson and Vallotton might craft answers in good faith sensitivity to the thorniest aspects of each challenge.

133. For a detailed treatment of this movement, see our book *A New Apostolic Reformation? A Biblical Response to a Worldwide Movement*.

134. Johnson and Farrelly, "Episode 6" (starting at the beginning). In *A New Apostolic Reformation?* we show that NAR is not some organization that churches do or do not belong to, but is a movement of churches and organizations who share specific beliefs. See the preface to this book, *Reckless Christianity*. When trying to ascertain whether a person or a group is NAR, the question is not whether any figure does or does not claim to be NAR. Very few claim to be NAR, and some actually deny being NAR. The determining question is this: does this person or that group hold to NAR beliefs and engage in NAR practices?

135. In *A New Apostolic Reformation?* we provide a detailed explanation of NAR beliefs.

136. Vallotton and Farrelly, "Does Bethel Church Belong." Vallotton expresses general agreement with core NAR beliefs but says that Bethel Church does not apply those beliefs in the extreme ways some critics have alleged. We demonstrate in the following chapters that Bethel is most certainly part of the New Apostolic Reformation because it promotes the core NAR belief that the church must be governed by present-day apostles and prophets who bring new revelation that is needed for the church to advance God's kingdom. We invite Kris Vallotton to state plainly any objections to our characterization and evaluation of the Bethel movement. And we invite readers to consider for themselves how radical or extreme the Bethel movement is.

Some viewers think the video series would not exist if something was not seriously amiss at Bethel Church. "Michelle" writes, "The fact that Bethel has to come out with this many videos defending themselves is already a problem."[137] What does it say about Bethel Church when a freight train of challenges and charges constrain its leaders to produce an extensive video collage of responses? What is it about the Bethel movement that attracts objections of the specific kind taken up in these videos? Considered collectively, the questions insinuate that Bethel Church is a mashup of the bizarre, the surreal, and the surreptitious.[138]

Yes, the many teachings and practices we've described in this chapter explain why Bethel Church has drawn so much attention and elicited a polarizing response. But love it or hate it, one thing about Bethel Church is certain: its influence is felt in churches worldwide. And it can't be ignored—first, because of its popularity, and second, because of its place in a broader movement that's transforming churches worldwide.

But Bethel can't introduce all their new teachings and practices into churches without first altering churches' authority structures. So, in the next chapter, we will look at the Bethel apostles and prophets who claim that they—not pastors—must hold the top posts.

137. For this comment, see Vallotton and Farrelly, "Does Bethel Church Belong."

138. Gurgling in the background are so many oddities that may never be addressed. For starters, what was Bill Johnson's role in the strange *Lord of the Rings* "prophetic" reenactment ceremony—complete with a wizard's cloak and staff—that was supposed to have banished the spirit of racism from the church? (Other influential "apostles" who took part in the ceremony, which was held at Bethel and broadcast on Bethel.TV, were Ché Ahn and Ed Silvoso. See Johnson, Ahn, Silvoso, and Barrett, "Gandalf Staff.") Also missing from the video archives is the explanation for Beni Johnson's teaching that Christians should try to wake "sleeping" angels—and why blowing a shofar was her preferred method for doing this. (See Beni Johnson, "Wakey, Wakey.") And nothing was said about Jenn Johnson's irreverent allusions to "farting contests" by angels around the throne of God. (See Jenn Johnson, "Black and White." Jenn is Bill Johnson's daughter-in-law and a senior worship pastor at the church. Her evocative comments implicating angels were made during a women's conference.) Jenn has described the Holy Spirit as a "sneaky" blue genie—"like the genie from *Aladdin*." (See Johnson, "Jenn Johnson—Holy Spirit Is Like.") To his credit, Bill Johnson has gone on record saying that he would not have used those words himself to describe the Holy Spirit. As far as he is concerned, they "crossed a line." Apparently, he spoke to Jenn Johnson about this and she said she was no longer using that analogy. (See Brown and Johnson, "Dr. Brown Interviews Pastor Bill Johnson" [24:00].) These are all reasonable questions that might be considered for future video installments. Imagine the ingenuity it would take to dignify each question with a serious reply.

—2—

The Bethel Apostles and Prophets Governing Churches

We embrace the biblical government of apostles, prophets, evangelists, pastors and teachers.

—Bethel Redding Website[1]

When the apostle, prophet, evangelist, pastor and teacher flow together and create a healthy governmental covering over the saints, this covering forms a kind of celestial vortex that creates strategic alliances with our heavenly allies. The implication of the word [the Lord gave me] was that the Lord was establishing the fivefold ministry in His Church, and that the outcome would be increased angelic activity manifested by extraordinary miracles rarely witnessed in the history of the planet.

—The prophet Kris Vallotton of Bethel Church[2]

---

1. Bethel Redding, "Our Mission."
2. Vallotton, *Heavy Rain*, ch. 5.

BILL JOHNSON WOULD HAVE us believe that bringing heaven to earth is what the church's mission is all about.[3] This apparently means that no sin or sickness or disease or depression or poverty, or anything else that can't be found in heaven, will be found on earth. But this mission can't be realized without the dramatic occurrence of miracles. (As we'll show in chapter 7, these must be miracles of unprecedented magnitude.) And that's the problem. Miracle-working power has been largely absent from the church—for at least a millennium and likely for nearly two millennia.

But why has the Christian church labored, for the most part, without the ministry of miracles? Why are miracles so infrequent? Should they not be both pervasive and impressive?

Johnson answers that miracles have been in abeyance because apostles and prophets have gone missing. These leaders hold the keys—the divine revelations—needed to equip Christians with miraculous powers to "pull" heaven to earth.[4] There must be a restoration of authoritative apostles—working together with prophets—to formal offices in church government.[5] Johnson believes that this restoration is now underway, as shown by increasing miraculous power at work in the church today. He writes:

> One of the evidences of this [restoration of apostles] is the rising "water level" for the miraculous in the church. This is just a byproduct of the restoration of that [apostolic] gift. Years ago, [the prophet] Bob Jones said, "I am waiting for the full release of the apostolic gift. I won't be able to work in the fullness of the miracle realm that God has called me to until the apostle is in his place." This was a man who experienced the supernatural in an astounding way. And yet, he said that there was an element

3. We explain Johnson's understanding of the church's mission in greater detail in chapter 6.

4. Johnson writes frequently about Christians' ability to "pull" or "release" heaven (or God's kingdom) into this world. See, e.g., Johnson, *When Heaven Invades Earth.*

5. Later in this chapter, we will show how Johnson views apostles as holding formal church offices. We note that some apostles, such as Randy Clark, believe that the office of apostle never ceased, and that those in the office who succeeded the original apostles were called "bishops." He also believes that other individuals through church history were "apostolic" in function, including Protestant Reformers such as Martin Luther and well-known missionaries such as Hudson Taylor and William Carey. So he says he does not believe (as C. Peter Wagner taught and as Bill Johnson seems to believe) that the office of apostle only recently has been restored to the church. (See Clark, "A Response," introduction.) Regardless, the fact remains that the office of apostle, in both name and function, has only recently gained growing acceptance in Protestant churches, and Clark does promote the present-day office and thus is NAR.

missing. He felt that, until the apostolic was restored, there was
a level of the miraculous that was not going to be released into
the world. New wine cannot be poured into an old wineskin.
The infrastructure of heaven needs to be in place to sustain a full
outpouring of God's presence.[6]

That "infrastructure of heaven" spotlights the essential, God-ordained
roles of apostles and prophets.

But this bold suggestion is controversial. Bethel leaders acknowledge the reluctance among Christians to accept apostles and prophets
who must play a leading role in fulfilling the church's mission. Johnson
states: "Apostle is a term that much of the Church rejects as they don't
believe the office still exists today." Kris Vallotton, the senior associate
leader at Bethel, recognizes this, too: "There's many people in the global
church today that don't believe that apostles and prophets are for today."[7]
In a series of messages given at Bethel Church in February 2020, he noted
with concern a rising "surge or a siege" against apostles and prophets in
the past twenty-five years. For a time they were becoming accepted, but
now "maybe a third of the questions I get on my own social pages has to
do with the validity of apostles and prophets."[8]

Johnson and Vallotton explain this reluctance with the suggestion
that some past individuals who claimed to be apostles and prophets had

---

6. Johnson, in the foreword to Ahn, *Modern-Day Apostles*.

7. Vallotton claims to have received several private visitations during which God
called him as a prophet to the nations. ("The Power of the Five-Fold Ministry," February 9, 2020 [30:00].) These visitations are important because, according to many NAR
leaders, prophets (as well as apostles) must receive a call from God during a private
encounter with him, in addition to receiving a public commission by church leaders.
Vallotton applies this requirement to prophets in another message also titled "The
Power of the Five-Fold Ministry." ("The Power of the Five-Fold Ministry," February
23, 2020 [20:00].) In his book *Understanding Spiritual Gifts*, ch. 18, Sam Storms argues that one requirement for being a present-day apostle includes "having received
a personal call from Christ or commission to the office (be it face-to-face, as with the
original Twelve, or by revelation, or by some other subjective means)." We do not
know whether Storms would consider himself to be a part of the New Apostolic Reformation, but he does acknowledge its existence and the controversy surrounding it.
He may wish to distance himself from this movement, but he quite openly teaches
that present-day apostles have an "office or position of authority to which one is called
by Christ Jesus himself." He also refers to apostleship as an "ecclesiastical position"
(*Understanding Spiritual Gifts*, ch. 17). Since the central feature of NAR teaching is that
present-day apostles must hold governing offices in the church, he is certainly in close
alignment with the NAR movement.

8. Vallotton, "The Power of the Five-Fold Ministry," February 9, 2020 (00:00).

failures, abused their authority, or were engaged in self-promotion and they gave the rest a bad name.[9] But the restoration continues: "We are in an hour where God is restoring the apostle in a way that reflects His beauty, while avoiding the pitfalls of prior generations."[10]

Bethel Church is ground zero for this controversial restoration.

The Apostles and Prophets Governing Bethel Church

The Bethel Redding website unabashedly declares, "We embrace the biblical government of apostles, prophets, evangelists, pastors and teachers."[11] This statement refers to a teaching in the New Apostolic Reformation known as the "fivefold ministry." This teaching is promoted heavily by Bethel leaders and is foundational to Bethel's theology.[12]

---

9. There is widespread acknowledgment by New Apostolic Reformation leaders that some who have claimed to be apostles or prophets had significant moral failures and abused their authority. See our comments in note 45 regarding the "Shepherding Movement." Also note that some who have claimed to be apostles or prophets have been caught in moral failures (or have promoted aberrant and even heretical doctrines), and yet they are still regarded as genuine prophets by many NAR figures, including Johnson. We discuss the case of Bob Jones in the next chapter. We describe William Branham's heretical teachings in Geivett and Pivec, *A New Apostolic Reformation?*, ch. 14. (We note Johnson's admiration for Branham and Jones in chs. 2, 3 and 7 of the present book.)

10. Johnson, in the Forward to Ahn, *Modern-Day Apostles*.

11. Bethel Redding, "Our Mission." This statement was featured on the Bethel Redding website for several years, until at least March 2022. (Sometime later, the site content was updated.) It is safe to assume their beliefs about church governance have not changed.

12. See, e.g., Johnson, *Open Heavens*, ch. 14; Johnson and Vallotton, "5-Fold Live"; Silk, "Setting the Five-Fold"; and Vallotton, "The Power of the Five-Fold Ministry," February 9, 2020. This last message was part of a monthlong series Vallotton delivered at Bethel titled "The Power of the Five-Fold Ministry." Take note that not all Christians who use the term "fivefold ministry" are referring to the NAR teaching that the church government consists of five governmental offices. Some Pentecostals and charismatics use the term to express belief that Christ has given the church the ministry *gifts* (not church *offices*) of apostle, prophet, evangelist, pastor, and teacher. The exercise of a gift must not be confused with NAR's teachings about offices. Not being aware of this critical difference has caused many people, unwittingly, to be susceptible to NAR teachings. Because of the origin and history of the term "fivefold ministry," and its customary association with NAR, we would caution people against using this term in a description of their own view unless they are indeed NAR. No one should be surprised if they are thought to be NAR as long as they insist on using this term or affirming the "fivefold ministry."

According to this teaching, Jesus, during his ascension, gave the church five ongoing governmental offices: apostle, prophet, pastor, evangelist, and teacher.[13] NAR leaders[14] believe this teaching is found in Ephesians 4:11–13, which states:

> And he gave the apostles, the prophets, the evangelists, the shepherds and teachers, to equip the saints for the work of ministry, for building up the body of Christ, until we all attain to the unity of the faith and of the knowledge of the Son of God, to mature manhood, to the measure of the stature of the fullness of Christ.

In the NAR interpretation of this passage, Jesus meant for church government to consist of apostles and prophets—not just evangelists, pastors (shepherds), and teachers. (Taken together with the NAR interpretation of 1 Corinthians 12:28, pride of place goes to the apostles and prophets.)[15] Furthermore, Jesus intended that their governing roles should continue until the church attains the maturity of Christ. Or, as Vallotton says, "until we all look like Jesus."[16] Regarding this lofty outcome, Johnson states, "We're not quite there yet."[17] Thus, governing apostles and prophets are still needed. Johnson concurs, saying, "These offices still exist, according to the will and design of God, the perfect creator. Their value and significance are becoming more and more clear, as the outcome spoken of by Paul cannot be accomplished any other way."[18] Most Protestant churches, however, are governed by pastors and elders, and they do not see a role for present-day governing apostles and prophets.

13. Ephesians 4:8 is cited by NAR leaders, together with Ephesians 4:11, to show that these offices are "gifts" Christ gave the church at his ascension. Thus, NAR leaders also sometimes refer to these offices as "ascension gifts" (though in their view, these gifts are offices). So, whenever a church leader makes reference to "ascension gifts," it is important to ascertain whether they are referring merely to spiritual gifts or to offices. (Bill Johnson refers to the offices. See Johnson, *Open Heavens*, ch. 14.)

14. A NAR leader is any leader of a group of people who accepts and teaches basic NAR beliefs. They may be recognized as an apostle within a network of organizations. They may be an elder in a Baptist church with a pastor who knows nothing about NAR.

15. According to NAR leaders, the words "first" and "second" in 1 Corinthians 12:28 show that apostles and prophets hold the first and second highest positions in church government. (See Geivett and Pivec, *A New Apostolic Reformation?*, ch. 5.)

16. Vallotton, "The Power of the Five-Fold Ministry," February 9, 2020 (6:00). In the context of Bethel teachings, to "look like Jesus" includes doing the miracles that Jesus did.

17. Johnson and Vallotton, "5-Fold Live" (3:00).

18. Johnson, *Open Heavens*, ch. 14.

To be clear, some non-NAR Protestant churches do refer to church planters or missionaries as "apostles." But they do not regard these apostles as governing leaders in the church. The same goes for Pentecostal and charismatic churches that refer to some individuals as "prophets" who are thought to have the spiritual gift of prophecy.[19] These types of "prophets" do not possess special governing authority. To clarify their stance, the Assemblies of God—the world's largest Pentecostal denomination with more than sixty-nine million members—has issued a position paper disputing the NAR teaching that churches must be governed by apostles and prophets.[20]

Contrast this view with Bethel's. Within the fivefold governmental structure there, Johnson is viewed as an apostle. Though he does not typically talk about himself this way, he is publicly referred to as an apostle by the church's other leaders. For example, during a Facebook Live session featuring teaching about the role of apostles in the church, Vallotton stated matter-of-factly, "Bill is an apostle." He went on say that although Johnson is viewed as an apostle at the church, they don't refer to him by that title. "We don't call you 'Apostle Bill.' We don't throw titles around." To this Johnson replied, "I prefer people just call me 'Bill,' honestly."[21]

Johnson's preference reflects a belief held by many in NAR that, when it comes to apostles and prophets, titles can be misleading since they can be brandished by any Joe Shmoe with a business card. In addition, titles aren't as important as functions. If someone is truly an apostle or prophet,

---

19. These usages of the terms "apostle" and "prophet" are vastly different, and much less controversial, than the NAR usages.

20. "Apostles and Prophets."

21. Johnson and Vallotton, "5-Fold Live" (4:00). And Senior Leadership Team member at Bethel, Paul Manwaring, called Johnson an apostle while teaching at Bethel Church about the role of apostles. He said of Johnson, "He's an apostle. He probably wouldn't necessarily say that. But we all know he is." A collective, knowing chuckle rippled through the room—punctuated by a woman's voice shouting, "Yeah!" Clearly, some in Manwaring's audience agreed with his assessment. (See Manwaring, "Apostolic" [5:00]). Johnson's ministry associates outside the Bethel bubble are equally clear about his apostolic role. This can be seen in the endorsements and forewords they've written for the front pages of his books, calling him a "true apostolic teacher" and, more explicitly, "Apostle Bill Johnson." (See Johnson, *The Way of Life* [updated 2019 edition]; Johnson, *God Is Good*.) The influential apostle Ché Ahn refers to Johnson as an apostle multiple times in Ahn's book *Modern-Day Apostles*; we note that Johnson himself contributed the foreword to Ahn's book. In doing so, Johnson tacitly accepts Ahn's weighty assessment. (See Ahn, *Modern-Day Apostles*, chs. 5, 12, 13.)

they need not demand that others use this title. If the title fits, one should not be rebuked for using it, nor should one deny that it applies.

Together, Johnson and Vallotton provide the apostolic and prophetic leadership for Bethel Church. Their tag-team approach to leadership is common in NAR. Apostles and prophets have complementary roles, and they will often hitch themselves together in ministry.[22] We should note, the three other "offices" alleged to be part of God's essential heavenly infrastructure—the evangelists, shepherds, and teachers—receive much less attention in NAR. Where one might rightly expect some kind of council of five offices working together on equal terms, what actually results is a *de facto* twofold ministry where the governing apostle and prophet are elevated far above the other positions. This elevation is fitting, they think, because both apostles and prophets—unlike the pastors, evangelists, and teachers—receive revelation from God. But Johnson, being the apostle at Bethel, reserves the decisive say. As he puts it, "I have the ability to lay down the final word, so to speak."[23] It's no secret that Johnson is head honcho at Bethel Church.

Yet it wasn't always this way.

Pastors Are the Problem

When Johnson became senior leader of the church in 1996, his ministry was, says Vallotton, a traditional "pastorate." But by the time Vallotton arrived in 1998 to launch Bethel School of Supernatural Ministry, Johnson's pastorate was well on its way to becoming an "apostleship."[24] Vallotton claims that Jesus told him directly that God intends for the church at

22. See Geivett and Pivec, *A New Apostolic Reformation?*, chs. 5, 11. Vallotton describes their divine partnership like this: "Bill is an amazing apostle with a mandate to reform the Church, and I am a prophet with a passion for cultural transformation." See *Heavy Rain*, ch. 5.

23. "Excerpts" (1:00). Immediately after making that comment, Johnson said he likes to make all decisions in consultation with Bethel's other leaders. He added that, "if God speaks to me absolutely and I know what we're supposed to do, I will listen to all input, but then I'll explain, if the counsel is contrary, I'll say, 'God said.' But you can't use that trump card all the time. I've done it, I think, twice since I've been here [at Bethel], in twenty-two years."

24. Vallotton, *Heavy Rain*, ch. 5. Danny Silk also recounts how Bill Johnson led Bethel Church from a traditional pastor-led church to an apostle-led church (*Culture of Honor*, ch. 8).

large to undergo a megashift in governance, from being pastor-led to being apostle-led, just as this had recently happened at Bethel.

> I was lying on the floor and praying one morning when the Lord spoke to me so clearly that it stunned me.
>
> He said, *There is a new epoch season emerging in this hour. Much like the Protestant Reformation, there is another reformation coming that will unearth the very foundation of Christianity. This move of the Spirit will absolutely redefine your ideologies and philosophies concerning what the Church is and how she should function.*
>
> I asked Him, *What will this transition look like?*
>
> He said, *My Church is moving from denominationalism to apostleships.*[25]

In other words, move aside, pastors—make way for the apostles. Apostles—not pastors—must sit at the helm of church government so they can lead the charge in transforming society.

> It is paramount in this new season that we clearly understand the apostles' mantle and mandate to transform culture. With this fresh revelation, we can lay governmental foundations in

---

25. Vallotton, *Heavy Rain*, ch. 1 (italics are Vallotton's). Vallotton explains that "moving from denominationalism to apostleships" includes moving from pastor-led churches to apostle-led churches. "I believe that much of the Church in our day is making a dramatic transition out of denominationalism and into apostolic families. This is often referred to as the emerging apostolic age. That is, in fact, the title of the next chapter. In the pages ahead, we will contrast the nature of traditional pastoral government with that of an apostolic structure. This will help us gain more insight into this new season we are entering" (*Heavy Rain*, ch. 4). Vallotton also shares the story of his encounter with Jesus in a message given at Bethel Church (see Vallotton, "Covenant Culture"). Note that Vallotton's teachings about God's transitioning of the church from denominational/pastoral governance to apostolic governance aligns with C. Peter Wagner's teachings (see, e.g., Wagner, *Changing Church*, ch. 2, which is titled "From Denominational Government to Apostolic Government"). The similarities between Vallotton's teachings and Wagner's teachings spoil the efforts of some to distance Bethel Church from the movement that Wagner dubbed the "New Apostolic Reformation." See chapter 3 of this book for our discussion of Michael Brown's attempts to do that. Brown is a radio host and founder and president of FIRE School of Ministry in Concord, North Carolina. His effort to clear his friends of any association with NAR is seriously amiss. Also, note that Vallotton has claimed that, in critiquing "denominationalism," he is not critiquing "denominations" (see Vallotton and Farrelly, "Church Denominations"). But given NAR/Latter Rain leaders' long history of critiquing the democratic system of church government found in denominations, it is certainly understandable that people would see his critiques of denominationalism in that same light.

the Church that empower, rather than restrain, today's apostles in their extraordinary calling.[26]

This calling to transform culture is very different from that of pastors, and it results in different priorities. Pastors shepherd their flocks by gathering people together, tending to their spiritual needs, and creating "safe places" for them. They are inward-focused and risk-averse.[27] In contrast, apostles value risk.[28] Vallotton writes, "Pastorates simply are culturally ineffective by design. Apostleships, on the other hand, are developed around the principle of training, equipping and deploying the saints to radically alter society."[29] He adds, "That is not to say that there is no place for pastors. But the key to making pastorates effective is that apostleships must empower pastorates. . . . The transition from a pastorate model to an apostolic form of church government does not eliminate the pastorate, but repositions it within the greater purpose of the apostolic mission."[30]

In late 2007, says Vallotton, Jesus spoke to him yet again about apostles and the pastors standing in their way.

> The Lord spoke to me and said, *Mankind has just entered into the new apostolic age. Yet the modern world has never experienced the true power of an apostle, because apostles have emerged in a pastorate form of government that restricts, constrains and often usurps their ability to govern.*[31]

But make no mistake: no one stood in the way of the apostles at Bethel. And in 2006—a year prior to Vallotton's word about pastors clogging up the pipes of governance at other churches—the apostleship at

---

26. Vallotton, *Heavy Rain*, ch. 4. Joseph Mattera, the convener for the United States Coalition of Apostolic Leaders, also writes about the need for apostles, not pastors or other church leaders, to take the lead in the church: "There is a reason why Jesus chose 12 apostles, instead of 12 prophets, teachers, pastors, and evangelists, to start His church. . . . The apostles are the entrepreneurs, multipliers, pioneers, church planters, movement catalysts, and generals called to possess territory for God." See Mattera, "Ten Reasons."

27. Vallotton, *Heavy Rain*, ch. 5.

28. Vallotton, *Heavy Rain*, ch. 2.

29. Vallotton, Kris. *Heavy Rain*, ch. 5.

30. Vallotton, *Heavy Rain*, ch. 5. On this same page, Vallotton teaches that an "apostleship" (or organization led by an apostle) may include multiple "pastorships" (i.e., churches) under its "covering." We discuss NAR teachings about "spiritual covering" later in this chapter.

31. Vallotton, *Heavy Rain*, ch. 5 (italics are Vallotton's).

Bethel blasted from the launching pad and expanded beyond governance of a single local church in Redding, California. Vallotton writes:

> In 2006 the Lord once again took Bethel Church to another level in the Kingdom. He gave us a word that drastically altered our governmental structure again. He said, *You have a church that has a movement, but the movement has outgrown the church. Consequently, your governmental structure, which was built for a previous season, is inadequate to lead in this epoch season. I want you to develop a governmental structure for a movement that has a church.*[32]

Bethel leaders took this prophetic word to heart. In response, they divided the church's apostleship into four separate categories: the local church, the movement, the school of ministry (the future Bethel School of Supernatural Ministry), and the church's businesses. As a result, Johnson and Vallotton have come to be regarded as "apostle" and "prophet" respectively, not only over Bethel Church, but over an international movement.

A Global Network and an Upline to Heaven

Today the two men lead an "apostolic family of leaders," which incorporates the senior leaders of churches and other Christian organizations beyond Bethel. Launched in 2018, the Bethel Leaders Network is an "apostolic network," with the oversight of an apostle (in this case Bill Johnson).[33] Other North American-based apostolic networks with a global reach include Harvest International Ministry (led by the apostle Ché Ahn), Global Awakening (led by the apostle Randy Clark), and Partners in Harvest (led by the apostle John Arnott).[34]

32. Vallotton, *Heavy Rain*, ch. 5. (Italics are Vallotton's.)

33. According to statistics provided in Bethel's 2019–20 annual report, the Bethel Leaders Network, launched in 2018, already had 855 members. See "Movement Impact."

34. It is important to note that the vertical structure of many apostolic networks has been described as "multi-level" and "pyramid-like," with an apostle overseeing a group of apostles, who oversee other groups of apostles, who oversee many churches and organizations (see, e.g., Christerson and Flory, *The Rise*, chs. 2, 3, 5, 6, 7). The Bethel Leaders Network does not share all the features of these networks. For example, unlike some apostolic networks, the Bethel Leaders Network does not allow churches to join the network or use Bethel's name; only church leaders may join Bethel's network. Yet it remains to be seen how this young network will develop. Bethel has tried

The Bethel Leaders Network was formed in response to a divine directive Vallotton says he received. This directive is referenced in an information packet for prospective members:

> I woke up in the middle of the night with a decree from the Lord. He said, "Create a place where leaders can belong." I came to our team and shared the word with them. Through my tears I said, "We must find a way to create a culture where leaders feel at home; welcomed, honored, celebrated, and known." Everyone was immediately on board. We realized that we needed to build a completely new structure to accommodate this divine mandate. After many more months of dreaming, the Bethel Leaders Network (BLN) was born.[35]

A major benefit touted for pastors and other leaders who join the Bethel Leaders Network is that they will "experience the blessing of alignment and spiritual covering with Bethel's apostolic five-fold ministry leaders, such as Bill Johnson, Kris Vallotton and other fathers and mothers of the Bethel and BLN family."[36]

This statement is loaded with lingo from the New Apostolic Reformation, which is immediately recognizable to movement insiders.

"Alignment" refers to the NAR teaching that all church leaders, including pastors, should be properly aligned with, or submitted to, the

---

different approaches to network structuring over the years. In 2005, prior to launching the Bethel Leaders Network, Bethel started another apostolic network called Global Legacy. Brad Christerson and Richard Flory speak of Global Legacy as a "horizontal" and "nonhierarchical" network because members were not required to make financial contributions to the network or participate in annual meetings or what have you. Any church or individual could join the network simply by creating an online profile on the Global Legacy website. Membership was free of charge. But the launch of the Bethel Leaders Network in 2018—after the publication of Christerson and Flory's book—signaled a shift toward a more "vertical"-style network, where the highest level of membership (called "Influence") requires leaders to submit applications, make annual financial contributions, adhere to a set of beliefs and core values, commit to specific standards, and complete an online course called "Introduction to Kingdom Culture," all within their first year of membership. For a more detailed comparison of horizontal versus vertical networks, see Christerson and Flory, *The Rise*, ch. 3. We note that, as of 2022, the Bethel Leaders Network had another level of membership which does not require an application and is horizontal in structure.

35. *Bethel Leaders Network Information Packet.*

36. *Bethel Leaders Network Information Packet.* Take note that—though Bill Johnson is the chief apostle at Bethel and Vallotton is the chief prophet—other Bethel leaders may also be viewed as apostles and prophets, albeit with less stature and authority at the church.

leadership of the "apostolic five-fold ministry leaders"—especially the apostles and prophets.[37] Thus, in the context of joining an apostolic network, leaders voluntarily submit to the authority of the network's apostles, along with its prophets. In the case of the Bethel Leaders Network, those apostles and prophets are Johnson and Vallotton, of course, along with the other "fathers" and "mothers" at Bethel. Note that the terms "fathers" and "mothers" are used frequently in NAR as euphemisms, insinuating familial intimacy and authority for spiritual leaders including apostles and prophets.[38] Those who come under their spiritual authority are referred to as their "sons" and "daughters."[39] By aligning with Bethel's apostles and prophets, church leaders come under their "spiritual covering," and thus they receive spiritual protection and blessings that trickle downward to them.[40]

And, of course, the blessings pastors receive from apostles trickle down to the pastors' respective flocks. Said another way, pastors are in the apostles' "downline," and churchgoers are in the pastors' "downline." Thus, to receive an apostle's blessings—the superlative blessings that God intends for all believers today—a believer must be sure to attend a church where the pastor is aligned with an apostle. It stands to reason that a believer who desires God's blessing will seek out a church that functions

37. NAR leaders frequently use the term "alignment" for a pastor's voluntary submission to the leadership of an apostle. It can also be used to describe a prophet submitting to an apostle or one apostle submitting to another apostle. See, e.g., Ahn, *Modern-Day Apostles*, ch. 8.

38. Bethel leaders defend their teachings about "fathers" and "mothers"—described in terms of "mentorship" (not heavy-handed leadership)—in Vallotton and Farrelly, "Episode 4" (32:00).

39. See these euphemisms employed in the *Bethel Leaders Network Information Packet*, 20: "We believe spiritual covering is accessed as individuals position themselves as sons and daughters to receive from spiritual fathers and mothers."

40. In his *Apostolic and Prophetic Dictionary*, Abraham S. Rajah defines "covering" as follows: "This refers to the spiritual covering or protection over a person or ministry. Covering is usually provided for by ministries or ministers who have matured in ministry and have been given authority in the spiritual realm by God. Apostolic and prophetic covering refers to the covering offered by apostolic and prophetic ministries. Covering can be obtained through submission under a ministry. It can also be obtained through service and obedience to the ministry or its leaders; also, by sowing financially and through prayer from the covering ministry. Only ministries who are matured and confirmed by God can qualify to cover others. This is because God has tested and proven them. Covering is used for two main reasons: (1) To receive the gifts, grace or anointing flowing from the head ministry and; (2) to receive protection from spiritual attacks." See Rajah, *Apostolic and Prophetic Dictionary*.

under the ultimate authority of an apostle. By parity of reasoning, you forfeit blessing if you do not align yourself with a church that has its own apostle or apostles, or that is aligned with an apostle higher up the organizational stream.

And the trickle-down blessings that pastors and their flock receive from apostles are nothing to sniff at. Bethel Senior Leadership Team member Danny Silk writes that miraculous signs and wonders are the norm in an "apostolic environment"—or in a church where the pastor is aligned with an apostle.[41] The expectations for signs and wonders in such a church are captured in an "offering reading," which is read aloud by congregants at Bethel before the offering plates are passed at the Sunday services. It states, in part[42]:

> As we receive today's offering we are believing You for: . . .
> miracles created
> Dreams and visions
> Angelic visitations
> Declaration, impartation, and divine manifestations
> Anointings, giftings, and calls . . .
> Provisions and resources.[43]

All these blessings and more will be enjoyed by those who submit to apostles—whether they submit directly as pastors, or indirectly through their pastors' submission to apostles.

---

41. Silk, *Culture of Honor*, ch. 2.

42. Silk, *Culture of Honor*, ch. 2. This ("Offering Reading #2") is one of four "Offering Readings"—or congregational declarations—Bethel Church congregants alternate reciting each Sunday morning prior to the passing of the offering plates. See Bethel, "Offering Readings." Another congregational declaration, "Offering Reading #1," reads in part: "As we receive today's offering, we are believing the Lord for: Jobs and better jobs, raises and bonuses, benefits, sales and commissions, favorable settlements, estates and inheritances." These offering readings reflect a prosperity gospel theology (which emphasizes God's desire for all believers to be wealthy and healthy) held by Bethel Church and promoted in Vallotton's book *Poverty, Riches, and Wealth: Moving from a Life of Lack into True Kingdom Abundance* (Bloomington, MN: Chosen, 2018). Vallotton defends his teachings by saying that his definition of prosperity includes not just money, but also successful relationships with God and other people. (See Vallotton and Farrelly, "Episode 5" [56:00].) To receive wealth and health in NAR, the practice of making "prayer declarations," such as those recited in Bethel's offering readings, is key, as we explain in chapter 6.

43. The declarations for "provisions and resources" line up with the church's prosperity gospel teachings.

The blessing of greater effectiveness in ministry is a particular draw to pastors, who want to see their churches succeed. They believe that, in aligning with apostles, they will be positioned in the splash zones of their apostolic "mantles," and thus they will experience the overflow effects of the apostles' special "anointings."[44] This teaching is reinforced frequently at NAR churches. For example, in a message Vallotton delivered at Bethel Church, titled "The Power of the Five-fold Ministry," he taught that those who are in a "covenant relationship" with an apostle or prophet can do everything that an apostle or prophet can do.

But what is a "covenant relationship" in the context of NAR teaching? It is a lifelong commitment (ideally speaking) to be in relationship with—and to serve—another individual, a spiritual leader, or a local church congregation. NAR leaders speak frequently of the need for believers to be in covenant relationships if they are to fulfill their destinies.[45] During his message, Vallotton referenced his own covenant relationship with Johnson, stating, "The apostolic well is not on my property. But I have all the water I need. . . . Everything Bill can do—in the apostolic way, I mean—I can do that, not because the well is on my property but because I'm in covenant relationship with someone who has one."[46]

44. A "mantle" in NAR refers to a "personal and unique anointing [i.e., supernatural empowerment], gifts [i.e., supernatural abilities] or grace [i.e., God's unmerited favor shown through the miraculous gifts of the Holy Spirit or an anointing]." See Rajah, *Apostolic and Prophetic Dictionary*.

45. Teachings about the importance of believers forming "covenant relationships" with their spiritual leaders were also central in the "Shepherding Movement" (also known as the "Discipleship Movement") of the 1970s and 1980s. This movement began in Fort Lauderdale, Florida, under the leadership of five charismatic leaders and gained as many as 150,000 followers. Many Christian leaders, including many contemporary NAR leaders, have criticized the Shepherding Movement's teachings and practices for being spiritually "abusive," indicated by excessive one-on-one control exerted by leaders over individuals' lives. See, e.g., Ahn, *Modern-Day Apostles*, introduction. NAR leaders stress the need to form covenant relationships with church leaders who provide a "spiritual covering" for their followers—though without the same formal, pyramid-like, organizational structure of the Shepherding Movement (a difference that does not fully ensure that abuse never arises).

46. Vallotton, "The Power," February 9, 2020 (30:00). That is what it means to be "apostolic" and "prophetic," according to Vallotton—people who are not apostles or prophets themselves, but are in covenant relationships with those who are. In his book *Destined to Win*, Vallotton describes the covenant relationship that he and Johnson have made with one another. Vallotton writes that God commanded him, "Make a covenant with Bill to serve with him the rest of your life!" (*Destined to Win*, 54–55). During another message at Bethel Church, Vallotton said, "And the Lord said to me, 'If you make a covenant with Bill to stay with him the rest of your life, I'll show the world

Indeed, being positioned to receive from an apostle's mantle is the key to spiritual success. Vallotton writes:

> If we don't understand how to recognize and *align ourselves under true spiritual authority*, we may build bigger armies, develop better strategies and buy more powerful weapons, but we will still lose. It just never occurs to us that if we support (honor) our leaders, we will inherit their victories. Yet this is how leadership is designed to work in an apostleship.[47]

Note Vallotton's use of the words "support" and "honor," which—in the context of Bethel teachings about a "culture of honor"—are loaded terms implying submission to apostles.[48]

And now we come to a real stunner. These folks presume to enlist the angels of heaven to achieve their epic aspirations. Yes, the trickle-down benefits from apostles to those in their downline include the authority to dispatch angels to carry out their prayer declarations.[49] Vallotton addresses this particular benefit of spiritual covering at length in his book *Heavy Rain*. In a chapter titled "Apostle Covering and Angel Help," he teaches that apostles' sphere of authority extends beyond the physical realm—their authority extends to the spiritual realm where it is recognized by angels.[50] And that authority over angels extends to those who come under the apostles' "covering." Angels at your behest. Vallotton writes:

> When we are under God's authority, which includes being under His appointed leaders, we also partner with the angelic hosts. . . . The angels heed the voice of His word. The Church is His voice that declares His word on earth. I don't think this means that

---

what I can build on apostles and prophets who live in covenant" (Vallotton, "Covenant Culture"). And Vallotton gives more background about how their covenant relationship began in Vallotton and Johnson, *The Supernatural Ways*, ch. 11.

47. Vallotton, *Heavy Rain*, ch. 3 (our emphasis). His words "align ourselves under true spiritual authority" indicate that alignment involves submission to a higher authority.

48. Recall our explanation of Bethel's "culture of honor" teachings in chapter 1.

49. See chapter 6 for our explanation of Bethel teaching about "declarations." Note that Mike Bickle also teaches that angels carry out believers' declarations or "prophetic decrees." (See chapter 6, note 24.)

50. Vallotton imagines support for this teaching in the letters John the apostle wrote to the seven churches in the book of Revelation. Vallotton says, "[John] was instructed to write the letters to the seven angels of the seven churches. Wow! What we learn from these letters is astonishing. We see that true apostolic ministries have angels assigned to them" (*Heavy Rain*, ch. 4).

we have to tell the angels what to do; I simply am saying that when we pray and prophesy in the name of the Lord, the angels hear the word of the Lord and go out to perform it. But we can only declare a word of the Lord that commissions and sends the angels *if we are under authority and therefore have authority.*[51]

Conversely, Vallotton employs a bizarre interpretation of 1 Corinthians 11:1–10 to teach that those who do *not* submit to apostles will not have their prayers answered.

> Do the angels always go out and answer everyone's prayers and prophecies? I don't believe they do because I believe they recognize people who are under submission to an apostolic mission. This is just a theory, but I think sometimes people pray the right prayers when they're in trouble, but their life isn't in submission and so the situation doesn't change. They want to have the benefits of the Kingdom, but they don't want to serve the King. I don't mean they're going to hell, but they haven't recognized and submitted to the people that the Lord has delegated to have spiritual authority in their lives. So, according to First Corinthians

---

51. Vallotton, *Heavy Rain*, ch. 4 (our emphasis). In that same chapter Vallotton writes, "It is my personal conviction that one of the essential elements that has ushered in this apostolic age is that the angels no longer recognize the performance-based authority of denominationalism. Paul teaches us that angels recognize true spiritual authority. In fact, it is the angels who answer our prayers and fulfill our prophecies. Angels are mentioned more than 180 times in the New Testament alone. Where have all the angels gone in the twenty-first-century Church? What would the world be like if we were suddenly to employ angelic help on this planet in the same degree as they did in the first century? I think that as we are reformed into this new apostolic wineskin, we are about to find out." Who, pray tell, "employed" angelic help in the first century, and to what end, and with what result? Despite all the references to angels and their actions in the book of Acts, not a single one reflects strategic use of angelic power at the behest of an apostle. On the contrary, angels, when they aren't giving words of encouragement and hope (Acts 1:10–11; 27:22–25), are the ones giving orders (Acts 8:26; 10:1–8, 30–32). On one occasion, when Peter was imprisoned and the church was earnestly praying for him, an angel of the Lord did come to his cell and deliver him. But we know that this was not in response to a prayer of declaration, for when Peter reached the house where the church was praying, nobody believed the servant's announcement that Peter was knocking at the door. They were gobsmacked to learn that Peter had been rescued. Peter himself thought he was dreaming, at first. Angelic rescue was not expected. (For the whole account, see Acts 12:1–19. We know from Acts 5:17–26 of a previous occasion when a group of apostles was delivered from prison in Jerusalem by an angel of the Lord; prayer for their deliverance is not mentioned.) Notice that in all cases recounted here, the angels speak directly to those present with whatever message is suited to the occasion.

11, they don't have a symbol of authority on their head and the angels hear their prayers and say, "Still not commissioned."

The Lord recognizes His own authority. You can say "in Jesus' name" until you're purple, but the angels aren't going to recognize you unless you have a symbol of authority on your head.[52]

Notice how he latches on to a reference to head coverings in 1 Corinthians 11:1–10 and attempts to make this passage a teaching about spiritual covering.

So angelic help and all other blessings that come from aligning with Bethel's apostles and prophets are dangled like a prize before pastors. And the *Bethel Leaders Network Information Packet* assures them they need not be in physical proximity to Johnson or Vallotton to receive from their special connection with God. That's because all the network's members will have the opportunity to "experience the inheritance of fathers and mothers who have forged a relationship with God and whose blessing transcends time and space."[53]

In addition to the church leaders who have aligned formally with Johnson and Vallotton through the Bethel Leaders Network, thousands of Christians around the world regard them as authoritative apostles and prophets. And they seek to tap into their anointings by reading their books, attending their conferences, and following them on social media. Some even seek to become prophets and apostles, themselves, by taking part in training events taught by Vallotton, Johnson, and other Bethel leaders—such as Bethel's School of the Prophets or classes in Wagner University, a NAR school where Johnson and Vallotton teach courses and are designated "core residential faculty."

What's in It for the Apostles and Prophets?

Spiritual protection and blessings flow from the apostles and prophets to their followers. But what's in it for those in the upline? Do Bethel's apostles and prophets have anything to gain from those who choose to align with them?

To be sure, the transactional relationship goes both ways. And the apostles and prophets receive two major benefits from providing a "covering": increased influence and treasure (also known as "money").

---

52. Vallotton and Johnson, *The Supernatural Ways*, ch. 16.

53. *Bethel Leaders Network Information Packet.*

The reach of Bethel's apostles and prophets extends to the churches led by pastors in the Bethel Leaders Network. That reach snowballs when an apostle joins the network, since an apostle may oversee multiple churches. Bethel leaders often receive invitations to speak at members' churches, opening doors for them to bring their teachings to new audiences. And during their travels to churches, they make beachheads in new cities where they can recruit other pastors and leaders to join the network—multiplying the network's members.

Of course, multiplied members results in multiplied funding sources. Those funding sources expand far beyond what would be possible outside an apostolic network. Sociologists Brad Christerson and Richard Flory, who researched apostolic networks for their book *The Rise of Network Christianity*, write:

> Recall that "spiritual covering" means power and authority flow down from the apostle, whereas financial support flows upward (and sometimes downward as well) along the pyramid. These multilevel vertical networks allow for much more expansive funding streams than would be possible in a single congregation. An apostle at the top of the pyramid receives donations from leaders and ministries that they may have very little contact with, thus multiplying their funding sources.[54]

Bethel leaders might object to the characterization of their network as a multi-level scheme. As we noted earlier in this chapter, Christerson and Flory did not characterize Bethel's apostolic network as multi-level; at the time their book was written, Global Legacy was a horizontal network, not a vertical one.[55] But since then, the Bethel Leaders Network has adopted a more vertical structure, albeit one that may not meet the criteria of a full-fledged multi-level organizational structure. However, while the Bethel Leaders Network does not include churches—and thus does not receive monthly donations from local congregations, as some other apostolic networks do—every leader who joins the network is required to make an annual financial contribution. In 2021, that amount was $1,980 per individual leader.[56] But the money stream doesn't end there. Christerson and Flory write about the other sources of revenue available to a network's apostle.

---

54. Christerson and Flory, *The Rise*, ch. 5.

55. See note 34 for explanations of horizontal and vertical networks.

56. *Bethel Leaders Network Information Packet.*

The pyramid also allows for heightened visibility and increased sales of books and other media from the apostle at the top of the pyramid, as well as increased registration at conferences where the head apostle is a marquee speaker. Leaders and ministries that are aligned with a particular apostle advertise and encourage their members to attend conferences when that apostle speaks, as well as purchasing books and other media created by the apostle.[57]

In short, when an apostle such as Bill Johnson headlines a conference, the cash flows as abundantly as the prophetic words and alleged miracles.

But the money motive is not the biggest concern for many of Bethel's critics. Most important to those who are concerned about Bethel's theology, the Bethel Leaders Network gives Bethel leaders a growing platform from which to spread the church's controversial teachings about apostles and prophets governing churches. We evaluate those teachings next.

---

57. Christerson and Flory, *The Rise*, ch. 5.

—3—

Evaluating the Bethel Apostles and Prophets Governing Churches

I encourage you to get as close as you can to the apostle
with whom you are aligned. What do I mean by being close? . . . It means submitting to his authority.

—The apostle Ché Ahn of Harvest
International Ministry[1]

When we come into submission to God's apostolic leaders, we are
known in heaven and feared in hell. True heavenly authority causes
angels to help us and causes demons to respect our influence.

—The prophet Kris Vallotton of Bethel Church[2]

SINCE THE RESTORATION OF apostles and prophets is the foundation of
Bethel leaders' teaching, it is important to understand what their scriptural support is. ⸺ the proof

---

1. Ahn, *Modern-Day Apostles*, ch. 8. We note that Bill Johnson provided the foreword for this book.

2. Vallotton, *Heavy Rain*, ch. 4.

In a previous book we explained the arguments and scriptures New Apostolic Reformation leaders have leaned on to support the movement's teachings about present-day apostles and prophets.[3] In brief, they argue that, since churches led by apostles are the fastest-growing churches in nearly every region of the world, they must have the "blessing of God" on them. And they point to three key passages: Ephesians 4:11–13; Ephesians 2:20; and 1 Corinthians 12:28.

In this chapter, we remind you that Bethel leaders likewise rely heavily on Ephesians 4:11–13 to support their teachings about apostles and prophets who govern churches. We also present some of their additional arguments from Scripture.

Following our evaluation of these arguments, we consider four specific defenses used by defenders of the present-day apostles to prove—contrary to their critics' portrayals of them—that they do not claim to exercise extraordinary authority. We show that these defenses fail, and that critics' concerns are justified.

Bethel Leaders Ramp Up Teaching Promoting Apostles and Prophets

Recognizing that many Christians do not approve of present-day governing apostles and prophets, Bethel leaders have vigorously asserted their defense of those two offices. And the prophet Kris Vallotton appears to be the front man chosen for this task.

Kris Vallotton and Bill Johnson Take to Facebook to Defend Present-Day Apostles and Prophets

On June 11, 2020, Kris Vallotton and Bill Johnson went live on Facebook to record the first of a five-part series of teachings about the fivefold ministry offices of apostle, prophet, evangelist, pastor, and teacher. The first installment focuses narrowly on the office of apostle. The video begins with a lament that many Christians deny the genuineness of the offices of apostle and prophet today. Johnson notes that these offices are rejected by others besides cessationists (i.e., those who believe the miraculous gifts of the Holy Spirit listed in 1 Corinthians 12, including speaking in tongues and prophesying, are no longer active in today's church). They

3. See Geivett and Pivec, *A New Apostolic Reformation?*, chs. 5, 11.

are also rejected by many continuationists (i.e., those who believe that the miraculous gifts *are* active today). Johnson says,

> There are a number who don't accept the gifts of the Spirit for today as we were saying—they don't think that healing is still for today, etc. But they also don't believe in the gifts of Christ, which is the fivefold [ministry offices]. But the strange thing is there's many who believe in the gifts of the Spirit but don't accept the fivefold.[4]

Vallotton then cites Ephesians 4:11–13 to show that *all* fivefold ministry offices—including apostles and prophets—have been given by Christ until the church attains spiritual maturity.[5] His point is unmistakable: since all Christians have not yet achieved maturity, apostles and prophets must still govern the church. His interpretation of this passage matches the standard NAR interpretation.

Vallotton's initial appeal to Ephesians 4:11–13 is to be expected, for it is the favored proof text for NAR teaching about apostles and prophets. Before turning to his second argument, he fields an objection—that, to be an apostle, one must have accompanied Jesus during his earthly ministry, since that was a requirement for admission to the company of Christ's twelve apostles (Acts 1:21). Vallotton replies, "Well, that would eliminate Paul. And there were 25 named apostles, actually named apostles, in the New Testament, including one woman named Junias."[6] Implication? In addition to the Twelve, there are individuals in the Bible who were called apostles, and these individuals had not accompanied Jesus; therefore, one could still be an apostle today. That one has not walked personally with Jesus is not disqualifying. We will evaluate this claim in due course.

Vallotton proceeds with his second argument—an argument from the lesser to the greater. He states that in the New Testament there is not a single person named as "pastor," though one is named as "evangelist," and five are named as "teachers." According to his calculations, twenty-five individuals are named as "apostles" and nine as "prophets." And yet, he observes, the church has no problem calling people pastors and evangelists today. How much more, then, should Christians be willing to accept

---

4. In Johnson and Vallotton, "5-Fold Live" (1:00). Note Johnson's teaching that the spiritual gifts are gifts given to individuals by the Holy Spirit and the fivefold leaders are gifts given to the church by Christ.

5. Vallotton, "The Power of the Five-Fold Ministry," February 9, 2020 (6:00).

6. In Johnson and Vallotton, "5-Fold Live" (3:00).

apostles and prophets? "So, it feels a little odd," he says, "that no one is saying, 'Well, there are no pastors today, there are no evangelists today,' when actually what the New Testament actually emphasizes—as far as titles, if we are going to call it 'titles'—is apostles and prophets."[7]

Thus Vallotton rests his case for contemporary apostles and prophets (in this instance, anyway). But this Facebook series is just one part of Bethel leaders' recharged campaign to defend their teachings about present-day apostles and prophets.

Vallotton Delivers a Sermon Series
Defending Apostles and Prophets

Four months prior to the launch of the Facebook Live series, Vallotton delivered a monthlong sermon series at Bethel Church titled "The Power of the Five-Fold Ministry." In one sermon, he confronts another objection to present-day apostles and prophets: the objection that apostles and prophets passed away. After citing Ephesians 4:11–13 in support of these offices, he states, "There is no passage, by the way, that says there will be no more apostles and prophets after the first century." In fact, he suggests, Scripture indicates the opposite. He argues that Jesus's warning about false prophets in the last days shows that there will be genuine prophets because "that would mean there should be some real ones."[8] Surely, if Jesus had intended to say that *all* prophets in the last days would be false, he easily could have said so. But he didn't. So, there must be true prophets in the last days, too.

Case closed? We think not. Vallotton's arguments falter under scrutiny. Let us explain.

---

7. In Johnson and Vallotton, "5-Fold Live" (4:00). Johnson argues, similarly to Vallotton, that the word "apostle" is used many more times than "pastor" in the New Testament; therefore, people should not fear individuals today who use the title "apostle." (See *Open Heavens*, ch. 14.)

8. Vallotton, "The Power of the Five-Fold Ministry," February 9, 2020 (6:00).

Evaluating Vallotton's Arguments for Present-Day Apostles and Prophets

Ephesians 4:11–13

Consider Vallotton's first argument, that Ephesians 4:11–13 makes it perfectly clear that Christ gave governing apostles and prophets to equip the church until the church reaches maturity. "If you just looked at Scripture, you're like, how could you not believe that?" Vallotton wonders aloud during the Facebook Live video.[9] Johnson nods in agreement and says, "yeah." They casually proceed as if the NAR interpretation of this passage is patently obvious and that their doctrine is firmly established. Not true.

The passage does mention five types of gifted leaders given by Christ to the church. But Vallotton and Johnson hold that this passage prescribes formal offices with a peculiar authority that most New Testament scholars would find startling, if not baffling. (Recall from the opening quotations in this chapter and chapter 2, for example, that angels are under the "heavenly authority" of apostles, and that a "celestial vortex" is formed when the five governmental offices are in place, resulting in "increased angelic activity" and "extraordinary miracles rarely witnessed in the history of the planet.") In addition, they insist that this passage teaches that these governing offices are in effect even now.

We're not convinced of these things.

First, the passage does not use the term "office" for these ministry functions. Certainly, Paul is not expressly teaching here that these ministry functions should be understood as special governing offices of the sort the Bethel leaders assert. That conclusion is inexplicably imposed on the text by Vallotton and Johnson. After a thorough search, we have yet to find any effort by Vallotton or Johnson to ground their claims in textual evidence. Instead, they pound the same old drum: Ephesians 4:11–13 *proves* that apostles and prophets, in each successive generation, must hold formal governing offices in the church. But to really make their case, they must *show* that NAR-type "offices" are what Paul had in mind here—it is irresponsible simply to *assert* that they are offices. Ephesians 4:11–13 is not the slam dunk that Vallotton and other Bethel leaders seem to think it is.

In addition, it is possible that Paul lists five representative ministry functions, without intending to be exhaustive (see, for example, the

---

9. In Johnson and Vallotton, "5-Fold Live" (2:00).

longer list in 1 Cor 12:28). Also, the first two functions Paul names in Ephesians 4:11 are said in Ephesians 2:20 to be "foundational." So the larger context of the epistle strongly suggests that apostles and prophets, unlike the other ministry functions, play a crucial role in founding the church, and the 4:11 passage may envision only these few foundational figures of the first century, even though other apostles and prophets are mentioned elsewhere in the New Testament. For the significance of other apostles, these other passages would need to be consulted.[10]

The Presence of "Other Apostles" in the New Testament

We have noted that before making his second argument for present-day apostles and prophets, Vallotton speaks to the objection that to be an apostle in the New Testament one had to have walked with Jesus. Vallotton observes that there were some apostles in the New Testament who had not walked with Jesus. Since being with Jesus evidently was not a requirement for them, the door is open for present-day apostles.

Well, yes and no.

All New Testament interpreters agree that there were, in addition to the Twelve, individuals who were designated "apostles." Pointing out a fact that is universally acknowledged does not establish Bethel's claim that present-day apostles must govern the church. Vallotton does not mention—perhaps because he does not know or because he does not consider it relevant—that scholars generally identify different *types* of apostles in the first-century church. The Greek word for "apostle" (*apostolos*)—like the English word "messenger"—could be applied in different ways, depending on a writer's purposes in designating the function of an individual. The word literally means "one who is sent." Those "apostles of Christ" who were sent directly by Christ—having received a personal commission from him—exercised distinct authority in the early church; this included the Twelve and Paul.[11] Though Paul did not "walk with Jesus" as the Twelve did, he did experience a personal appearance from Christ, at which time he received a personal commission from him. At that time, the Twelve were still living and were able to vouch for Paul's status as an apostolic equal (Gal 1:11–21).[12]

10. For details see chapter 7 of our book *A New Apostolic Reformation?*

11. Geivett and Pivec, *A New Apostolic Reformation?*, ch. 6.

12. We explain why this point is crucial in Geivett and Pivec, *A New Apostolic Reformation?*, ch. 9.

There were others who were not personally commissioned by Christ, namely, the "apostles of the churches." These apostles were sent out by churches as missionaries and as representatives of churches for particular tasks. Notably, they did not hold authoritative offices.[13] Anyone who claims to be an apostle today, lacking a direct commission from Christ, can only be regarded as an apostle of this lesser, non-authoritative type. But, of course, Bethel leaders are not arguing for non-governing apostles who fulfill special ministry functions at the behest of individual churches. Their apostles must call the shots in churches. They are the principle decision makers and they exercise the highest levels of leadership. They also receive critical new revelation. They should, therefore, meet the requirements stipulated for any "apostle of Christ." This includes a literal visitation from Jesus Christ that could be corroborated by witnesses with the stature of the Twelve. The only alternative is to invent an altogether new class of apostles, unknown to the New Testament.[14]

Argument from the Lesser to the Greater

Now back to Vallotton's second argument, from lesser to greater: the church accepts pastors and evangelists today, so why not also "apostles" and "prophets" since many more of them are referenced in Scripture?

This is supposed to be a rhetorical question. But notice that the question assumes that these are *governing* apostles and prophets, and it assumes that their chief function is not that of *founding* the church.

13. See Geivett and Pivec, *A New Apostolic Reformation?*, 67–74.

14. And this NAR leaders have done. Daniel Kolenda, for example, argues for a category of governing apostles with less authority than the Twelve, yet still possessing governing authority, along with miracle-working power. He refers to this alleged category as "five-fold apostles." See Kolenda, "Are There Apostles" (20:00, 2:00:00). Kolenda holds that the Twelve apostles had a uniquely authoritative and non-continuing role in the church, but he argues that the other apostles in the New Testament (including Paul) had a role in the church that carries on to the present day. (Kolenda identifies a class of apostles that includes Paul and others, but he unaccountably cedes to Paul something of a higher standing within this group.) So Kolenda, who falsely accuses all of his critics of being cessationists, acknowledges that the peculiar role played by the Twelve has ceased—which makes him a cessationist of sorts. Kolenda also argues that, since present-day apostles do not have the authority of the Twelve to write Scripture or to give authoritative teaching, criticisms of them are unfounded. He says, "Beyond some debatable semantics, this [i.e., what we have designated as NAR] is pretty conventional Christianity" (13:00). But we have demonstrated that NAR is anything but "conventional Christianity." And NAR leaders do present their revelations and teachings as authoritative, even if they don't use that word to describe them.

But what, exactly is his point? He's begging the question: Are *governing* apostles and prophets for today?

Suppose we grant that Paul, in Ephesians 4:11–13, addresses the present and ongoing structure of the church.[15] Then, this verse would support the continuation of apostles and prophets—in terms of church planters and prophetically gifted individuals—along with evangelists, pastors, and teachers.[16] (This would be to treat the apostles and prophets of 4:11 as inclusive of, but not limited to, the foundational figures of 2:20.) In any case, the passage speaks of apostles and prophets who fulfill certain *functions* in the church; it does not speak of individuals who hold formal, hierarchical positions in church government. And the fact that numerous people are named as apostles and prophets in the New Testament hardly makes the case that all those apostles and prophets had a *governing* function. As noted earlier, there were different types of apostles, including non-authoritative (and non-foundational) apostles. And there is no evidence that prophets ever held governmental offices in the church.[17] It remains, then, for Vallotton to show why we should suppose that all those who are named as apostles and prophets governed *and* that their governing offices were ongoing. This he has not done.

No Proof Text Showing that Apostles and Prophets Have Disappeared

What of Vallotton's point that there is no proof text for the disappearance of apostles and prophets? In the sermon we have cited, he observes that Scripture nowhere specifically states that governing apostles held a *temporary* office that eventually disappeared. But this does not negate what can be logically inferred. There *are* passages of Scripture describing the unique callings of, and criteria for being, the apostles of Christ.[18] And there is additional evidence that the calling of these apostles was unique

15. See Geivett and Pivec, *A New Apostolic Reformation?*, ch. 5; compare Arnold, *Ephesians*, 256.

16. However, we believe it is wise, and permissible, to avoid labeling anyone today an "apostle" because of the confusion that would inevitably result. Since NAR leaders promote present-day apostles who govern and receive critical new revelation for the church, other types of present-day "apostles" may inadvertently be seen as making the same claims of themselves.

17. Geivett and Pivec, *A New Apostolic Reformation?*, ch. 13.

18. Geivett and Pivec, *A New Apostolic Reformation?*, ch. 6.

and temporary. They did not appoint any new apostles to succeed them; rather, they appointed elders to a position of considerable authority and responsibility that is rather more fully delineated and apparently unexcelled (Titus 1:5; 1 Pet 5:1–3; Acts 14:23).[19] With the disappearance of the apostles of Christ, all of them known to have been eyewitnesses of Christ, leadership of the church is entrusted to elders. Of course, there would come a time when these apostles would be gone. Other arrangements for church leadership were needed, and provisions were made. Two points: First, the apostles make much of having been eyewitnesses (Acts 1:21–22; 3:15; 4:20; 10:39–41; 13:31). And Paul vigorously defends his apostleship and clearly viewed himself as having a level of authority equal with the Twelve (2 Cor 11; Gal 1:10–24; 2:11–14). The Twelve also recognized his authority as equal to theirs, though his commission differed (Gal 2:1–10). Second, it's significant that John, thought to be the last living apostle, was entrusted with the lately revealed prophecy we have in the book of Revelation, and that its message is intended to address concerns that no doubt would have been uppermost in the minds of saints living at the time. John was the sole remaining apostle, and he was old. His departure, we suppose, was imminent. What did God have in store for his church? How were they to carry on in the absence of Christ's apostles? John's message is given in part to prepare them for this circumstance.

Recall, as well, that there are other types of apostles, gifted in the ministry of church planting as the church expands globally. There is every reason to believe that this gift continues to be called for and is exhibited today. But this is not the sense of ongoing apostleship that our Bethel friends are most intent on defending.

And, contrary to Vallotton's claim, Jesus's warning about false prophets in the last days does not prove that there will also be genuine prophets. It simply proves that there will be false prophets; it says nothing one way or the other about whether there will be genuine prophets. Vallotton argues weakly from silence when he claims that Jesus could easily have said all last-days prophets would be false. At most, what Jesus actually said leaves open the *possibility* of future genuine prophecy. More to the point, even if Jesus's warning did logically entail that there would

19. Matthias was appointed as a replacement for Judas after his early death, but once his vacant office was filled and the circle of Christ's twelve apostles was completed, there was no attempt to replace any of the apostles of Christ after their deaths (Acts 1:24–26).

definitely be genuine prophets (which it does not), this would not be evidence that those prophets would hold formal, authoritative offices. And it would be no help in determining when legitimate prophets could be known to have arrived. There could, as well, be a lengthy hiatus between Jesus's warning and the eventual emergence of genuine prophets, whereas false prophets might be at large during the entire interval leading up to the last days. Let us at least take Jesus at his word and believe that there will certainly be false prophets in the last days, and let us weigh every prophetic claim today in light of this warning. For after all, Jesus also said that even the elect will be vulnerable to the blandishments of false prophets, since they will impress with signs and wonders (Matt 24:24).

So much for Vallotton's case from Scripture that apostles and prophets must govern today's churches.

Bethel Leaders Dodge Their Critics' Challenges to Their Use of Scripture

Bethel leaders generally do not acknowledge the above challenges to their arguments from Scripture. Instead, they routinely change the subject and assert that the reason many Christians do not accept governing apostles and prophets is because of the past moral failures and spiritual abuses of people claiming to be apostles and prophets.[20] That certainly is *one* reason to be cautious when our contemporaries claim to be apostles or prophets, and we can thank NAR leaders for reminding us (however inadvertently) of the need to test such an extraordinary claim. But this is by no means the primary reason for suspicion, since most simply do not see support in Scripture for present-day offices of apostle and prophet, as defined by Bethel)

Let us not pass too quickly over this matter of spiritual abuse by people who have claimed to be apostles and prophets. Some readers may recall that Jim Jones—of the infamous "Jonestown Massacre" in 1978—claimed to be a prophet when he led more than nine hundred of his followers to commit suicide. Our mention of Jones in this connection has special relevance: unbeknownst to many, he participated in the post-World War II "Latter Rain" movement, the theological forerunner to NAR. The influence of Latter Rain teachings on Jones—especially those

---

20. Johnson and Vallotton, "5-Fold Live" (2:00). Vallotton says, "Maybe people sometimes react to abuse by developing a new theology as opposed to just dealing with the abuse itself." This remark is ironic, since it is NAR leaders who have manufactured a new theology—not their critics.

of the "prophet" William Branham—appears to have persisted throughout his life.[21] With or without a connection to the Latter Rain movement,
contemporary claims to have apostolic and prophetic authority have
proven to be effective tools of deception among unsuspecting people. In
South Africa, apostles and prophets have reportedly abused their followers in terrible ways: spraying deadly insecticide in their faces, commanding them to eat grass, and raping them.[22]

To be clear, we are not suggesting that Latter Rain teachings were
responsible for Jones's evil actions. Nor are we suggesting that today's
NAR leaders would necessarily use their authority for such heinous ends
as Jones or the prophets and apostles from South Africa we mention. But
we would be derelict if we did not point out the serious abuses that have
occurred at the hands of so-called apostles and prophets and the very
real possibility of more such abuses. Again, Jesus's words of warning were
meant to alert us to abuse by false prophets and encourage caution, which
begins with the demand for evidence of authenticity.

As another case in point, consider the spiritual abuses that came to
light in 1991, committed by the influential US prophet Bob Jones, who
has been very influential on NAR leaders. Jones, who was accused of
"encouraging women to undress in his office so they could stand 'naked
before the Lord' in order to receive a [prophetic] 'word,'" admitted to
abusing his prophetic office.[23]

---

21. Collins, *Jim Jones.* Branham—despite his heretical teachings—is revered as a
powerful prophet by many of today's NAR leaders, including Johnson and Vallotton.
See Johnson, "Stewards of Revival"; "False Teachers"; Geivett and Pivec, *A New Apostolic Reformation?*, ch. 14. According to former Bethel elder Mark Mack, Bill Johnson
asked all the elders to read three books about William Branham during Mack's three-
year term as an elder (showing just how important a figure Branham was to Johnson).
(Mack and Kozar, "Behind the Scenes" [41:00].) So it pays to consider the nature of
Branham's legacy for a scurrilous cult leader like Jim Jones, and be wary of dangers
that may be latent in his influence more generally. NAR admiration for a false teacher
like Branham is disconcerting, to say the least. We also note that Jim Jones's wife and
Jim Jones himself stated that he used religion as a means to promote a Marxist political
agenda. See Carter, "9 Things You Should Know about Jim Jones." Whether he actually believed Latter Rain theology or merely used it to further a political agenda, his
followers viewed him as a prophet and obeyed him as such, allowing them to become
victims of spiritual abuse. For more information about Branham and Bethel leaders'
admiration for him, see chapter 7.

22. "South Africa's 'Doom Pastor'"; "Eight More Women"; Kaya, "Apostle Arrested
for Rape."

23. See Geivett and Pivec, *A New Apostolic Reformation?*, ch. 14.

And we have not yet referenced the abuses that are less overt and have received less media attention. The sheer volume of the stories we have been told personally speaks to the reality and extent of this problem. Many have shared with us the harm they experienced because they or a loved one felt pressured to obey the words of an apostle or prophet—whether that involved breaking off contact with family members, working countless hours for a church leader without pay, or going on mission trips at the risk of piling up debt.[24] Former church members and church staff also have described being pushed out of churches after questioning an apostle.[25] In many of these cases, the apostles and prophets are not known outside their own cities or smaller networks, so their alleged mistreatment of churchgoers have not received much notice. Nevertheless, these churchgoers report experiencing real injury.

The potential for abuse by present-day apostles and prophets is greater than the potential for abuse by other church leaders because they claim to speak directly for God and to exercise unique authority. And there is no independent means of verifying the veracity or authority of their claims to be apostles and prophets.

Four Defenses Mounted on Behalf of Present-Day Apostles

In defense of present-day apostles (and the prophets working with them), some have said that these leaders have been misrepresented by their critics and that most do not claim to exercise unique authority. One of these individuals is Christian radio host and author Michael Brown, a leader in the charismatic movement and one of the most vocal defenders of present-day apostles and prophets.

Defense No. 1: The Apostles Do Not Claim Any Special Authority

During a podcast debate about the New Apostolic Reformation with the authors of this book, Brown challenged the notion that NAR is a major,

---

24. We have received numerous stories over the years from many people who have contacted us. We share some of those stories in our books *God's Super-Apostles* and *Counterfeit Kingdom*.

25. Pivec, "Is It Too Late"; Lewis, Rowntree, and Miller, "Fired from NAR Church."

worldwide movement, and he denied that the leaders we have identified as NAR hold to the extreme teachings that many, including ourselves, associate with the NAR movement.[26] He said the idea that apostles and prophets are "constantly looking for new revelation . . . that's just bogus."[27] He also said the apostles he knows—including Bill Johnson and Ché Ahn, whom he mentioned by name during the debate—function similarly to church planters and the leaders of denominations and do not claim any special authority. He said:

> Every so often in 46 years of ministry I've run into someone that thought that they were some modern-day apostle that had special authority over the church. Every so often. But I've never heard it from any of the people involved nor would anyone I know think like that. . . . And you'd never hear them get up and speak of apostolic authority to do this or that any more than you'll hear a pastor talk about leadership authority that they have.[28]

26. We document the massive size and influence of the NAR movement and its key teachings in Geivett and Pivec, *A New Apostolic Reformation?* Note that not all leaders we have identified as being NAR accept the NAR label, though some do embrace it, including the apostle Ché Ahn. (See Ahn, *Modern-Day Apostles*.) Yet specific leaders Ahn associates with NAR, in his book, include leaders we associate with NAR as well: Bill Johnson, Heidi Baker, and Mike Bickle.

27. Alisa Childers Podcast, "NAR" (26:00). (We will argue to the contrary in the next chapter. And, in chapter 7, we show that Bethel leaders teach that God will give the church new revelation, in the form of divine strategies, to find solutions to the world's most perplexing problems.)

28. Alisa Childers Podcast, "NAR" (22:00). Starting at about thirty-one minutes, Brown acknowledges that "yes, Peter Wagner felt that he was operating under certain apostolic authority" during a commissioning ceremony for Todd Bentley he led at the Lakeland Revival in Florida in 2008. Brown also said, "What happened in Lakeland was a mess. . . . That was an embarrassment. It was ridiculous." (Soon after the ceremony, multiple moral failures on Bentley's part became known, causing many NAR leaders to the view the ceremony as an embarrassment.) But what Brown doesn't say is that, during the ceremony, Wagner also presented Ché Ahn, John Arnott, and Bill Johnson as apostles possessing special authority. Wagner went so far as to compare their role in the commissioning ceremony to events in the book of Acts when James, Cephas, and John extended the right hand of fellowship to Paul and Barnabas. He also referred to them as "apostolic pillars of today's church." Notably, Ahn, Arnott, and Johnson did not show any objection to Wagner's characterization of their apostolic authority but appeared to accept it, and they participated fully in the ceremony. (See Geivett and Pivec, *A New Apostolic Reformation?*, 209–11.) So, one may wonder why Brown acknowledges that Wagner "felt that he was operating under certain apostolic authority," but he seems to let Ahn, Arnott, and Johnson off the hook, though they also allowed themselves to be publicly depicted as apostles with special authority.

Yet Brown's portrayal of these present-day apostles conflicts with the words of those apostles and of prophets working with them. Consider, for example, these words from Ché Ahn, one of the apostles Brown appeared to defend during the debate. Addressing the revelation being received today by apostles, including himself, and by prophets, he writes: "I'm constantly trying to hear what the Spirit of God is saying to the church at large. It is one of the reasons why I host a prophetic conference once a year. We hear from prophets in our stream such as Patricia King, but I also want to hear from prophets who are not in our stream. Every year, we invite prophets from other streams to come. We've had Kris Vallotton and Bobby Conner. They are not part of HIM, but we want to hear from them. Let me encourage you to regularly inquire of the Lord and to surround yourself with godly prophets so that you can receive revelation."[29] Yet, recall, that Brown called the notion that apostles and prophets are constantly looking for new revelation "bogus."

And, to Brown's statement that the apostles and prophets he knows do not claim any special authority, recall that in chapter 2 we noted the explicit language Vallotton uses to depict the authority of apostles, strongly indicating a special governing authority that exceeds that of mere pastors.

> In late 2007, the Lord spoke to me and said, *Mankind has just entered the new apostolic age. Yet the modern world has never experienced the true power of an apostle, because apostles have emerged in a pastorate form of government that restricts, constrains and often usurps their ability to govern.*[30]

Elsewhere in his book *Heavy Rain*, Vallotton highlights one thing that sets apart the unique authority of apostles from that of pastors. While contrasting pastor-led churches with apostle-led churches, he writes that "miracles happen in pastorates, but they are infrequent and inconsistent."[31] An apostle's special authority includes an ability to work miracles that simply is not as available to pastors.

Conspicuously, Vallotton also directly challenges the comparison of apostles with church planters—a comparison Brown made during the debate—stating, "For the most part, the Church has only empowered apostles to plant churches. But apostles were never meant merely to be

29. Ahn, *Modern-Day Apostles*, ch. 18.

30. Vallotton, *Heavy Rain*, ch. 5. (Italics are Vallotton's.)

31. Vallotton, *Heavy Rain*, ch. 5.

church planters: they were called to be world changers!"[32] This stands in direct contrast to Brown's statement.

Special apostolic authority extends beyond the churches' walls, according to Vallotton. For apostles also possess authority in the angelic realm; this is a "heavenly authority" with considerable scope. "When we come into submission to God's apostolic leaders, we are known in heaven and feared in hell. True heavenly authority causes angels to help us and causes demons to respect our influence."[33]

Clearly, Vallotton's apostles enjoy unique authority—an authority that even angels and demons acknowledge. And he's not the only one whose elevated view of present-day apostles stands in stark contrast to Brown's more modest portrayal of them. The apostle Ché Ahn teaches that apostles have "extraordinary authority." In his book *Modern-Day Apostles*, in a chapter titled "Apostles Have Extraordinary Authority," Ahn notes that apostolic authority functions at a "different level" than pastoral leadership. One difference, according to Ahn, includes the authority to perform miraculous signs and wonders. He writes: "I want to talk about the authority that God has given apostles because, of course, apostles move in signs and wonders, too. Paul performed extraordinary miracles in Acts 19. There's a different level of authority."[34]

Apostles also have a special authority to wage spiritual warfare and make "apostolic decrees," according to Ahn. In chapter 6 of the same book, he claims that apostles' decrees can even alter the weather—such as a decree that the prophet Lou Engle told the apostle Ahn to make, that allegedly caused it to stop raining during a 2002 stadium event in Seoul, South Korea, titled The Call. Ahn recalls,

> Lou and I understood that prophets hear from God, but apostles are the ones to make the decree. So, I said okay. I went up to the microphone and I said, "Brothers and sisters, wherever you are, just stop walking and let's just agree and pray that it will stop raining." There are 60,000 witnesses of what happened next. I prayed a very simple prayer, and within a matter of minutes—not ten minutes, not fifty minutes, I'm talking about less than maybe three, four minutes—it stopped raining. The clouds parted and a beautiful sunray came right down on the stadium for the rest of the day. The most amazing thing about it is that it was raining all around the stadium but not over the stadium.

32. Vallotton, *Heavy Rain*, ch. 5.

33. Vallotton, *Heavy Rain*, ch. 4.

34. Ahn, *Modern-Day Apostles*, ch. 5.

And don't forget the "apostolic decree" made at Bethel Church by Ahn, Bill Johnson, and Ed Silvoso to cast out a spirit of racism in the global church (referenced in chapter 1, note 138).

Ahn also teaches that the authority of apostles is not limited to the church. It can extend to the state and society. He refers to this extension of authority in a book that is endorsed by Johnson and bears a foreword by Johnson. Johnson's endorsement of the book is important because it indicates agreement with its major teachings. In this book, Ahn writes: "We must also recognize that apostles have the authority to govern on all seven mountains of culture, whether it's in the church, government, education, business, media, arts, and entertainment, or family."[35]

Those familiar with NAR teaching will know that Ahn's reference to the "seven mountains of culture" affirms a controversial revelation concerning the "Seven Mountain Mandate"—a strategy for taking dominion over the whole of society. According to this revelation, NAR apostles must rise to the top of society's seven major institutions, called "mountains": government, media, family, business, education, church, and the arts. Once they hold the top posts in each domain, they can cast out the high-ranking demonic spirits (called "territorial spirits") that are believed to rule over these institutions.[36] They find support for this strategy in an odd amalgamation of Old Testament Scriptures: Israel's mandate to conquer seven nations before it could enter the promised land (Deut 7:1), and the prophecy of Isaiah 2:2: "Now it shall come to pass in the latter days that the mountain of the LORD's house shall be established on the top of the mountains."[37] This mandate is closely related to the Bethel teaching that God has given apostles different "spheres" of influence or "metrons" to govern.[38] Importantly, their assigned metrons may be inside or outside the church, including the dominant sectors of

35. See Ahn, *Modern-Day Apostles*, ch. 15.

36. Vallotton is one NAR leader who believes that casting out of territorial spirits is pivotal to fulfilment of this mandate (see Vallotton and Farrelly, "Episode 4"). For more information about this mandate, see Geivett and Pivec, *A New Apostolic Reformation?*, ch. 15.

37. Isaiah 2:2 is cited in the New King James Version in Wallnau and Johnson, *Invading Babylon*, ch. 2. See also Geivett and Pivec, *A New Apostolic Reformation?*, ch. 15.

38. Vallotton, *Heavy Rain*, ch. 4. Bethel teaching about metrons is consistent with NAR teaching—including the teaching of C. Peter Wagner—that apostles have different, limited "spheres" of authority. See also Geivett and Pivec, *A New Apostolic Reformation?*, ch. 5.

society.[39] The notion that apostolic authority reaches to the realm of politics is especially controversial, for it raises concerns that NAR apostles are working to establish a theocracy, something they adamantly deny.[40] Yet even Christ's original apostles governed only within the church. So, remarkably, present-day apostles are claiming an authority that even the Twelve and Paul did not have.

Wrapping up, Vallotton and Ahn's descriptions of present-day apostles' authority—an authority to work miracles not available to pastors and an authority that extends to major societal institutions, as well as the angelic realm—conflict sharply with Brown's claim that they do not claim any special authority.[41]

---

39. According to Vallotton, the metron of some apostles may encompass their own city or a specific industry, such as music or business. See Johnson and Vallotton, "5-Fold Live" (6:00).

40. See these denials, for example, in Wagner, *Dominion!*, introduction, and Kolenda, "What is the N.A.R.?" (45:00). Instead, they say they want the church to exert influence over society through democratic means and the preaching of the gospel. Kolenda also defends the Seven Mountain Mandate, but suggests it's merely about Christians having a positive influence in the major sectors of society. In this he neglects to mention the controversial aspects of this mandate, including the crucial role of apostles and the casting out of territorial spirits.

41. It is true that many NAR apostles have stated that they do not view themselves as having the prominence or stature of Christ's twelve apostles who were eyewitnesses of Jesus and were personally chosen by him. See, e.g., Ahn, *Modern-Day Apostles*, introduction. And virtually all present-day apostles agree that they cannot write new Scripture. Yet, despite their words, they do claim similar authority and functions to Christ's apostles, including the authority to govern the church and to give critical new revelation. But, as we've argued in *A New Apostolic Reformation?*, those functions were the prerogative of the apostles of Christ (ch. 6). And, as we've shown in this chapter, influential present-day apostles claim even greater authority than Christ's original apostles, including the authority to govern beyond the church—within societal institutions and even in the angelic realm. In contrast, the authority of the apostles of Christ did not extend beyond the church or include the authority to make declarations that dispatch angels. Furthermore, the revelations of many present-day apostles—though not physically affixed to the pages of the Bible—are treated on a par with Scripture, as we will show in chapter 5. And finally, it's not clear why they would deny that they could be recipients of scriptural revelation today, since that would seem to require an argument for cessation of a specific form of revelation that we have not seen developed in any of their work.

Defense No. 2: The Apostles Do Not Teach a Hierarchy

During the same debate, Brown also had this to say in defense of the teachings of his apostle friends: "There is hardly some hierarchical thing where everyone has to be under an apostle. It exists here and there. But it is hardly a large-scale thing." And regarding Bethel specifically, he states:

> Their emphasis, as I understand it, [is] the importance of having
> fathers and mothers in the faith and having honor and respect
> for one another as opposed to you must come under the apostle's
> authority and by coming under the apostle's authority you will
> be blessed. I've never heard any such teaching from them, nor
> am I aware of that coming from others.[42]

Brown also says—regarding the teaching about the necessity of all churches having an "apostolic covering"—that he rarely hears of it.[43] That teaching is not common in apostle-led churches, according to Brown. But we will show that Bethel leaders do, in fact, teach a hierarchy, and it is closely tied to their teachings about apostolic covering.

Bethel Teachings Promote a Hierarchy

In the last chapter, we recalled Johnson's claim that, as an apostle, he has the "final word" at Bethel. We note that his claim undercuts an oft-repeated defense made by himself and other NAR leaders, namely, that apostles are not operating in a hierarchical role.[44] The point is reinforced in their use of certain metaphors, like this one by Vallotton: "We need the entire fivefold ministry working in harmony together like a beautiful orchestra, with the apostle being the conductor."[45] And the hierarchy

42. Alisa Childers Podcast, "NAR" (26:00).

43. Alisa Childers Podcast, "NAR" (57:00).

44. See, e.g., Johnson and Vallotton, "5-Fold Live" (2:00). Johnson states, "It's thought of as a hierarchy—it's like to call yourself an apostle or evangelist or whatever is a self-appointed title of esteem. And it's just not. Paul said the apostle is the least of all."

45. Vallotton, *Heavy Rain*, ch. 5. Vallotton has used another, equally telling, metaphor. Speaking to a group of leaders at a Youth with a Mission base in Chico, California, he said that God, speaking directly through him, told the leaders, "We're moving from a round table to a rectangular table" (Vallotton, "God has called"). He went on to decipher the message for the leaders. He told them it meant that, in God's kingdom everyone is not equal; there are leaders, whom others must submit to. Though he didn't name apostles in that moment, his message was clear: the church government

teaching is even more explicit in a book written by Bethel Senior Leadership Team member Danny Silk. In *Culture of Honor*—which is required reading for students in the Bethel School of Supernatural Ministry—Silk teaches about God's "order of priority" in church government, where the offices of apostle and prophet are "first" and "second."[46] Silk also says that the church at large has empowered the wrong leaders (i.e., pastors, teachers, and administrators) to be the "primary leaders." He refers to this improper empowering of pastors and others as "the critical flaw" in current church structure and government and he states that "the roles and relationships of leaders are out of order according to Scripture." He also writes the following (in a section tellingly titled "Governmental Shifts"):

> Once again, one of the primary things we must confront is the issue of order in the House of God, and we do that with Scripture:
> *And God has appointed in the church, first apostles, second prophets, third teachers, then miracles, then gifts of healings, helps, administrations, various kinds of tongues.*
> I'm still not sure how this got passed over for so many years in our approach to governing God's church. I am not sure how Paul could make it clearer than "first . . . second . . . third." Where did that go?[47]

Silk's teaching, that apostles must sit at the top of church government, could not be more straightforward.

Controversially, Silk acknowledges that the church government he describes is non-democratic:

> I realize that the kind of government I am describing, in which there is a clear order of priority in the various roles, is difficult to understand and embrace in American culture. Our American style of democratic government is designed to keep all its governing members in a system of checks and balances, where each branch of government must be accountable to another branch so that no one legislator, judge, or president can gain control of the whole government. I understand that and value this in an earthly model. Nonetheless, it is there in the Scripture: "first apostles, second prophets, third teachers. . . ." I believe that

is a hierarchy. That teaching is made more explicit in his book *The Supernatural Ways of Royalty*, in which he gives the same metaphor of the rectangular table and explains that it is about "levels of honor" in the "government of God" and that apostles and prophets are the highest spiritual authorities (see chs. 10 and 16).

46. Silk, *Culture of Honor*, ch. 2.

47. Silk, *Culture of Honor*, ch. 8.

much of the Church has ignored this Scripture and has been using templates gleaned from earth's governors in an attempt to replicate Heaven. But only Heaven's template can reproduce Heaven on the earth.[48]

Clearly, apostles top out a hierarchy, according to Bethel leaders' teaching, despite any denials to the contrary. And this perspective is undergirded by Bethel's teaching about "apostolic covering"—a teaching we documented in the last chapter but one that Brown says he rarely hears.

It is true that Bethel leaders do not deliver their teachings in such bald terms as, "You must submit to us or else." Nonetheless, submission to the authority of apostles and prophets as a requirement for receiving divine blessings is emphasized by them, often couched in their teachings about "alignment" and "covering," as we showed in the last chapter. And sometimes they are quite explicit, as we see in this statement from Vallotton: "Because of how authority works, when we come into submission to an apostolic leader and are commissioned to serve their mission, we can operate with their authority. That is probably the broadest and most fundamental level of our spiritual covering."[49]

Once these teachings have been accepted by their followers, Bethel leaders don't always need to push hard with overt calls for submission; their followers have already stepped in line with a posture of submission.

Other NAR Leaders Associated with Bethel Also Teach a Hierarchy

Bethel leaders are not alone in promoting a hierarchy led by apostles. Teachings about apostolic authority, submission, and spiritual covering are also emphasized by NAR leaders outside Bethel who are nevertheless closely associated with Bethel leaders.

Ché Ahn, in his book *Modern-Day Apostles*, writes:

> I encourage you to get as close as you can to the apostle with whom you are aligned. What do I mean by being close? It means carrying the heart of the apostle. Following him as he follows Jesus. *It means submitting to his authority.* The closer you are with your apostle, *the more you will receive the blessing of the corresponding grace and favor that comes with the alignment.*[50]

48. Silk, *Culture of Honor*, ch. 2.

49. Vallotton and Johnson, *The Supernatural Ways*, ch. 16.

50. Ahn, *Modern-Day Apostles*, ch. 8 (our emphasis). Recall that Bill Johnson provided the foreword to this book.

Of course, this is hierarchical. And there's more. Ahn holds that apostles, not pastors, are the highest authority in the church. He recalls a conversation he had with the NAR apostle C. Peter Wagner that made him realize that apostles are the highest authority in the church and, thus, that they are the key to revival.

> As we study this verse [1 Cor 12:28], it is clear that it is God who has given extraordinary authority to apostles.
>
> As we read in Matthew 28:18, "All authority has been given to Me in heaven and on earth," and God has delegated that authority first to apostles.
>
> One day, Peter Wagner and I were discussing the various prayer initiatives in support of the 10/40 window. These initiatives were led by pastors and the vision that was given to the pastors. There were a lot of prayer gatherings, and in some places revival did break out, especially in developing nations, but in America it didn't happen.
>
> Peter said, "The reason why I don't think it happened is because pastors are not the ones with the highest level of authority in the church. It's apostles. Now if apostles came together and prayed, what would that look like?"
>
> I realized that wherever revival has broken out it was because an apostle led that revival. This was true whether it was John Arnott in Toronto; John Kilpatrick in Brownsville; or me in Pasadena at Mott auditorium, where we had nightly meetings for three years; or Bill Johnson in Redding, California. It was true for a lot of places. I believe the reason why Harrisburg, Pennsylvania and Life Center is another hot spot in America is because of the apostolic leadership of my good friend Charles Stock.
>
> When apostles take the initiative, when they pray, and when they bring others in the five-fold ministry together, things do shift. These revivals are just a few examples of the extraordinary authority that God has given to apostles.[51]

Driving this teaching of hierarchy home, Ahn describes the relationship between pastors and apostles as one of submission. "Apostles provide a spiritual covering to pastors who are in their sphere of influence and who agree to submit to the authority of the apostle."[52]

(Potential for abuse of authority (forming a cult, unquestioning following)

51. Ahn, *Modern-Day Apostles*, ch. 5.
52. Ahn, *Modern-Day Apostles*, ch. 15.

Clearly, Bethel leaders and their close associates do teach a hierarchy, even though Brown insists that they do not.[53]

Defense No. 3: The Authority of Apostles Is Kept in Check by Elder Boards

[handwritten note in margin: I how did it work? was it work?]

Some defenders of present-day apostles argue that the apostles could not possibly exert extraordinary authority since their churches are governed by boards of elders to whom they are accountable. So, how could they exercise excessive authority and yet submit to such a governing board? This particular defense was made by Elijah Stephens, who teaches classes for the Bethel School of Supernatural Ministry and acts as an unofficial spokesman for Bethel and an apologist for Bethel and NAR teachings.[54] During an interview with Remnant Radio titled "The New Apostolic Reformation: Is Bethel NAR? Questions for Bethel Leadership," Stephens asserted that Bethel isn't part of NAR since, after all, Bill Johnson must answer to an elder board.

> Bethel doesn't run under this "the apostle is in charge of everything." We have an elder board. And so, we take members of our fivefold ministry—Bill, Kris—and they operate in their office on that elder board. . . . And so, as a church that has an elder board, one of the things you need to know is that if he [Bill Johnson] falls into heresy, if there's financial misconduct, they can fire him. And so, it's not this absolute authority thing. According to our bylaws, he is able to hire staff. But our board of

---

53. In a video of a show on GOD TV, Ché Ahn tells Brown he believes Brown is an apostle in the body of Christ who carries "authority." Ahn then asks Brown to make "decrees" and "declarations" for revival. Brown does not correct Ahn during the show or dispute that he is an apostle and proceeds to make several declarations based on his presumed authority as an apostle. See the video embedded in this article by Churchwatcher, "Watch Dr. Michael Brown." But we note that, during a public dialogue with the authors of this book, Brown denied that he considers himself an apostle. See Alisa Childers Podcast, "NAR" (48:00). In light of Brown's conspicuous acquiescence to Ahn's portrayal of him, it's understandable if some are confused about how Brown truly views himself.

54. Stephens has taken part in multiple interviews defending Bethel Church's teachings and practices. He clarified that he was not sent by the church but acted in an unofficial capacity. He also raised more than $130,000 to produce a documentary, titled *Send Proof*, purporting to present medical evidence for alleged miracles and featuring interviews with NAR leaders including Bill Johnson, Heidi Baker, and Randy Clark. See our concluding chapter (including note 20) for more about this documentary.

elders, essentially, sets budget, and they control the doctrine, as a board. So, it's not just one guy going up there and saying, "Hey, the Bible teaches this." . . . And so, it's got the protective layer of eldership going on that doesn't fit the criteria for NAR.[55]

Stephens has also characterized Johnson's relationships with the other elders as one of "mutual submission."[56]

But the fact that Bethel has a board of elders does not mean that Johnson doesn't exercise unique authority. Nor is his authority necessarily diminished by the fact that these other elders have some measure of authority in relation to Johnson. Here are three reasons why.

All Tax-Exempt Charities in the United States Have Boards, but They Don't Necessarily Negate an Apostle's Authority

First, it is not surprising that Bethel Church would have a governing board made up of multiple individuals. It's not surprising because all nonprofit, tax-exempt charities in the United States are required to have a board of directors. In other words, Bethel would not be able to obtain tax-exempt status and to receive donations that are tax-deductible for the church's donors if it did not have a board of directors (a board known at Bethel as the "Council of Elders"). Take note that Harvest International Ministry—the apostolic network led by the apostle Ché Ahn—is also registered as a nonprofit, tax-exempt charity and, thus, has its own board of directors. Yet recall what Ahn unabashedly teaches about the "extraordinary authority" possessed by apostles; he is one of the most outspoken proclaimers of such authority. So—despite Stephens's defense of Bethel—having a board of directors/elders does not preclude claims by an apostle to possess extraordinary authority.

Bethel's Elder Board Faces Charges of Nepotism

Second, concerns have been raised about the makeup of the Council of Elders at Bethel and, in particular, concern about conflicts of interest. News reporter Annelise Pierce is a graduate of the Bethel School of Supernatural Ministry and a former member of Bethel Church. In her

---

55. Lewis, Rowntree, and Stephens, "The New Apostolic Reformation" (22:00).

56. Lewis, Rowntree, and Stephens, "The New Apostolic Reformation" (28:00).

article "The Really Big Business of Bethel: Part 2—Who's in Charge,"
Pierce shares the results of her research into the composition of the board
in July 2019, when her article was published:

> Interestingly, the Board [of Directors/Council of Elders] is
> comprised of many of the same members as the Senior Leader-
> ship Team it oversees, with almost half (five out of 11) of its
> members holding positions on both groups. Bill Johnson serves
> as Senior Elder on the Board that oversees him and decides his
> salary, while his close friend Kris Vallotton is his associate Se-
> nior Associate Elder on the Board. Eric Johnson, Dann Farrelly
> and Charlie Harper also all play a role on both teams, de facto
> supervising themselves. Other members of the Board of Direc-
> tors include Andre Van Mol, Mike and Julie Winter, Josh and
> April LaFrance, Gene and Nell Nicolet, and Ron Rock. These
> eight independent members of the Board/Elders are also less
> independent than one would expect; six of them are in a spousal
> relationship to another member of the Board/Elders and Andre
> Van Mol is the supervising physician to Nurse Practitioner (and
> Redding Mayor) Julie Winter.[57]

Of her findings, Pierce concludes: "Is nepotism alive and well at Bethel
Church? Obviously. What about cronyism? No doubt at all."[58]

Thus, serious doubt hangs over the claims that Bethel's elders will
keep Johnson in check and would fire him, if necessary.

Would a Board Ever Fire an Apostle?

Third, setting aside questions about alleged nepotism at Bethel, having a
board still doesn't diminish Johnson's authority. He could theoretically be
fired, but would he be?[59] Would the other elders fire the apostle? Pierce

57. Pierce, "The Really Big Business of Bethel Church, Part 2." According to Bethel's
website, the members of the board of elders, at the time of this book's writing, are Bill
Johnson, Kris Vallotton, Dann Farrelly, Charlie Harper, Steve Moore, Josh and April
LaFrance, Ted and Michelle Thompson, Mike and Julie Winter, and Andre Van Mol.

58. Pierce, "The Really Big Business of Bethel Church, Part 2."

59. According to Bethel Church's bylaws (as approved February 13, 2018), if the
Council of Elders votes to remove the senior elder (i.e., Bill Johnson) then the council
must notify an Apostolic Intervention Committee (consisting of five previously selected Christian leaders from outside of Bethel) and this committee is authorized to
restore the senior elder's position after holding a hearing. If the committee does decide
to restore the senior elder's position, then all the elders who voted to remove the senior
elder must submit their resignations. (See Bethel Statement of Purpose.) This provision

asks, "In a ministry where God himself speaks to the top leader or leaders, who are their Board/Elders to tell them otherwise?"

Good question.

It's a rhetorical question. And two sociologists, Brad Christerson and Richard Flory, would likely concur with the implied answer. They found, through intensive research into apostle-led churches, that included interviews with leaders and participants in many such churches, that, "although most leaders and their ministries have boards to maintain their nonprofit status, it is clear that if an apostle thinks a particular course of action is what God wants, there is rarely any resistance to that declaration from the board."[60] These researchers' findings line up with Johnson's own words, cited in the last chapter: "If God speaks to me absolutely and I know what we're supposed to do, I will listen to all input, but then I'll explain, if the counsel is contrary, I'll say, 'God said.'" Johnson does not view his relationship with the other elders as one of "mutual submission." It does not matter that his spokesman, Elijah Stephens, says otherwise.

Most important, to go against the apostle—even for one of the elders—would risk loss of the personal blessing and protection that results from being under the apostle's "covering." Opposing God's chosen leader—in this case, Bill Johnson—is *hazardous*, according to explicit Bethel teaching.[61]

---

in the bylaws raises a question: When it comes to firing the senior elder, are the elders at Bethel Church truly the ultimate authority or are the members of the Apostolic Intervention Committee the ultimate authority? And who are the members of this committee? Are they apostles (as the name of the committee implies)? If so, would they be sympathetic to restoring the position of a fellow apostle?

60. Christerson and Flory, *The Rise*, ch. 6. Former Bethel elder Mark Mack says he did not seek to re-up his term as elder after serving for three years because he believed the board was becoming a group of yes-men. See Mack and Kozar, "Behind the Scenes" (47:00).

61. The apostle Randy Clark is a NAR leader who defends present-day apostles with the claim that they do not exert legally binding authority. Their authority is not derived legally; rather, it is "relational." That is, apostles develop relationships with those they lead and seek to build consensus. See, e.g., Lewis, Rowntree, and Clark, "The NAR Debate!" (27:00). But we say that it's the relational exploitation of their authority that is the problem, and all the more so because people would generally and quite naturally be maximally deferential toward an apostle.

Defense No. 4: Apostles Do Not Interfere in Local Churches

One other defense of Bethel's apostles is that they do not interfere in the decision-making of the local churches who join the Bethel Leaders Network. So any notion that Johnson is flexing his apostolic muscles in churches is totally off base. Stephens has said:

> When you're inside the Bethel network . . . there's no authority to make a decision at a local level other than, like, let's say, you sit down with Bill and he's like, "Here's some advice as a pastor." But every pastor has that relationship with leaders, and you can reject it and still be a part of the network. . . . And so, trying to use heavy-handed authority to achieve an agenda is just outside of the scope of what we're trying to do as a movement.[62]

Stephens's statement does seem to be supported by what is said in an information packet for the Bethel Leaders Network. This packet delineates what the network does not do for local churches.

BLN covering does NOT include:

- Direct, personal connection or access to Bethel Senior Leaders.

- Personal or organizational direction, management or oversight from Bethel leaders. (We expect every BLN member to have a healthy support system in place to successfully manage their organization's finances, ministry, and conflict resolution.)

- Vetting or endorsement of a church. BLN is a place for leaders to belong.[63]

If the apostle is "hands off"—as the information packet describes—it seems like he is prevented from telling a pastor what to do in his or her own church.

Lest there by any confusion, it appears that the Bethel Leaders Network does not have the organizational mechanisms to provide formal governance for local churches. And, apparently, Bethel leaders generally do not seek to tell pastors what to do when it comes to hiring, firing, and other matters related to governing their own congregations. Even if they had the desire to do so, they likely would not have the time to provide such oversight. There are too many leaders in the Bethel Leaders

---

62. Lewis, Rowntree, and Stephens, "The New Apostolic Reformation" (26:00).

63. *Bethel Leaders Network Information Packet.*

Network for direct governance of their churches by the apostles to be feasible. In that respect, then, the Bethel Leaders Network is no different from other large apostolic networks that state they "will not violate the autonomy of each local congregation."[64]

Notice, however, that nothing impedes a Bethel leader from *advising* a pastor. Recall that Stephens himself expressly allows for this possibility, although he suggests that any advice Johnson might give would simply be the advice of one pastor to another. Peer to peer. Words from an equal. Stephens even says that Johnson's advice could be rejected by a pastor, and the pastor would still be permitted to maintain membership in the Bethel Leaders Network. But it is a gross mischaracterization to portray Johnson's advice as somehow on a par with the advice of any other pastor. Within the Bethel Leaders Network, Johnson is simply not viewed as a pastor among pastors; he's also considered an apostle with a rightful claim to divine authority. The same goes for Bethel's other apostles and prophets. And Bethel leaders have made it clear that yielding to such apostles and prophets is necessary. Pastors are moved to join the Bethel Leaders Network chiefly because they recognize the apostles' and prophets' authority and they desire to "align" with it and come under the apostles' and prophets' "coverings," thereby receiving all the attendant benefits. Could a pastor disagree with Johnson and rebuff his advice? Sure, he could. But *would* he? That's highly unlikely. He'd undoubtedly forfeit the divine blessing that was initially sought through membership in the Network.

Let us not forget Bethel and NAR teaching about "covenant relationships," which we explained in the last chapter. This term, laden with special hierarchical significance, appears twice in the Bethel Leaders Network information packet—signaling to pastors who join that they are entering a committed relationship with Bethel leaders and other members of the network.[65] The specific nature of the pressure to remain in the Network—as with any other apostolic network—may not be readily

64. Geivett and Pivec citing Harvest International Ministry, in, *A New Apostolic Reformation?*, ch. 5.

65. *Bethel Leaders Network Information Packet.* The packet states that, in joining the Network, church leaders will have the opportunity to "experience mutual covering, strength, and support by partnering in covenant relationships with other BLN members." Also, under "Core Values," the packet states: "In covenant relationships, we purposely grow our capacity to trust and be trusted as we empower and confront one another in order to live out who we truly are." A high level of accountability is enjoined on members.

apparent to those who view NAR from the outside. But it is surely apparent to those who are versed in Bethel and NAR teachings. And if a NAR pastor did choose to leave the Bethel Leaders Network, and thereby remove himself or herself from Johnson's covering, that pastor would likely feel the need to find some other apostle to align with so as to enjoy his or her protective covering and its attendant blessings.

In short, apostles could exert considerable influence in local churches, despite what their defenders have said. But let us bear in mind that the main reason apostles must govern, in NAR teaching, is not so they can micromanage local churches—it is so they can bring new revelation needed by the church to develop miraculous powers for realizing God's kingdom on earth. So even if Bethel apostles do not directly interfere with the decision-making of local churches, they still have an influence on those churches' teaching and practice through their new revelations. Apostles' and prophets' revelations are delivered directly to churches when they speak at churches in the Bethel Leaders Network. And their revelations are channeled to far-away members of the Network through media, books, and other teaching materials promoted by the Network. It is primarily for the purpose of delivering these new revelations that apostles and prophets must govern the church.

We turn in chapter 4 to examine their claims to give crucial new revelation.

—4—

The Bethel Apostles and Prophets Giving New Revelation

The call of the apostle is to release the blueprint of heaven
into the earth, equipping the saints to join the vision.

—Bill Johnson[1]

AT BETHEL AND OTHER NAR churches, apostles and prophets have been restored to a governing capacity that God has intended all along.[2] They can now provide Christians with the new revelation needed to transform society, take dominion, and "bring heaven to earth."[3]

The apostle Bill Johnson writes about the new revelation God has entrusted to apostles, referring to it as "the blueprint of heaven."[4] Bethel

---

1. Ahn, *Modern-Day Apostles*, foreword. Note that Johnson wrote these words in the foreword he provided for this book.

2. We describe what NAR leaders mean by apostles who "govern" churches in chapter 2.

3. Recall from chapter 1 that "bringing heaven to earth" is Bill Johnson's (and Bethel Church's) revisionist understanding of the Great Commission. We discuss this understanding in detail in chapter 6.

4. Ahn, *Modern-Day Apostles*, foreword. Note that Johnson wrote these words in the foreword he provided for Ahn's book.

Senior Leadership Team member Danny Silk refers to the revelation apostles have received as "blueprints."

> It is as though God Himself has given blueprints to certain individuals to reproduce Heaven on the earth. Along with this blueprint, the anointing of the apostle contains a quality that stimulates and draws to the surface the diverse anointings in the people around him. As those around the apostle begin to manifest their own unique anointings, it creates an environment of "sub-contractors" who help the "master builder" to realize the blueprints of Heaven.[5]

Note that Silk writes of "blueprints," a "master builder," and "subcontractors." This is the language of building and construction. Johnson uses it, too. Why do they favor this terminology?

In Bethel teaching, apostles and prophets have a supernatural ability to perceive what is going on in heaven—how God "structures" things there—and to recreate those "blueprints" on earth.[6] Indeed, overseeing the establishment of heaven on earth is the "primary objective" of the apostle.[7] Silk refers to the apostles as the "master builders" because these individuals develop strategies for churches and Christian leaders to transform society, primarily through their miraculous powers, and build God's kingdom in their various spheres of influence, or "metrons,"

5. Silk, *Culture of Honor*, ch. 2. For the definition of an "anointing," see chapter 2, note 44.

6. Silk, *Culture of Honor*, ch. 2. According to Johnson, an apostle receives a perception of the way God structures things in heaven and then implements that in his or her *metron*, or sphere of authority. See Johnson and Vallotton, "5-Fold Live" (5:00). See also the *Apostolic and Prophetic Dictionary*, which states, "Apostles are strategists in that they are able to build on earth according to the blueprints they receive regularly from heaven." (See the entry titled "Apostolic Strategy" in Rajah, *Apostolic and Prophetic Dictionary*.)

7. Silk writes: "When Jesus taught the disciples to pray, He brought a key phrase into their core values. He told them to pray, 'Your Kingdom come. Your will be done on earth as it is in heaven.' His instructions taught them to long for Heaven on earth. I believe this core value is the primary objective of the apostle's ministry. Apostolic leaders are focused on Heaven, and their mission is to see Heaven's supernatural reality established on the earth. They long to see the evidence of Heaven's touch in the environment they lead or influence. Having this motivation at the foundation of a church leads to an entirely different emphasis in the church's governing priorities. The apostle will make the presence of God, the worship of God, and the agenda of Heaven the top priorities in the environment. An apostolic government is designed to protect these priorities." (See Silk, *Culture of Honor*, ch. 2.)

using the "blueprints" they have received.[8] And the leaders who have "aligned" with the apostles—along with those leaders' followers—are regarded as "sub-contractors."[9] That's because, once they enact the strategies and develop their own miraculous powers by following the teachings and practices of the apostles, they can assist the apostles in replicating heaven on earth.

So what types of revelation, or "blueprints," do apostles and prophets convey, and what kind of content do they contain?

Types of New Revelation Given by Bethel's Apostles and Prophets

In NAR, prophets and apostles deliver revelation for individuals, local churches, the broader church, and nations. We have explained these types of revelation in more detail in our previous work.[10] Here we summarize and give specific examples of each type of revelation given by Bethel's prophets.

Revelation for Individuals

NAR prophets (as well as apostles)[11] may prophesy to individuals, revealing their spiritual gifts, confirming a call to one of the fivefold ministry offices—whether that is to be an apostle, a prophet, an evangelist, a pastor, or a teacher—and disclosing God's will about major life decisions, such as whom to marry or where to live and work.[12]

In his book *Developing a Supernatural Lifestyle*, Kris Vallotton describes a time when he prophesied to two men—both were unbelievers, and Vallotton stresses that they were homosexuals—who were sitting next to him on a flight. He told one of the men, a fellow named Tony, that

---

8. See chapter 3, notes 38 and 39.

9. See chapter 2 for an explanation of Bethel teaching about the importance of "aligning" with apostles.

10. Geivett and Pivec, *A New Apostolic Reformation?*, ch. 11.

11. The apostles are specially tasked to interpret and implement the revelation, whether it comes through a prophet who is not an apostle, or through an apostle.

12. Geivett and Pivec, *A New Apostolic Reformation?*, ch. 11. NAR prophets also sometimes guide secular businesses. For example, Shawn Bolz said he is a "spiritual advisor" in contract with two multinational companies. See "Excerpts."

God had gifted him with artistic ability and created him to make a living producing art. He told the second man, Frank, that God had given him the ability to fix mechanical things. It turned out that both men were talented in those specific areas, and they were encouraged by his prophetic words, according to Vallotton.[13] His revelation revealed the men's giftings and, at least in the case of Tony, disclosed God's will for his vocation.

Another example of a prophetic word given to an individual is from Steve Backlund, the senior associate director of the Bethel Leaders Network. While speaking at Hope Church in Virginia Beach, Virginia, in 2015, Backlund pointed to a woman seated in the third row, wearing yellow, and he tossed to her a free copy of a book written by his wife, Wendy, titled *Living for the Unseen*. Then he asked the woman her name. She replied, "Ann." He told her:

> Ann, you are a great influencer. . . . Even tonight I just saw the Lord, [and] He wanted to just say, "Thank you—thank you for not quitting, thank you for loving well." . . . And you've got such a powerful ministry to people, and it's gonna increase. . . . The story that you have in your life, you're gonna get clarity on how to communicate that at a level like never before, and it's gonna set people free like never before.

Then Steve Backlund's wife, Wendy, added to his prophetic word for Ann, saying:

> I feel like God wants you to know that you've actually had a lot more victories than failures, but the Enemy's only highlighted the failure part. And, in fact, you're known as a courageous warrior in heaven. That's your persona in heaven. . . . You've won some inner battles that are huge, and He's just very proud of you.[14]

These are a couple of examples of revelation for individuals given by Bethel leaders. We will evaluate their revelation for individuals in the next chapter.

Revelation for Local Churches

NAR prophets and apostles also receive revelation for local churches. This may include revelation into what a particular church's vision and

13. See Vallotton, *Developing a Supernatural Lifestyle*, ch. 5.

14. Steve and Wendy Backlund, "Contagious Hope" (29:00).

purpose should be, when demons have been sent to thwart the work of a church, and confirmation that a pastor is God's choice for a church.[15]

In chapter 2, we explained how prophetic words have guided Bethel Church leaders over the years, including their decision to change the church's organizational structure and to form the Bethel Leaders Network. And, according to Bethel Senior Leadership Team member Danny Silk, many other influential prophets have given words directing Bethel's "course and destiny." The list reads like a who's who of influential prophets, including Bob Jones, Bobby Conner, Dick Joyce, Dick Mills, Mario Murillo, Michael Ratliff, Jill Austin, John Paul Jackson, Paul Cain, Patricia King, Larry Randolph, Mahesh and Bonnie Chavda, Iverna Tompkins, Cindy Jacobs, Wes and Stacy Campbell, and Rolland and Heidi Baker.[16]

In chapter 2, we also explained that Bethel's prophets are regularly invited to speak in churches that are part of the Bethel Leaders Network, where they give revelation to those churches. For example, during a Zoom call, Vallotton gave the following revelation to one church leader, who is part of the Bethel Leaders Network. The man reported:

> Kris prayed over me two calls ago, that there would be a tangible increase in miracles and that our church would be born in the supernatural. And he said, "I'm gonna release over you the miracles and the signs and wonders of God." And since then, everyone that I have prayed for has gotten healed.[17]

❧ Revelation for the Broader Church

Vallotton and Johnson are seen by their followers as recipients of vital revelation, not just for individual churches, but for the church at large. This can be seen, for example, in the endorsements featured on the front pages of their books. The endorsers, including influential apostles and prophets, laud the books for presenting "a highway of revelation to what the Spirit is doing in this coming apostolic age," for releasing "revelation into the army

---

15. See Geivett and Pivec, *A New Apostolic Reformation?*, ch. 11.

16. See Silk, *Culture of Honor*, ch. 2.

17. Bethel Leaders Network, "What Leaders" (1:00). The type of prayer Vallotton gave during the Zoom call is called a "declaration" (described in chapter 6). We explain, in chapter 5, that declarations are viewed as a form of prophecy by many NAR leaders, including Vallotton.

of God that moves it into the kingdom work," and for containing "hidden truths and revelation being shared in these last days."[18]

Vallotton claims that Jesus spoke to him directly about the new revelation he was going to give to the broader church. But Jesus would not give it to "denominational" churches, led by pastors—only to "apostleships," or churches led by apostles.[19]

> The Lord also told me, *I am about to open up the vaults of heaven and reveal depths of My glory that have never before been seen or understood by any living creature.* He explained that this glory was going to be revealed to, and through, His Church in what can only be called a new epoch season. Then He stated, *If I pour out new revelation into the wineskin of denominationalism, it will rip the wineskin and the wine will be lost* (see Luke 5:37–39).[20]

This alleged revelation contains a veiled threat: you'd better hurry because the offer is going fast. You're going to miss out if you don't jump on the apostle bandwagon.

Vallotton has recounted this particular divine encounter a number of times, embellishing somewhat as the occasion calls for it. In a sermon he gave at Bethel Church, Vallotton said the Lord told him that the revelation He was going to pour out to the church through apostleships had been kept in the vaults of heaven "for the eons of ages."[21]

That's a very long time the church has been waiting for apostles to rise and receive this revelation. Consider how extraordinarily privileged Vallotton must be to have been selected as the vehicle of revelation in this case!

---

18. These samples are from Vallotton, *Heavy Rain*, and Johnson, *When Heaven Invades Earth*. They are representative of the type of thing commonly exhibited in endorsements for books by prophets and apostles of NAR.

19. In chapter 2, we explain Vallotton's teachings about the necessity of the church transitioning from "denominationalism" (including pastor-led governance) to apostle-led governance. Denominations are not only anachronistic, poised for replacement by apostleships today, but are an inferior form of church life and organization. See our explanation of NAR teachings about new truths/restored truths in Geivett and Pivec, *A New Apostolic Reformation?*, ch. 11.

20. Vallotton, *Heavy Rain*, ch. 1. (Italics are Vallotton's.)

21. Vallotton, "What Is an Apostle?" (13:00).

Restoring Lost Truths

It's important to understand that, in NAR, revelations received by apostles and prophets are sometimes referred to as "new truths." However, specific "new truths" are also simultaneously described as lost truths that are presently being restored, making them appear to be "new." In line with this NAR teaching, Johnson teaches explicitly about critical truths that have been lost by the church over the centuries and need restoring.[22] For example, in *When Heaven Invades Earth*, he writes:

> We are the most to be pitied if we think we've reached the fullness of what God intended for His Church here on earth. All Church history is built on partial revelation. Everything that has happened in the Church over the past 1900 years has fallen short of *what the early Church had and lost.* Each move of God has been followed by another, just to restore what was forfeited and forgotten. And we still haven't arrived to the standard that they attained, let alone surpassed it.[23]

Johnson's statement raises the questions, when, where, and how did the early church lose crucial revelation? And is there some place in the Bible where we can turn to see what was revealed but has since been lost or neglected? There should be evidence of earlier revelation for each truth that has been lost. Where is that evidence? Without adequately answering these questions, Johnson persists in his claim that the church has lost pivotal truths.

> When truth came to the early Church, it was to increase and be passed to the next generation. It was only meant to go in forward motion, yet that didn't happen. . . . I have no finger to point or bone to pick. But there were realms of God that were entered into in past generations that were neglected. Who knows the reasons? I don't even care. All I know is that there are realms of God, realms of past triumphs and victories that the Church entered into that are not a present day experience. It's a tragedy because He said, "The things that are revealed are yours and your children's forever."[24]

22. It is noteworthy that Johnson's claim that the church's original beliefs need restoring is similar to claims made by cults of Christianity, including the Church of Jesus Christ of Latter-Day Saints and Jehovah's Witnesses.

23. Johnson, *When Heaven Invades Earth*, ch. 17 (emphasis ours).

24. Johnson, "Recovering Our Spiritual Inheritance," ch. 4.

So, Johnson doesn't know and doesn't care how the church lost such vital truths over the centuries. He simply asserts there has been a falling away. But he hasn't proven his starting point—that the things he speaks of were once revealed to the church. This is a huge hole in his teaching—an apostasy of the gaps. Notice that his claim implies that he has received revelation of two forms: first, revelation that the things he describes are meant by God to be realized in the world today, and second, revelation that these truths were once possessed by the church and have been lost. He says he "knows" that this is true. How does he know it? By means of revelation he has received. — *which nobody can challeng*

Johnson, of course, is not alone in having received such critical revelation for the church. He credits certain individuals for restoring lost truths. These trailblazers include Smith Wigglesworth, Aimee Semple McPherson, A. B. Simpson, John Wesley, John G. Lake, and his own father, M. Earl Johnson. Of these and other "giants of the faith," Johnson has written:

> And so they began to possess territory that had not been possessed by anyone continuously since the days of the apostles. They did it at great personal risk and sacrifice, and entered into things that were *completely unknown to the Church at that time* [emphasis ours]. But what was gained by [these] past generations has not been occupied and advanced by those who followed. . . . We were never intended to start over from scratch every two or three generations. . . . Inheritance helps us to build truth on top of truth. Instead of starting over each generation, we inherit certain truths that allow us to move forward into new areas. . . . We are in the beginning stages of the season called *accelerated growth* [emphasis Johnson's]. I believe it is possible under the mercy and grace of God to make up for several hundred years of failure in these areas. It is possible, if we are willing to pour ourselves out, to lay the groundwork for another generation to come and use our ceiling as their floor, to build upon it, to bring things of the Church into a place where it must come to.[25]

(fair comment)

Johnson claims that Wigglesworth, McPherson, Simpson, and others have recovered truths that have been lost "since the days of the [Christ's] apostles." And he describes the recovery of these truths as necessary if the church is to counteract "several hundred years of failure." His portrayal of church history is grim, indeed. And it is based on special knowledge he has received through revelation.

25. Johnson, *The Supernatural Power*, ch. 11.

or they could see the need to reorganise or redirect the church of their times.

In contrast with the hapless digression of the church historically, he portrays the modern apostles and prophets as heroes of the faith who have recovered lost truths, bright stars shining against the church's black backdrop, saving the church from oblivion.

Completely New Truths

Johnson believes that God is in the process of restoring lost truths to the church through key individuals. But he also hints that God intends to reveal completely new truths to the church, truths never before revealed—not even to the early church. Teasingly, he writes about a special destiny for the present generation of the church—a destiny not attained, even, by the early church. Apparently, today's church must receive altogether new revelation if it is to fulfill its destiny.

> Each move of God has been followed by another, just to restore what was forfeited and forgotten. And we still haven't arrived to the standard that they attained, *let alone surpassed it. Yet, not even the early Church fulfilled God's full intention for His people. That privilege was reserved for those in the last leg of the race. It is our destiny.*[26]

proof?

Recall Vallotton's words, cited earlier in this chapter, specifically referencing "new revelation" Jesus desires to pour out, revelation that has "never before been seen or understood by any living creature" and has been held in heaven "for the eons of ages." His choice of wording suggests that the new revelation will not be restored truths, but truths that even Christ's apostles had not known. *— teasing his followers to be in on all this.*

Prophetic Illumination

But how will God give apostles and prophets these truths—whether they be brand-spanking "new truths" or dusted-off and polished "restored truths"?

 According to Bethel leaders, He will reveal new understandings of Scripture that have previously been hidden to Scripture's readers. John- son writes:

---

26. Johnson, *When Heaven Invades Earth*, ch. 17 (our emphasis).

As wonderful as our spiritual roots are, they are insufficient. What was good for yesterday is deficient for today. . . . It's not that everything must change for us to flow with what God is saying and doing. It's just that we make too many assumptions about the rightness of what presently exists. Those assumptions blind us to the *revelations still contained in Scripture*.[27]

(?)

Of these "revelations still contained in Scripture," he also writes:

We've gone as far as we can with our present understanding of Scripture. . . . In this hour the *experience* [of miraculous signs] will help to open up those portions of Scripture that have been closed to us.[28]

(what would again)

An example of one such revelation is the new understanding Johnson claims to have received of Isaiah 60:1–3.[29] He spoke on Sid Roth's *It's Supernatural!* television program about the exact moment he received the epiphany. It happened during what he called a "power encounter"—or a supernatural experience of God—that he described as "revelatory."

I was reading Isaiah 60:1: "Arise, shine; for your light has come, the glory of the Lord has risen upon you." . . . Even though I couldn't have explained it to anyone, I didn't have the insight to explain it, yet I knew that this was life to me. I could feel the breath of God on those verses. . . . So, I took that verse, I shared it to our church on Sunday. I said, "I feel like this is a word for us right now." *(but it might not be)*

What was the new understanding? Johnson told Roth's viewers:

This is a present-day word that the people of God are to rise because the glory of God will be seen upon us. . . . [God] is saying, "You rise, and the glory will be seen. I will answer your posture with heaven's invasion. I'll put my sign of presence upon you if you'll take your right place."[30] *(whipping up the crowd)*

The insight Johnson claims to have received about this verse happens to align with his dominion theology—that Christians are to "rise" and take their "right place" in society, resulting in "heaven's invasion" (or

27. Johnson, *When Heaven Invades Earth*, ch. 17 (our emphasis).

28. Johnson, *When Heaven Invades Earth*, ch. 11 (his emphasis).

29. For another example of prophetic illumination Johnson claims to have received regarding a specific Scripture verse (Rev 19:10), see Johnson, "How Your Miracle."

30. Roth and Johnson, "Impact the World" (18:00).

the arrival of God's kingdom). In relating his new insight, he did not acknowledge the original Israelite audience, or how they may have understood those words at the time, but simply declared that the verse is a "present-day word" for Christians.[31] And we have more to say about his alleged illumination of this verse in the next chapter. *(cherry-picking texts)*

Johnson claims to receive such prophetic illumination as he is delivering messages in the pulpit. He does not use prepared notes when he preaches—in fact, he believes God "prohibited" him from doing so.[32] Instead, he desires to "impart what [the Father] is saying in the moment." But in a telling concession, Johnson states that his words, at these times, are not "infallible" and are not equal to Scripture, though they always represent his "best attempt." *(good)*

Johnson's teaching that revelation will come to the church through hitherto unknown understandings of Scripture is not original to him. This teaching is known as "prophetic illumination" and it's taught by other leaders in the New Apostolic Reformation.[33] They teach that, since Martin Luther's recovery of the truth of salvation by grace through faith during the sixteenth-century Protestant Reformation, God has been progressively restoring other lost truths to the church through apostles and prophets. We have listed several of these "truths" in an earlier book.[34] They include many taught by Bethel leaders and discussed in this book, such as Word-of-Faith-type prayer "confessions" (also known as "declarations") and other prosperity gospel teachings, the need for the "activation" of miraculous gifts in believers, and the restoration of the governmental offices of apostle and prophet. They also include the Seven Mountain Mandate, which is widely regarded as a new revelation given by NAR apostles and prophets to the broader church.[35]

---

31. Johnson states that the clause "your light has come," in Isaiah 60:1, is a reference to Jesus, whom John the apostle said "is the light that came into the world" (John 1). So, since Jesus has already come, the command to "arise" applies to present-day Christians, according to Johnson. See Roth and Johnson, "Impact the World" (20:00). But his failure to consider the original audience is either a hermeneutical faux pas, or it is irrelevant because of the status of Johnson's interpretation as authoritative new revelation. *(conceit again)*

32. Johnson and Farrelly, "Episode 2" (27:00).

33. See our explanation and evaluation of NAR teaching about prophetic illumination in Geivett and Pivec, *A New Apostolic Reformation?*, chs. 11, 13.

34. See Geivett Pivec, *A New Apostolic Reformation?*, ch. 11.

35. See our description of this revelation in chapters 1 and 3.

All the "truths" that have been given to apostles and prophets to date (through prophetic illumination) are often referred to as "present truth."[36] And NAR churches seek to teach the entirety of present truth.

New/Restored Truths Taught by Bethel Church Leaders

What are specific new/restored truths that Bethel leaders claim God has either given them or given to other present-day apostles and prophets, for the broader church? Following are six examples of new revelations they teach.

- *Transition from Pastors to Apostles:* As we explained in chapter 2, Vallotton claims to have received direct revelation from Jesus that God is transitioning churches from being pastor-led to apostle-led. He and other NAR leaders teach that the church at large must embrace this critical truth if it is to experience miraculous power, transform society, and bring God's kingdom to earth.[37]

- *Heaven on Earth/The Lord's Prayer:* Johnson teaches a novel interpretation of the Lord's Prayer—that it's a battle plan for the church to bring heaven to earth through Christians' spoken "declarations." We explain his interpretation, and the practice of declarations, in chapter 6.[38]

- *The "Billion-Soul Harvest":* Johnson, like many other NAR leaders, teaches that the largest revival the world will ever experience is about to occur, fueled by unprecedented miraculous signs and wonders to be performed by the apostles, prophets, and their followers.

---

36. Geivett and Pivec, *A New Apostolic Reformation?*, ch. 11.

37. The idea that apostles must be restored to the church government is the core belief of NAR, so it's no surprise that many apostles and prophets claim to have received revelation about it, including Bill Hamon and Rick Joyner. See, e.g., Hamon, *Apostles, Prophets*; Joyner, *The Call*; and, Joyner, *The Apostolic Ministry*.

38. As far as we know, Johnson has never stated that he received this interpretation of the Lord's Prayer directly from God. But he does teach that many Christians have missed the true meaning of the Lord's Prayer as Jesus intended it to be understood. He also states that a renewed emphasis on the prayer—including multiple songs that recently have been written about it—is "a great sign of the times for us because we're in the beginning of a reformation." See Johnson, "Pastor Bill Johnson Sermons" (12:00). That reformation—informed by this novel take on the Lord's Prayer—will empower the church to finally fulfill its mission. So it does seem that Johnson views his interpretation as a critical truth that has been restored for the present generation.

They believe this end-time "great harvest of souls" is a major truth that has been restored to the church.[39] It has been restored through "prophets," including Bob Jones and Paul Cain. We explore these teachings in chapter 7.

- *The "Goodness of God" (as It Relates to Physical Healing)*: Johnson claims that God gave him a "mandate" to write a book about his special insight into God's goodness—that God's goodness entails that he never causes or allows sickness or suffering, and that it is always his will to heal a person.[40] (We explained his teachings about God's goodness and healing in chapter 1.) He also claims that the first Christians shared his view of God's goodness, a view that was lost by subsequent generations. "A major change in theology has taken place over the past two thousand years," he writes. "When Jesus walked the earth, all sickness was from the devil. Today a large part of the Body of Christ believes God either sends sickness or allows it to make us better people by building character and teaching us the value of suffering."[41] But this truth—that the goodness of God requires that it is always his will to heal a person—is now being restored by Johnson and other NAR leaders.[42]

- *"Victorious Eschatology"/"Apostolic Eschatology"*: NAR leaders teach that God is revealing to the church at large a new view of the last days, which they have referred to as a "victorious eschatology" and also an "apostolic eschatology." For example, Vallotton claims he received direct revelation from God about this new doctrine: "In the winter of 2007, the Lord spoke to me, saying, *The spirit of fatalism and the spirit of martyrdom are holding back the apostolic age.* . . . The

(or, we don't know why)

---

39. Hamon, *Apostles, Prophets*, 107.

40. Johnson writes about this mandate in Johnson, *God Is Good*, introduction.

41. Johnson and Clark, *The Essential Guide*, ch. 5.

42. The influential prophet James Goll writes (in an endorsement for Johnson's book): "With every historic movement of the Holy Spirit, a truth becomes illuminated concerning the nature of God. Five hundred years ago the Great Reformation was spearheaded by Martin Luther. A fire was lit when the Holy Spirit highlighted a verse in the Book of Romans: 'The just shall live by faith.' Progressive revelation came tumbling forth and church history was altered. In the past twenty years, another aspect of the nature of God is being highlighted by the Holy Spirit once again. This time it centers around the goodness of God." (See Johnson, *God Is Good*, Endorsements.) Note that Goll's depiction of the Holy Spirit's "highlighting" of specific doctrines aligns with NAR teaching about how God is restoring lost truths to the church through prophetic illumination of Scripture, a teaching we described earlier in this chapter.

Lord went on to tell me that He was going to give us an 'apostolic eschatology.'"[43] Without this new view of the end time, Christians will not believe they can, or even should attempt to, bring heaven to earth (which, as we explain in chapter 6, NAR leaders understand to be the Great Commission).[44]

- *Jesus Emptied Himself of His Divine Powers:* Johnson teaches that Jesus did not work his miracles when he was on earth as God, but as a man fully dependent on the Father and empowered by the Holy Spirit. This he did, ostensibly, so that he would be a model for all of his followers to work miracles pretty much as he did. Johnson sees this teaching as another critical truth that must be "recaptured" to make "possible a full restoration of the ministry of Jesus in His Church."[45] Thus, it is in line with the types of new/restored truths today's church is to expect, according to NAR leaders.[46]

---

43. Vallotton, *Heavy Rain*, ch. 15.

44. See chapter 6, note 38 for more about NAR's "victorious eschatology." See also our discussion in Pivec and Geivett, *Counterfeit Kingdom*, ch. 6.

45. Johnson, *When Heaven Invades Earth*, ch. 2.

46. This is a version of kenotic Christology. Johnson says all of Jesus's miracles were performed this way, but that seems flatly wrong. At least some of his miracles were performed with his own direct, divine power, including the calming of the sea, the raising of Lazarus from the dead, Jesus's transfiguration, the healing of the paralytic (in demonstration of his divine authority to forgive sin!), and his own resurrection (John 2:18–22; Rom 1:4; 8:11). Johnson is fond of saying that "Jesus modeled what it looks like to be full of the Holy Spirit." See Johnson, "Jesus, Full of the Holy Spirit." But this is misleading. At his baptism, the Holy Spirit descended upon Jesus, and, in that moment, a voice from heaven declared, "You are my beloved Son; with you I am well pleased" (Luke 3:21–22). Shortly after this, being "full of the Holy Spirit," Jesus left the Jordan and was led by the Spirit into the wilderness to be tempted by the devil (Luke 4:1–2). Following the temptation, Jesus returned to Nazareth, and taking the Isaiah scroll, he quoted these words: "The Spirit of the Lord is upon me, because he has anointed me to proclaim good news to the poor. He has sent me to proclaim liberty to the captives and recovering of sight to the blind, to set at liberty those who are oppressed, to proclaim the year of the Lord's favor" (Luke 4:18–19, quoting Isa 61:1–2). Jesus then said, "Today this Scripture has been fulfilled in your hearing" (Luke 4:21). This whole sequence of events attests to a unique and favored role that Jesus occupied in relation to the Spirit. In virtue of that relationship, Jesus was God's uniquely authoritative spokesman. It is a mistake to assume that we may be filled with the Spirit *in the same way* Jesus was in this instance, and that we can therefore do all that Jesus did in dependence on the Spirit. For further study, see Acts 10:34–39; Matt 12:28; Luke 5:17. See our brief critique of Johnson's teaching about Jesus emptying himself of his divine powers in Pivec and Geivett, *Counterfeit Kingdom*, ch. 6.

To be sure, Johnson and other Bethel leaders do not necessarily claim these revelations were given first, or exclusively, to them. Other apostles and prophets teach them, too. But they are seen by Bethel leaders as indispensable truths for the present generation of the church, derived from new insights into Scripture taught by contemporary apostles and prophets. Thus, they match their description of the types of new revelation the church is to anticipate. And because of Bethel leaders' influence, they've played a key role in popularizing and spreading these new truths throughout the world. And, of course, they believe they have the same direct "prophetic" insight into the relevant passages of Scripture themselves, which reinforces their confidence in their promulgation of these lost or hidden truths.

Revelation for Nations

Besides giving revelation to individuals, local churches, and the broader church, some NAR prophets and apostles also prophesy to cities and nations and to national leaders. Bethel's Vallotton is one of those. He states:

> In 1985, I had an encounter with the Lord that changed the trajectory of my life forever. The call of God on my life to be a prophet to the nations was clear; I could not deny it if I wanted to. Jesus walked into my bathroom amid my evening bath and told me, "I have called you to be a prophet to the nations. You will speak before kings and queens. You will influence prime ministers and presidents. I will open doors for you to talk to mayors, governors, ambassadors, and government officials all around the world."[47] *(what conceit & arrogance!)*

In light of this revelation so dramatically delivered to Vallotton, we wonder if he is the prophet Bill Johnson referred to when Johnson was a guest on Sid Roth's television program. During that interview, Johnson said that a prophet from Bethel Church was contacted by an unnamed politician from outside the United States. The politician was thinking about running for president in his home country and was "fishing for feedback." But the prophet told him, "You're asking the wrong question. God wants to know what kind of man are you going to be? Are you going

---

47. Vallotton, "Prophetic Gifting." This is a remarkable claim. Consider the implications of Vallotton's testimony of his encounter with Jesus if false.

to be faithful to your wife, or are you going to continue your relationship with your mistress?"[48]

Prophets also may deliver prophetic words at the national level and about nations, such as predicting earthquakes and other catastrophes of nature, economic upheavals, and the outcomes of elections.[49] The highly publicized "Trump Prophecies," of the 2020 US presidential election, are a notorious case in point.

The "Trump Prophecies" and the End of COVID-19

Prior to the election, numerous NAR prophets claimed that God informed them that President Donald Trump would win a second term in office.[50] Vallotton was among them.[51] While giving a message at Bethel Church on December 8, 2019, Vallotton said that God had revealed to him that Barack Obama would have two terms as president and that Trump would win the 2016 election. He said the Lord also told him He would "step into the impeachment process" against Trump, "bring it to a close," and would give him another term as president "because the Lord wants it."[52]

Of course, Vallotton was wrong about Trump winning a consecutive term in 2020. But it's an example of a prophecy given by a Bethel leader pertaining to a nation. Another example of such a prophecy—this one with an international scope—was given by Shawn Bolz, who speaks frequently during Bethel church services and conferences. Like Vallotton, Bolz prophesied Trump's 2020 reelection.[53] He also made another prediction while speaking in South Africa at a conference in February 2020—with Bill Johnson standing on the stage with him. Bolz prophesied the COVID-19 outbreak would soon end and that it would not become a major pandemic.[54] That, of course, was not to be.

48. Roth and Johnson, "Impact the World" (8:00).

49. Geivett and Pivec, *A New Apostolic Reformation?*, ch. 11.

50. Duin, "The Charismatic Christians."

51. Blair, "God Is Going to End."

52. Vallotton, "Sovereign Providence" (starting at 36:00).

53. Bolz, "Any response."

54. Parke, "Christian Pastor Shawn Bolz."

Damage Control

How did these prophets address the fallout when their prophecies about Trump's reelection and COVID-19 did not come to pass?

PUBLIC APOLOGIES

When it became clear to Vallotton that Joe Biden had won the 2020 election, he released a video online with this public apology: "I really want to apologize, sincerely apologize, for missing the prophecy about Donald Trump. . . . I was completely wrong. I take full responsibility for being wrong. There's no excuse for it. I think it doesn't make me a false prophet, but it does actually create a credibility gap."[55]

Other prophets issued their own apologies. But, like Vallotton, they maintained that they are still genuine prophets of God despite missing the mark by a long shot. One of those prophets was Bolz. In an apology posted to Facebook, Bolz wrote that, to hold himself accountable so he wouldn't prophesy wrongly again, he would refrain from giving "public political prophetic words" for a "season" and put his focus on growing in his "closeness to Jesus."[56] Yet he did appear to leave the door open for giving future prophecies of a political and national nature. (He did not say whether God had revealed to him that he needed to adopt this policy.)

"PROPHETIC STANDARDS" STATEMENT

These apologies were not enough for others. The failed "Trump prophecies" and failed "end-of-Covid prophecies" received attention in the media, creating major embarrassment for Christian leaders who believe there are genuine prophets today and are convinced that the "prophetic ministry" is to be greatly valued. So, to clean up the mess left behind by the failed prophecies, which had given present-day prophets a "bad name," a number of high-profile NAR, Pentecostal, and charismatic

---

55. Vallotton, "My Apology," January 8, 2021. Vallotton originally posted this apology video on November 7, 2020, but removed it shortly after posting it, referencing concerns from many of his followers that he had apologized too soon since the election results were being contested. He reposted it after the US Congress certified the Electoral College vote.

56. Bolz, "Any response."

leaders released a "Prophetic Standards" statement in April 2021.[57] Its purpose is to provide "scriptural guidelines" for prophets to follow prior to delivering prophecies (including never charging money to deliver a prophetic word) and steps to take in the aftermath of any failed prophecies (including making a public apology if an erroneous word has been delivered publicly).[58] Vallotton was among the ninety-one "initial signers" of the document, which also included other influential prophets and apostles: Patricia King, Stacy Campbell, John Kelly, Mark Chironna, Jeremiah Johnson, James Goll, Jennifer LeClaire, Joseph Mattera, and Randy Clark. And well-known pastors who signed it included Robert Morris (of Gateway Church in Southlake, Texas) and Mark Driscoll (of The Trinity Church in Scottsdale, Arizona).[59] Conspicuously, the signers also included the respected Bible commentators and theologians Wayne Grudem, Craig Keener, and Sam Storms—lending their respectability to the document.

Efforts to hold prophets to a biblical standard are commendable. But this document has some significant flaws. In the next chapter, we will pinpoint some of those flaws as we evaluate the Bethel apostles and prophets claiming to give new revelation.

57. "Prophetic Standards." This document was initiated by two individuals, Joseph Mattera—the convener for the United States Coalition of Apostolic Leaders (US-CAL)—and USCAL member and radio host Michael Brown. See Brown, "A Unified Call" and Mattera, "The Need for Prophetic Standards."

58. In chapter 5, we explain and critique the NAR view—a view also held by many charismatics—that prophets can make mistakes in their prophesying, yet still be genuine prophets of God. Continuationists need not be fallibilists, and we maintain that they should not be.

59. This is the same Mark Driscoll who, in 2014, resigned as the pastor of Mars Hill Church in Seattle, Washington, (another church he founded) following allegations of abusive leadership. See Welch, "The Rise and Fall."

—5—

Evaluating the Bethel Apostles and Prophets Giving New Revelation

When prophecy fails, evangelicals go ballistic!

—Holy Koolaid's YouTube Channel
(238,000 Subscribers)[1]

IN THE LAST CHAPTER, we showed that Bethel's apostles and prophets—similar to other apostles and prophets in NAR—claim to deliver divine revelation for individuals, local churches, the broader church, and nations. In this chapter, we evaluate those claims on the bases of Scripture and careful reasoning.

Revelation for Individuals and Local Churches

(19 pay for a course)

First, in Bethel teaching, *all* believers can *learn* to prophesy by taking part in "prophetic activation exercises," as illustrated in their use of the Prophetic Uno game we described in chapter 1. Scripture does not teach that miraculous gifts, such as prophesying, are latent powers that can be activated by individuals at will. They are distributed directly by the

---

1. Holy Koolaid, "Evangelicals Freak Out."

97

Holy Spirit to individuals as he alone decides (1 Cor 12:11). And these gifts are not apportioned equally to all. They are variously distributed in accordance with God's will. The idea that people can learn to prophesy through the type of classroom training offered in BSSM has been challenged by Pentecostal and charismatic leaders, including the Pentecostal-charismatic historian Vinson Synan.[2]

Second, Bethel leaders teach that making "declarations" about individuals is a type of prophesying. We explain declarations more fully in chapter 6; in short, they are words, spoken in faith, that are believed to create reality. So when someone with the gift of prophecy offers a prophetic word about the future to someone, according to Bethel leaders, this is not always a matter of merely "telling the future," in the way that predictive prophecy is usually understood. Often, they are "causing the future."[3] That is, speaking the words aloud actually sets their fulfillment in motion. Later in this chapter, we share an example where Kris Vallotton claims to have prophesied in just this way. But the idea that prophetic words do not merely reveal information about the future, but actually bring it to pass, is a new NAR view of prophecy.

Third, Bethel leaders emphasize that, whenever a person with the gift of prophecy gives a prophetic word to someone (especially if that word comes from a person who does not hold the formal office of prophet) that word should always be "positive" and "life-giving" for the recipient.[4] These prophecies should be about "finding the gold" in people's lives—to

2. See Synan, "2000 Years of Prophecy," 55. In NAR teaching, there are two main ways that individuals can begin "operating" with a miraculous gift: through "activation" of a latent gift or "impartation" of a new gift. According to the *Apostolic and Prophetic Dictionary*, impartation "refers to the act of transferring anointing, [miraculous] gifts or grace from one person to another. While activation is done within a believer, impartation is deposited from one believer to another." An impartation is often done through the "laying on of hands" (i.e., "the act of a believer physically putting hands on someone as a point of contact in order to release faith for something to happen to or for that person"). See Rajah, *Apostolic and Prophetic Dictionary*.

3. Vallotton and Farrelly, "Episode 5" (12:00). Vallotton refers to causing the future as "forthtelling." This reflects a NAR redefinition of "forthtelling," which, outside of NAR, has referred to divine revelation about something from the past or the present (as opposed to revelation about the future, i.e., "foretelling"). The way they "cause" the future is by angels hearing the spoken declarations and carrying them out. (See chapter 6.) For more on how Johnson believes prophecy can cause the future, see Johnson, "How Your Miracle."

4. Pivec, "The Problem."

use a common Bethel catchphrase.[5] "The gift of prophecy convicts [people] of the greatness, the goodness, God has placed in every person" and reveals their "divine destiny," according to Vallotton.[6] So its role is not to expose sin in people's lives or to pronounce judgment. But while Scripture teaches that prophesying "speaks to people for their upbuilding and encouragement and consolation," it does not set the parameters that Bethel leaders have. And since prophecy is a gift given by the Holy Spirit, Bethel leaders, in effect, have placed parameters on God (or "put God in a box," to use a popular NAR expression of disapproval when they believe others have placed undue constraints on God's power).

Furthermore, surely a person may be edified and encouraged by a prophetic word that convicts them of their sin, if that word leads them to repentance and restoration in their relationship with God and stops destruction in their life. One Assemblies of God pastor reports that he has seen prophecy work effectively in this way, when one of his close friends was privately given a prophetic word that exposed hidden sin in his life. His friend confessed his sin, which resulted in his going to jail as punishment for his sinful acts. But the course of his life was changed for the better.

We also note that there is a big difference between those Pentecostals and charismatics who merely claim to have the spiritual gift of prophecy and those NAR apostles and prophets who claim to hold formal, governing offices invested with extraordinary authority.[7] Thus, when Bethel leaders prophesy to individuals or local churches, their words are seen as having divine authority. Unlike those who have a *gift* of prophecy, prophetic *office*-holders may pronounce judgment or expose sin in another's life, as the unnamed Bethel prophet did with the politician (an incident we described in chapter 4).

Because prophets in the office possess divine authority, there is a danger that the people or churches to whom they prophesy will view their words as the very words of God. How can someone resist a prophet's injunction to buy, to sell, to go, to stay, to change the very course of their life, despite warnings and pleadings from friends and family? To disobey the prophet, who speaks for God, is to disobey God.[8]

5. Vallotton and Farrelly, "Episode 5" (51:00).

6. Vallotton and Farrelly, "Episode 5" (54:00).

7. We have argued, in chapter 3, that there is no scriptural basis for present-day governing apostles and prophets.

8. The "Prophetic Standards" statement, released in April 2021, states: "We reject any threatening words from prophets today, warning their followers that judgment

Further, they face serious consequences if the prophets are wrong. Many people have shared stories with us of NAR prophets advising them, or people they know, to invest in specific publicly traded stocks (that later tanked), to undertake risky businesses endeavors (that didn't succeed), and to go on mission trips (that required the individuals to accrue more debt, which they later regretted). And prophecies by Bethel leaders that the church and the surrounding city of Redding would become a cancer-free zone have prompted cancer patients to travel to Bethel in expectation of being healed; yet even Bethel leaders admit that many are not.[9] Who can calculate the harm the sick and infirm have experienced after entrusting themselves to Bethel's apostles and prophets? Traveling, sometimes very long distances to a remote city, often calls for families to make financial and other sacrifices. In addition is the painful emotional toll for those whose ill-grounded hopes are shattered because they have not been healed as expected.

The consequences for local churches may be even greater than for individuals. The negative consequences of an erroneous prophecy delivered to a single individual are mostly confined to that individual, but the toxic effects are magnified when a false prophecy is issued to an entire congregation. Consider, for example, the prophecy Vallotton gave to that pastor in the Bethel Leaders Network—the prophecy that his church would experience "a tangible increase in miracles." (We mentioned this prophecy in the last chapter.) The pastor claims that the prophecy was fulfilled and that every sick person he has prayed for since that time has been miraculously healed.[10] It is striking that, in NAR delivering this type

---

will fall on them if they fail to obey the prophet's words. We see this as a dangerous form of spiritual manipulation." ("Prophetic Standards.") Despite this statement, there is no escaping the fact that prophets, in NAR, are seen as having special divine authority and their followers naturally do feel compelled to take their words very seriously. And why shouldn't they if they believe they have a sure word from a genuine prophet? Signatories to the "Prophetic Standards" statement are here telling recipients of such prophecy not to heed the warnings of their prophets. By what authority do these signatories override the words of a prophet who is thought to be speaking for God? Do the signatories simply know that any prophet who issues warnings of judgment upon the disobedient is issuing a false prophecy? What is the basis for this stricture? What authority does it have?

9. Flinchbaugh, "Ignite the Fire"; Yoars, "The Radical Revivalists."

10. Bethel Leaders Network, "What Leaders" (1:00). The type of prayer Vallotton gave during that Zoom call is called a "declaration" (described in chapter 6). We explain, in this chapter, that declarations are viewed as a form of prophecy by many NAR leaders, including Vallotton.

of prophecy is a prerogative reserved for prophets and apostles, and it is evidence of the "extraordinary authority" we associate with their conception of apostles and prophets. It is a kind of authority that is extraordinary in the sense of what it entitles them to do. But if this is a truthful account of the effect of Vallotton's prophecy, what possible harm could come from such a prophecy?

The content of Vallotton's prophecy contains implicit direction for the church. For example, it purports that miracles ought to be a major focus of this church. What does that mean? And would such a focus be healthy and biblical? Do we see anything like this set forth as desirable in the New Testament?

Vallotton's prophecy has significant doctrinal and practical implications. It implies that miraculous healings are normative and that such healings are a sign of God's favor on a church. But what if churchgoers determine that genuine healings are not occurring normatively there? What then? Will they become disheartened, wonder where they've gone wrong, and look for another church where miracles *are* happening? Will leaders in the church double down on their efforts to develop miraculous powers—adding classes in healing and prophesying, and inviting more Bethel apostles and prophets to the church to impart miraculous powers, until they finally see their efforts bear the miraculous fruit that Vallotton's prophecy has led them to expect?

At the very least, we see that, despite the claim that Bethel's apostles and prophets do not interfere with the affairs of local churches, their prophecies do set priorities and establish direction for those churches.[11]

When considering how conspicuously mistaken Vallotton and other NAR leaders have been about their revelations for nations—about US President Trump's reelection, for example—we wonder why anyone would trust their revelation for individuals or local churches. Why should the pastor of a church trust Vallotton's words about God's plan for his church when Vallotton's confident words about God's plan for the United States cannot be trusted?

---

11. See chapter 3, where we discuss Bethel leaders' claims that they do not interfere in the decision-making of local churches.

Revelation for the Broader Church

Bethel prophets don't limit their prophecies to local congregations; some claim to reveal "new truths" (or to restore "lost truths") to the church at large.

Johnson offers a radically new interpretation of the Lord's Prayer; but he also audaciously insists that all Christians must accept his interpretation of the Lord's Prayer—or miss their role in bringing God's kingdom to earth. The same holds for his conception of God's goodness. He declares that all Christians must embrace his understanding of God's goodness lest they be guilty of misrepresenting God and neglecting the assignment he has given them, since otherwise they will not seek to heal every sick person they encounter. And he has primed his followers to anticipate other novel interpretations of Scripture, as we showed in the last chapter. Recall his words about "revelations still contained in Scripture" and "portions of Scripture that have been closed to us" that will be opened up.[12]

Surely, if Johnson wishes to allege that critical truths have been lost by the church, he must show why anyone should accept his claim. For example, when it comes to his peculiar interpretation of the Lord's Prayer, he should not just *claim* that the first Christians saw prayer that way. He must *show* that this was their understanding of prayer. Or regarding his understanding of God's goodness, he must offer substantial evidence that the first Christians held a view of God's goodness entailing that it is *always* God's will to heal sickness. Since he has not offered such evidence, it is fair to wonder whether he expects his followers simply to accept his interpretation because he says so. Certainly, many of his followers seem inclined to do just that. Such uncritical acceptance of Johnson's teaching imperils their approach to Scripture. If they don't understand some passage of the Bible, they naively trust pronouncements based on prophetic illumination, presumed to be specially available to an apostle or prophet, who thereby has access to the true meaning of Scripture. Indeed, this is what people are taught, as we showed in the last chapter.

Recall that Johnson claims to receive such prophetic illumination as he is delivering messages in the pulpit, though he admits that revelation could be fallible. This is puzzling, and troubling for a variety of reasons. First, like many NAR prophets and preachers, Johnson likes to hedge his

---

12. Johnson, *When Heaven Invades Earth*, chs. 11 and 17.

revelation claims. "I *feel like* this is a word for us right now," he'll say.[13] This language is inherently tentative. And yet, when Johnson and other NAR preachers talk more generally about God's ongoing revelation to them, they are quite sure of themselves and they don't qualify their terms. So in their general teaching that God is continuing with revelation for the church, they aren't tentative; but in concrete situations when they deliver actual revelations, they seem to feel a necessity to express themselves with less confidence. It may not matter much to their typical audience when they do this. Many people probably don't even hear the tentativeness in their statements. It's just vernacular for them. But it is striking to us. The homiletical hedge spoils the prophetic edge.

Second, Johnson studiously avoids Bible study in preparation for his preaching, favoring instead the frisson of spontaneity and new revelation emanating from the pulpit. But this only increases the chances of getting it wrong. A preacher's task is to explain the word of truth correctly, and best practices include careful study (see 1 Tim 2:15). It's inconceivable that a preacher's "best attempt" at getting it right can simply set aside this responsibility.

Third, Johnson's message derives, in some sense, from Scripture—Isaiah 60:1, in the example we're considering, is the springboard for his claim.[14] It's virtually a proof text for his message. "I could feel the breath of God on those scriptures," he says (without explaining what that means). But his message is not equal to Scripture. The new truths are somehow contained in Scripture, but in a way that is accessible only by special insight (i.e., revelation; like an "inner light," of some sort, available only to select individuals). So, on the one hand, the message is supposed to be there in the text; but on the other hand, the message is fallible because it's a novel product of the preacher's encounter with the text. While the message, linked to a specific passage, is somehow made transparent by Johnson's subjective experience of the breath of God, this work of God in the moment does not ensure infallibility.

Fourth, while Johnson allows that his message is not infallible, there are no independent tests that his audience could apply to confirm its accuracy or check up on the likelihood that it comes from God. You cannot simply consult the passage he cites and apply a standard hermeneutic, since the message is a novel layer of truth that is only tenuously

---

13. See chapter 4.
14. See chapter 4.

connected with the passage and is ultimately subjectively revealed to a particular individual. Johnson is his own authority. His audience is left depending on how right the message feels to him.

On close inspection, it appears that the novel layer of truth picked up by Johnson while reading a passage of Scripture may be explained less by any special work of God in the moment of (fallible) revelation, and more by the underlying NAR theology that informs Johnson's preaching and writing.

So we should practice pressing for good reasons to accept anyone's interpretation of Scripture—even if that individual claims to be an apostle. We might even say, *especially* when that person claims to be an apostle! When the apostle Paul brought new teachings to the Jews in Berea, they did not automatically accept his words because he claimed to be an apostle. They examined the Scriptures daily to see if his teachings had their support (Acts 17:10–14).

The notion that the church is to look for critical new revelation from present-day prophets and apostles is nowhere endorsed in Scripture. Notice that the apostle Paul, toward the end of his life, instructed his young protégé Timothy to take the teachings he had learned from Paul—the apostolic teachings—and "entrust [them] to faithful men who will be able to teach others also" (2 Tim 2:2). Paul did not advise Timothy to expect and rely on new truths from prophets and apostles. He instructed Timothy to recall truths *already revealed* through the apostles of Christ—those first-century apostles who had seen the resurrected Christ and received a personal commission from him when he appeared to them.[15] Once the truths of the Christian faith were preserved in Scripture, Christians weren't to expect new truths from future prophets or apostles. Rather, they were admonished to safeguard the truths that had already been revealed—once and for all (Jude 3).

In contrast to NAR teachings about the ongoing revelation of new truths, Protestant Christians have held that all teachings and practices that are essential for the health and success of the church can be found in Scripture (2 Tim 3:16–17). And in contrast to NAR teachings about the revelation of new interpretations of Scripture, Protestants have emphasized the perspicuity of Scripture, the doctrine that, its teachings on essential truth are clear, plain for all to see, if they can but read the Bible for themselves. This tradition of the church stands opposed to the NAR view

---

15. Geivett and Pivec, *A New Apostolic Reformation?*, ch. 14.

that a prophet or apostle with a special office is required to give the church new revelations or set forth previously hidden interpretations of Scripture.

While Johnson insists that all believers ought to accept his revisionist understandings of biblical truths, he states that he would never equate the revelation he has received with Scripture.[16] He also observes that when God speaks to him, it is through God's Word, not in addition to it: "This needs to be said. Some might think that adding to the Bible is okay. It's not okay. Ever. And then there are some who accuse us of adding to God's Word, simply because we believe God still speaks. Neither is true or healthy."[17] So Johnson maintains that new revelation is not on a par with Scripture and does not supplement it. This is initially reassuring. But the value of this caveat is completely neutralized by his teaching that, through prophetic illumination, the church will be given new understandings of Scripture. When he urges all believers to accept his new understandings of Scripture, is he not, in effect, claiming that his words are equal to Scripture? He believes that his audience must embrace the new and improved interpretation of key passages in Scripture, or miss out on what God wants to do through them in the world.

With their novel conception of biblical interpretation, subject to the authority of prophetic illumination, NAR leaders like Johnson are clearly at odds with cardinal Protestant doctrines of the sufficiency and perspicuity of Scripture—despite their claims to uphold the Protestant tradition.

Revelation for Nations: The "Trump Prophecies" Up Close

In addition to giving revelation for individuals, churches, and the broader church, some Bethel leaders claim to give revelation to nations. To demonstrate the problems that can be associated with such national prophecies, we examine their failed predictions about Donald Trump.

In chapters 1 and 4, we referenced a prophecy Vallotton gave about a national election—that US President Donald Trump would be reelected. Vallotton was among the numerous NAR prophets who inaccurately prophesied Trump's reelection, having a pie-in-the-face effect for those who believe in the validity of present-day prophets.[18] Their embarrass-

16. See Johnson, "March 15, 2020" (1:32:00).

17. Johnson, *The Way of Life*, ch. 14 (updated 2019 edition).

18. Duin, "The Charismatic Christians." For a video compilation of prophecies given that Trump would be reelected, see Lewis and Rowntree, "Testing the Prophets."

ment was addressed by New Testament scholar Craig Keener in an article he wrote for *Christianity Today* magazine. Keener, who identifies himself as a charismatic Christian in the article, wrote, "The failed prophecies of Donald Trump's reelection may have damaged the credibility of the US independent Charismatic wing of evangelicalism more than any event since the televangelist scandals of the 1980s."[19] Anyone who recalls those scandals, and the ensuing fallout, grasps the significance of Keener's statement. But the damage from these failed "Trump Prophecies" went beyond the reputation of charismatics, according to Keener. He writes, "They have led some outsiders to criticize Christianity itself and rightly call us [charismatic Christians] to introspection."

Notably, even a mainstream evangelical leader, Eric Metaxes—a *New York Times* best-selling author and conservative radio show host— was bewitched by the prophets' predictions about Trump. Metaxes forced eyebrows up on other evangelicals when, during an interview with Charlie Kirk, he said, "People I know and trust well have heard from God that Trump will have a second term. . . . I know that sounds insane to people, but I'm at a point where I don't care."[20] Clearly, he trusted these prophets. Yet other influential Christian leaders, including Rod Dreher, publicly expressed alarm at Metaxes's uncritical acceptance of the prophets' forecast. Dreher shared a concern expressed by his own wife that, if Trump failed to get a second term, many Christians would question their entire faith. He writes: "If Joe Biden is sworn in, does that mean God has failed, or abandoned us? Or, if Christian authorities were wrong about Trump getting a second term, what else are they wrong about? Are they wrong about who Jesus is?"[21]

Sobering questions, indeed.

Unsurprisingly, with so many prophets prophesying Trump's reelection, the mainstream media and liberal pundits took notice. YouTube videos mocking all evangelicals because of these failed prophecies received millions of views. The description of one video, titled "Evangelicals Freak Out," lumps the NAR prophets together with all evangelicals, making no distinction between them. It declares:

> After Trump loses the election, evangelicals go nuts! Pastors and prophets incorrectly prophesied Trump would win the election and get a second term. When the Trump prophecies failed, the

19. Keener, "Failed Trump Prophecies."
20. Dreher, "Eric Metaxes's American Apocalypse."
21. Dreher, "Eric Metaxes's American Apocalypse."

evangelicals (some of whom sit on Trump's evangelical advisory committee, like Paula White and Kenneth Copeland) had an absolute ballistic meltdown going into denial. When prophecy fails, evangelicals go ballistic! Here is a compilation of some of the best evangelical freak-outs. Enjoy![22]

High-profile media outlets that reported on the predictions include *Politico, Newsweek, USA Today,* the *Washington Post,* and the *New York Times.*[23] Like the YouTube video, many of these articles implicated all Christians for the false predictions. They did this by referring to the NAR prophets as "Christian prophets," "Christian leaders," or as "evangelicals"—not as the fringe leaders of a theologically aberrant movement. The derisive edge in some of these reports is palpable. One article, titled "What Happens after Christian Prophets Admit They Were Wrong about Trump?," likens the prophets to psychics, tarot card readers, and astrologers. It also notes that hundreds of thousands of people had watched their predictions on YouTube. And it points out that many of the prophets' followers clung to their predictions even after the prophets themselves admitted they were wrong! It states: "If you read the comments below social media posts by prophets who have reckoned with and apologized for their incorrect predictions, many of their followers won't accept the backpedal. The followers assure them they didn't get it wrong. Be patient. Trump's win will come to pass in God's time."[24]

Neither could prominent atheists pass on the opportunity to mock the prophets and their failed predictions. Blogger Hemant Mehta, known in the blogosphere as the "Friendly Atheist," has more than 550,000 followers on Facebook. He wrote an article linking to a video compilation of the prophets' predictions about the election on YouTube. Knowing the failed predictions would tickle his atheist audience, he wrote:

> You deserve something nice. So here are 12 Christian preachers—including some self-described "prophets"—declaring with *absolute certainty* that Donald Trump would win re-election. I can't wait to watch the video where they all attempt to explain

22. Holy Koolaid, "Evangelicals Freak Out."

23. Duin, "The Christian Prophets"; Lemon, "Christian 'Prophet' Claims"; Hafner, "Meet the Evangelicals"; Boorstein, "For Some Christians"; and Graham, "Christian Prophets."

24. Stankorb, "What Happens."

how God's Word got mistranslated along the way. The rain inter-
fered with it or something. I'm sure that's it.[25]

Mehta reports prophetic missteps with glee. And of course he would.
They provide more fuel for his anti-religion-reporting bonfire.

Sadly, all Christians are caught in the crosshairs of media fire when
NAR prophets' predictions go haywire.

And so it happens, with their failed prophecies about Trump's reelection, NAR prophets disappointed their followers, damaged the reputation
of the church at large and fostered greater suspicion of Christian leadership generally. And they have made it much more difficult for Christians
to share the gospel going forward. These are important reasons why false
prophecy is so egregious and rightly condemned in Scripture (Deut 18:20;
Jer 14:15–16; 23:9–40; Ezek 13; Matt 7:15–16; 24:11; Mark 13:22). How
timely are the words of Jeremiah, "Do not listen to the words of the prophets who prophesy to you, filling you with vain hopes" (Jer 23:16), and of
Ezekiel of old, "Woe to the foolish prophets who follow their own spirit,
and have seen nothing!" (Ezek 13:3). Jesus said that future false prophets
 would be known by their fruits (Matt 7:16). He also warned that eventually many will be led astray by false prophets (Matt 24:11).

These NAR prophecies about Trump are not the only failed prophecies about the United States in 2020. Or so that was the determination
of the hosts of Remnant Radio, a webcast on YouTube with more than
seventy thousand subscribers. Joshua Lewis and Michael Rowntree aired
a special New Year's Day eight-hour marathon on December 31, 2020,
for the specific purpose of testing the prophecies that had been given
by the prophets in 2020.[26] Both hosts are continuationists (that is, they
believe in the contemporary gift of prophecy), and their show promotes
charismatic theology. Commendably, they felt it was necessary to obey
Scripture's injunctions to test prophetic words. And, prior to the marathon, they beseeched their followers, far and wide, to send in, for their
evaluation, the most accurate prophetic words they had heard given that
year. After combing through more than eighty hours of video footage—
and evaluating prophetic words given by influential NAR prophets, such
as Chuck Pierce, Robert Henderson, and James Goll—the hosts shared

25. Mehta, "Here Are 12" (his emphasis).

26. Special guests interviewed during this marathon—who helped evaluate the
prophetic words—included well-known continuationist Christian leaders (Michael
Brown, Craig Keener, Sam Storms, Ken Fish, Jack Deere, Joel Richardson, and Mike
Winger).

their findings with a "heavy heart."[27] Rowntree said, "We came into this actually rooting for a substantial portion of these [prophecies] to be right."[28] Yet they weren't:

> You would think in eighty hours of footage, just if you were guessing about what would happen in 2020, you might hit 20 percent or 30 percent. We're estimating that something like 1 percent or less, maybe 0 percent, of the prophecies over 2020 were actually, for sure, fulfilled in 80 hours of footage. . . . What most would label as the worst year on record in a long time, the prophets said, essentially, would be the best year. *(sooth sayers)*

And, in response to the remarkably low number, if any, of accurate prophecies, Lewis replied, "That would be unacceptable."[29]

We agree, it is unacceptable. But it is not surprising. The notion of present-day prophets who give revelation to nations has no biblical support, as we have argued elsewhere.[30]

It is sobering to recall the severe words God had for the prophets of Jeremiah's day who spoke presumptuously and recklessly, leading his people astray.

> Therefore, behold, I am against the prophets, declares the LORD, who steal my words from one another. Behold, I am against the prophets, declares the LORD, who use their tongues and declare, "declares the LORD." Behold, I am against those who prophesy lying dreams, declares the LORD, and who tell them and lead my people astray by their lies and their recklessness, when I did not send them or charge them. So they do not profit this people at all, declares the LORD. (Jer 23:30–32)

 These long-ago prophets were charged by God with stealing their prophecies from one another. That is, rather than receiving revelation directly from God, they were merely repeating what other prophets said. One might wonder if the same can be said of the NAR prophets today, given that so many of them got it wrong about the US election *collectively*. How

27. Lewis and Rowntree, "Testing the Prophets" (7:26:00).

28. Lewis and Rowntree, "Testing the Prophets" (7:29:00).

29. Lewis and Rowntree, "Testing the Prophets" (7:26:00).

30. Geivett and Pivec, *A New Apostolic Reformation?*, chs. 12, 13. Notable exceptions are John the Baptist and Jesus, who prophesied to national Israel, pre-Pentecost. And the two witnesses in the book of Revelation strike the earth with plagues (Rev 11:6). But, according to a futurist interpretation of this book, these two witnesses won't appear until just before Christ's return.

does that happen? Where were the prophets who got it right, who rightly predicted that Trump would lose? Did any? Was it ten to one?[31]

We should ask, if these NAR prophets did not receive divine revelation, why did they believe what they predicted? What is the real reason? An agenda? Wishful thinking? A theology that entails the rise of a Trump-like leader whom they see as instrumental to the fulfillment of their prophecies about bringing God's kingdom to earth through the so-called "Seven Mountain Mandate?"[32]

Whatever the reason, damage has been done, as some of the prophets themselves seem to recognize.

Public Apologies

To be sure, Vallotton apologized for his off-the-mark predictions about Trump, as did several other NAR prophets.[33] But they were remarkably cavalier about it, even claiming that they could make false predictions and yet still be considered genuine prophets of God. Thankfully, we have no record of a single apology ever issued by a legitimate New Testament prophet. We doubt that the world of New Testament times could have been turned upside down in an atmosphere of prophetic chaos like we've seen in recent years (Acts 17:6). There is simply no basis in Scripture for defending contemporary apologies. These confessions, forced on recent prophets by actual events, should be accompanied by candid acknowledgments that they are not true prophets.

Now, some Christians today believe that prophecies, since the New Testament era, can be mistaken—unlike the prophecies given by the great Old Testament prophets (such as Moses, Isaiah, and Jeremiah), which were expected to be 100 percent accurate (Deut 18:22). Wayne Grudem has popularized this view of fallible New Testament prophecy, which he refers to as "ordinary Christian prophecy."[34] Other scholars, such as

---

31. After the election, Ron Cantor claimed that God told him Joe Biden would win the election, though he only shared his "revelation" privately. Obviously, this does not count as a public prophecy, if it was even prophetic at all. See Cantor, "What (I Felt)." (We note that a correct guess or an accurate hunch is not a fulfilled prophecy.)

32. See chapters 1 and 3 for our description of this alleged mandate.

33. Lea, "Ministry Leaders Apologize."

34. See Grudem, *The Gift of Prophecy*, ch. 4. Grudem does not believe the actual prophecies God gives err; rather, they become contaminated in reception or transmission by their human recipients. There is zero evidence for this in the New Testament.

(an excuse)

Thomas Schreiner and Robert Saucy, deny that New Testament prophecy can err and argue strenuously that Grudem and others who promote that view are mistaken.[35]

Let us, for the sake of argument, allow for the moment that Grudem's view is defensible. It nonetheless happens that very specific novel prophecies about events at the national level and among nations, as in the case of prophecies concerning Trump's re-election, are not your garden-variety prophecies. Prophecies of this type are common in the Old Testament, less so in the new.[36] But failed prophecies of this Old Testament kind are unequivocally disqualifying.

Furthermore, the spiritual gifts, including the gift of prophecy, are bestowed for the edification of the church (Rom 12:4–8; 1 Cor 12–14). In contrast, failed prophecies regarding the election brought shame to the church, injured its witness to the world, and undermined the faith of believers. Surely, it brought shame to those Christians who embrace the contemporary spiritual gift of prophecy. This fact was tacitly acknowledged by the drafters of the "Prophetic Standards" statement, who sought, by crafting an official statement, to restore credibility to the practice of contemporary prophecy and to rein in those making inaccurate predictions, including Vallotton.

"Prophetic Standards" Statement

We mentioned that Vallotton signed the "Prophetic Standards" statement. And we are compelled to ask, should his agreement to abide by the standards set forth in this document diminish concerns about his claim to be a prophet, in light of his failed public prophecy? We think it should not, for we believe the standards are an inadequate tool for determining whether someone is, indeed, a prophet or for evaluating contemporary prophecies. Here are four flaws we see in this document.

It is not taught and there are no clear cases. And the very concept is puzzling. The very God who reveals is thought to do so by an utterly unreliable method that might easily result in confusion, false belief, and unwise decision making—all things that legitimate prophecy is meant to guard against.

35. Schreiner, *Spiritual Gifts*, ch. 7. Saucy, "An Open but Cautious Response to C. Samuel Storms."

36. See Geivett and Pivec, *A New Apostolic Reformation?*, ch. 13.

The Statement Equivocates between So-Called "Ordinary
Christian Prophecy" and the Governing Office of Prophet/
Authoritative, Old Testament-Type Prophecy

The statement affirms both the present-day "gift of prophecy" and "the five-fold ministry of the prophet." Yet it allows that *all* prophecies may, at times, be erroneous—whether they're given by any lay believer with the mere gift of prophecy or by a prophetic minister who claims to hold a formal, authoritative office in church government.[37] Both types of prophets are allowed to err. And the statement goes further. It allows for prophetic ministers to give revelation for entire regions and nations, and not only for individuals and local churches. Thus, the statement grants extraordinary authority to certain present-day prophets.

This depiction of present-day prophets who hold governing offices and give prophecies about nations is troubling for at least two reasons. First, the statement nowhere makes the case that there is a present-day church *office* of prophet—or, indeed, that such an office *ever* existed. It merely assumes there is biblical support for such an office, effectively smuggling in a disputable office alongside the less disputable gift of prophecy. Second, by allowing that contemporary prophets may give prophecies to nations, the statement portrays those prophets as fulfilling a function characteristic of Old Testament prophets, and not in much evidence among New Testament prophets. This is a problem because the document purports to defend present-day prophecy and prophets patterned after those in the New Testament.

But prophecies at the national level, and about nations, are Old Testament-type prophecies, whether or not they are introduced with such Old Testament formulaic language as "Thus says the LORD." The introductory wording does not matter as much as the nature of the prophecies. Thus, even if one exercising the New Testament gift of prophecy may err—as Grudem argues—prophets who purport to prophesy to nations and function in other ways like Old Testament prophets should be held to the Old Testament standard of total accuracy.

---

37. The word "office" does not appear in the statement, but it seems to affirm an office of prophet. For example, it states that "prophetic ministers"—in distinction from those who merely have the spiritual gift of prophecy—must meet the scriptural qualifications for elders as found in 1 Timothy 3:1–8 and Titus 1:5–9. Thus, they appear to hold a formal office on an authoritative par with the office of elder. Also, many of the document's signers, including Vallotton, claim to hold the office of prophet.

On this point, the "Prophetic Standards" statement seems to concur. Though the document does not recognize that prophecies to nations were typically the domain of Old Testament prophets (not of New Testament prophets), it does state: "Those wanting to use Old Testament prophetic texts to exercise influence or authority over their followers should remember that inaccurate prophecy under that same Old Testament standard was punishable by death." So they agree that contemporary prophets cannot have it both ways—pronouncing dire judgments on those who refuse to listen to them, yet expecting only a slap of the hand when they get it wrong; or, putting the point differently, expecting their followers to view their words as authoritative as the words of Old Testament prophets, but wanting to be held to a lesser, allegedly New Testament standard.

By oscillating indiscriminately between types of prophecy—between a *gift* of prophecy and prophecy as given by a prophet in a formal, authoritative *office*—the document creates confusion and treats these two types of prophecy similarly, when there are supposed to be substantial differences. It also allows individuals, such as Vallotton, to operate according to Old Testament type, with authority comparable to that of Old Testament prophets, without being held to the same exacting standard of accuracy and reliability.

2) *The Statement Does Not Provide Adequate Tests for Prophets and Their Prophecies*

As we've shown, the document adopts a different standard for testing a New Testament prophet than was applied when evaluating the claims of an Old Testament prophet. But we must ask, what, then, is the proper response when a leader today gives an inaccurate prophecy? Here's how the document answers that question:

> Finally, while we believe in holding prophets accountable for their words, in accordance with the Scriptures, we do not believe that a sincere prophet who delivers an inaccurate message is therefore a false prophet. Instead, as Jesus explained, and as the Old Testament emphasized, false prophets are wolves in sheep's clothing, in contrast to true believers who might speak inaccurately (see Matt. 7:15–20; Jer. 23:9–40; Ezek. 13:23). Thus a false prophet is someone who operates under a false spirit masquerading as the Holy Spirit.

– and how can this be proved?

We therefore recognize distinctions between a believer who gives an inaccurate prophecy (in which case they should acknowledge their error), a believer who consistently prophesies inaccurately (in which case we recognize that this person is not a prophet and we urge them to stop prophesying), and a false prophet (whom we recognize as a false believer, a lost soul, calling them to repent and be saved).[38]

In other words, a contemporary prophet may occasionally give an inaccurate prophecy and still be a bona fide prophet.[39] There are various problems with this statement, and vagueness is one of them. What is an "inaccurate prophecy," according to the document's drafters? Do they require that a prophecy should be specific enough to be meaningfully testable? What ratio of false to true prophecies is permitted? The standard as stated here only says that if one never gets it right, then one surely is not a prophet. But what if he gets it right only 1 percent of the time? That would have us wondering whether an individual's purported "prophecies" were merely guesses. And that is another problem. One hundred percent accuracy is some protection against the charge that a supposed prophet is merely guessing when he gets it right. What counts as a bad enough track record to warrant the urging of a prophet to cease and desist? Should prophets with a dismal track record also "repent"? If so, what sin have they committed? And what penalties are in place for those who do not desist, or do not acknowledge their error? And are any penalties recommended for those who follow after sketchy or false prophets? What is the difference between a false prophet and a prophet who "consistently prophesies inaccurately"?

Apparently, the test for determining whether someone is a genuine prophet of God has something to do with the proportion of accurate prophecies in that person's portfolio of prophesies. Perhaps they may pass as true prophets as long as they are accurate more often than not. Those who do not meet this rather relaxed standard are not to be viewed as genuine prophets, though this does not necessarily make them false prophets.

---

38. "Prophetic Standards."

39. We also note that prominent signers of the "Prophetic Standards" statement teach that prophetic words may not come to pass if the individual receiving the word has "very little faith in the word." See Vallotton, "Common Misconceptions" (2:00). So prophets always have an out, even if they do appear to give an inaccurate prophecy: they can claim that the recipients of their prophecy did not have enough faith in the prophecy.

Further questions follow hard after these. Why should anyone ever trust the pronouncements of a prophet whose track record is hit-and-miss? On what basis can they expect their followers to believe them the next time they claim to have a word from God? What degree of confidence should someone have in their words after they've been mistaken? Twenty-five percent? Fifty percent? Seventy-five percent? And belief is only one dimension of the challenge to any recipient of a prophet's message. We call prophecy that calls for action of one sort or another "actionable prophecy." But if a recipient of some prophet's message knows in advance that the prophet is fallible—that is, if the prophet could, on any given occasion, be mistaken in what he or she represents as truly prophetic—then what sort of action is called for? This is a practical problem of knowing what to believe or how to act in response to any prophetic word, since it is considered fallible even when uttered. Is it really actionable if it could be mistaken? Notice, we assume that a prophecy is not actionable if it is known to be mistaken. But we suspect that, as a matter of practical Christian living, it is not actionable as long as it is *possible* that it is mistaken. This is one of the most severe challenges to the whole notion of fallible prophecy. Commentators like Grudem have saddled an entire class of prophecy, really, all New Testament and all contemporary prophecy, with the unfortunate reputation of being "possibly mistaken." A red flag waves over every prophecy given today. For all intents and purposes, a prophecy comes with a warning label: "This may not actually be a word from God."

For convenience, we distinguish between "false prophecy" and "fallible prophecy." False prophecy is prophecy that is false when uttered, regardless of what happens. An individual may prophesy a future event that does not come to pass. That would be a false prophecy. But an individual might also presume or pretend to prophesy an event that does actually come to pass. It does not follow that he has *prophesied* correctly or accurately. For his message to count as genuine prophesy, his insight into the future and his message about it must have been given to him by God. So a false prophet might make an accurate "prediction." This is not evidence that he has prophesied truly. The prophet of God does not just utter a statement of fact about the past, the present, or the future. The prophet does so *on God's behalf*. The genuine prophet speaks for God. So when uttering any statement (whether it is about the past, the present, or the future), implicit in that statement—if the individual is speaking in the persona or role of a prophet—is always the tacit claim to be speaking for

God. The words "Thus says the Lord" are implied. And that, also, is either true or false. So for an individual to prophesy truly, both the specific content of his message (about the past, the present, or the future) *and his or her tacit claim to be speaking for God* must be true.

Now, what becomes of the force of this tacit claim to be speaking for God if the message, from the moment it is uttered, is under the shadow of fallibility? It is under the shadow of fallibility insofar as it remains possible that it is mistaken. You might think that the shadow dissipates for those prophecies that prove to be accurate. But this is doubly worrisome. First, such a prophecy is not fully actionable until it is known to be accurate, which is only possible in the event that a predictive prophecy comes to pass. By then it may well be too late to be actionable in the usual sense associated with valuable prophecy. Second, if a predictive word comes to pass, this attests to the accuracy of the *content* of the prediction; but it does not automatically corroborate the prophet's tacit claim to speak for God. So even should a fallible prophecy come to pass, it will not be obvious that people had received genuine prophecy.[40] This is why it is so important that we consider the need for any prophet to produce evidence that he or she truly is a prophet of God. An uncanny ability to get it right every time would surely help to alleviate any natural concern about the authenticity of a prophet's claim. As we've noted elsewhere, a track record of producing miracles that confirm the authority of a prophet's message would also weigh significantly. And a prophet's general skillfulness in teaching already revealed truth with accuracy and insight, in accord with proven standards of responsible interpretation, must be considered, as well.[41]

The fallibility principle, accepted by far too many in the continuationist camp, creates a giant loophole for false prophecies to escape

40. On the view that now prevails among NAR prophets, and too many who stand more generally in the continuationist camp, a prophet today should rather say, not "Thus says the Lord," but "Maybe the Lord is saying . . ." But we wouldn't place too much confidence in a prophet who is forever consigned to wearing training wheels and is never able to assure me that God has indeed spoken. It seems that I would always be justified if I did not quite believe the prophet's message, or act on the basis of it. On a separate point, those continuationists who chide cessationists (sometimes calling them "aberrant") for seeing a change in how God works without evidence of any such change, but embrace this doctrine of fallible prophecy, are cessationists themselves. And yet they have no compelling case that God shifted dramatically from utilizing prophets with unimpeachable credentials to utilizing individuals who cannot say for sure whether God has indeed spoken. Continuationism needs defenders who will hold the line and insist on a divine standard of accuracy for predictive prophecy.

41. See Pivec and Geivett, *Counterfeit Kingdom*, ch. 4.

detection. And it defrauds the church, for it hamstrings its capacity to act responsibly on the basis of whatever is revealed in truth to a legitimate prophet of God. In the aftermath of the United States presidential election, NAR prophets defended themselves by claiming to have accurately predicted other past events. In other words, they point to a track record. For example, Shawn Bolz wrote on Facebook, "In the same season of such a big miss I have had some of the most marvelous fulfillment of prophecies in my entire career." But what "marvelous" fulfillments was he referring to? He didn't say. Surely, he was not referring to the prediction he made that COVID-19 was ending and would not become a major pandemic.[42] That was another major miss on his part.

Yet, even if Bolz has made accurate predictions in the past, that still does not prove his legitimacy as a prophet. Notice, the Old Testament cites failed predictions as a *negative* test for prophetic authority: if the prophecy fails, then the prophet is not the real deal (Deut 18:20–22). Failed prophecy *disconfirms* the individual's claim to be a prophet. But the test of accurate predictions cannot be used by itself to *confirm* that one is a prophet of God. This point is made clear in Deuteronomy 13:1–5, which warns that, even if a so-called prophet makes a prediction that comes to pass, they must not be listened to if their prophecies are accompanied by false teaching. Indeed, prior to Grudem's popularization of the notion that New Testament prophecy is fallible, it was the consensus among Christians that, according to Scripture, one failed prophecy is sufficient to show that a person is not a genuine prophet of God.

Grudem's critics argue that his proposal—namely, that New Testament prophets, in contrast to Old Testament prophets, erred—simply isn't credible.[43] They aren't moved by Grudem's argument that Agabus made a mistake—when he said the Jews would bind Paul and deliver him to the Romans (Acts 21:11).[44] Nor are they persuaded by his other arguments.[45]

---

42. We referenced this prophecy in chapter 4.

43. See, e.g., Schreiner, *Spiritual Gifts*, ch. 7.

44. Schreiner, *Spiritual Gifts*, ch. 7.

45. Schreiner, *Spiritual Gifts*, ch. 7. One of Grudem's other arguments is that, in the New Testament, prophecies are judged, not the prophets themselves. He bases this argument on 1 Corinthians 14:29 and 1 Thessalonians 5:20–21. But Schreiner points out that, in the Old Testament, the only way to evaluate a prophet—whether he was true or false—was by his prophecies, and Schreiner notes that 1 Corinthians 14:29 and 1 Thessalonians 5:20–21 demonstrate that same means of evaluation; they don't do away with it. Another of Grudem's arguments—based on Acts 21:4, 13–14—is that sometimes prophecies in the New Testament were disobeyed and such disobedience

Since there is nothing to suggest that the standard of accuracy changed between the Old Testament and the New, we conclude that it stands. Like Old Testament prophecy, New Testament prophecy cannot be a mixture of truth and error. Yet the drafters of the "Prophetic Standards" statement reject the historic consensus and follow Grudem's permissive view that allows for inaccurate prophecies to be given by legitimate prophets. Notably, Grudem is one of the document's signers.[46]

watered down + confusion

Their rejection of the standard of total accuracy has left the door wide open to false prophets to prance in and out without detection. Jesus and the apostle John warned the church in advance about the coming of false prophets. They said there would be "many" false prophets, and they would not be easy to distinguish from true believers (Matt 7:15; 24:11; 24:24; Mark 13:22; 1 John 4:1; Rev 16:13; 19:20). In light of their warnings, Thomas Schreiner observes, "Those who claim that New Testament prophecy is fallible don't account well for the need to discriminate between true and false prophets, for making such judgments would be terribly hard if the words of true prophets contain both truth and error."[47] Hard, indeed. And because they have done away with the "one strike,

---

was not sinful, indicating that New Testament prophecies were understood to be errant and less authoritative than Old Testament prophecies. In response, Schreiner argues that Paul did not disobey a prophecy, but disregarded a mistaken inference drawn from the prophecy. Because of a prophecy by Agabus, Paul was warned by the believers that he was with not to travel to Jerusalem. They thought that because Agabus had prophesied trouble for Paul if he were to go there, Paul should steer clear of the place. But Paul, though he agreed with the prophecy, and no doubt expected the trouble that it portended, decided that he should go anyway. And so he did. And while he was there, the details of the prophecy were fulfilled with precision. While verse 4 says that "through the Spirit," Paul's companions urged him not to go to Jerusalem, they do not say that this was the Spirit's direction (see v. 12); on the contrary, they deferred to Paul and said, "Let the will of the Lord be done" (v. 14). They were sensitive to the Spirit throughout the exchange with Paul, but they received no explicit instructions from the Spirit that Paul should not go. Paul had already determined that he was constrained by the Spirit to go to Jerusalem, despite the trials he could anticipate (Acts 20:22–23). The Spirit was not leading Paul to adopt one course of action, and then cancelling that through contrary advice from his companions.

46. Grudem argues that New Testament prophets did not hold a formal, governing office in contrast to many of the document's other signers and in contrast to the document itself, which appears to assume a present-day prophetic office modeled after the New Testament prophets (although it does not use the word "office"). Grudem, *The Gift of Prophecy*, ch. 10.

47. Schreiner, *Spiritual Gifts*, ch. 7.

you're out" criterion, the document's drafters have had to resort to other more subjective tests.

Certainly, the Prophetic Standard Statement does recognize the reality of "false prophets." It states that "a false prophet is someone who operates under a false spirit masquerading as the Holy Spirit" and is "a false believer, a lost soul."[48] But, having already excluded the possibility of appeal to the fulfillment test for predictive prophecy, it does not suggest any other means of identifying such a deceiver. And if we turn to criteria for identifying false prophets given by influential prophets who have signed the statement, for example, Kris Vallotton, they are not especially helpful. In his book *Basic Training for the Prophetic Ministry*, Vallotton lists three characteristics of false prophets: they have an "evil heart" (one that does not know and obey God), they misuse Scripture to support their own agendas, and they seek influence to draw people to themselves. While these all are marks of false prophets, as criteria for testing prophets they are rather impressionistic and vague, and their usefulness for testing a prophet is limited. Suppose Vallotton (or any other one of the document's signers) is a false prophet. Using the criteria set forth by Vallotton, would it be possible for them to reach this verdict?

If we suppose that genuine prophets can err (as allowed by the statement's drafters), how are their individual prophetic words to be evaluated for accuracy? The document answers: "We can only believe the prophetic word if it is not contrary to Scripture, it is not factually in error, and our own spirit bears witness with it."[49] It also states that prophecies "should be evaluated by other mature leaders" in addition to the prophetic minister who delivers it.

These tests are not adequate. The first two tests—as we noted above regarding failed predictions—are negative tests that can disconfirm a prophecy: if a prophecy contradicts Scripture or contains elements that are factually in error, then it cannot be a true prophecy.[50] But passing these tests does not confirm that a prophecy is true. Presumably, that is the point of the third test that "our own spirit bears witness with it." This test is presented in the document as a confirming test, but it is highly subjective and oddly spiritualistic, and, therefore, almost totally useless.

48. "Prophetic Standards."

49. "Prophetic Standards."

50. In our previous work, we explain why "not contradicting Scripture" is too low of a bar for testing prophecies. See Geivett and Pivec, *A New Apostolic Reformation?*, ch. 9.

And we have to ask, where is this test ever given in Scripture? How did they come up with this test? Moreover, the test of having mature leaders evaluate prophecies does not resolve these problems. All this so-called test does is move back a step the process of testing prophecies. What criteria do mature leaders use for this purpose?

Finally, when it comes to testing present-day prophets and their prophecies, the document addresses only what prophets actually say; it does not address what they *don't* say—which can be just as telling. For example, no major prophets saw COVID-19 coming.[51] One might wonder, of what use are prophets to nations who did not foresee one of the most significant events to occur in recent history—a global pandemic that disrupted the entire world and even led to strife within churches as they responded to government regulations? Nor did any well-known prophets we are aware of foresee the 2022 Russian invasion of Ukraine. And, as the war unfolded, they were conspicuously quiet as to its outcome. A hush descended on the prophetic community in an apparent community-wide plague of laryngitis.[52] Their silence was deafening. It was a prophetic blackout. But those were precisely the sorts of situations when you would expect them to be outspoken. After all, a favored NAR proof text for claiming that God always reveals his plans (including major world calamities) to his prophets in advance is Amos 3:7: "For the LORD God does

51. On January 26, 2020, Vallotton "prayed" (i.e., made a "declaration") for the people in China who "are having such a struggle with an outbreak of virus there" and that there would be "no more deaths." He spoke of the virus as if it was a threat only to China. He was, obviously, unaware of the global pandemic to come. See Vallotton, "Covenant Culture." Perry Stone claims he prophesied COVID-19 in advance, but his words—in the August 19, 2018, sermon clip he presents as evidence of his prediction—do not provide any specific details about COVID-19, the date of its appearance, or that it would become a global pandemic. They only refer to the devil trying to create "a new strain of virus like eboli [*sic*] and other kinds of strains of flu that is [*sic*] virulent against medical treatment." See Prince, "Joseph Prince Prophesied." (The very fact that he would have to replay his prophecy, on video, to his followers to prove he had predicted it seems odd; people would not need reminding of an amazing prediction of the sort he claims to have made. Otherwise, what would be the purpose of a prophecy no one recalled? Even in retrospect, it does not appear to be a prophecy that was of actionable value at the time.) No influential apostles and prophets made specific predictions that were clearly about COVID-19. For example, a leading council of prophets known as the Apostolic Council of Prophetic Elders, led by Cindy Jacobs, released its "Word of the Lord for 2020," which said nothing about a virus or pandemic. Cindy Jacobs, "ACPE."

52. Mocking failed prophets is an Old Testament tradition! (1 Kgs 18:27; Isa 28:7–8; 56:10)

nothing without revealing his secret to his servants the prophets."[53] Yet they don't prophecy when it's expected, on their own assumptions and past practice. This is another negative test they have failed.

3) *The Statement Does Not Address the Novel, NAR-Type of Prophecy Known as Making "Declarations"*

Many of the statement's signers promote a novel type of prophecy, yet the statement says nothing about this newfangled class of prophetic utterances. Let us explain.

Historically, Christian prophecy has been understood as revelation from God. Yet, influential NAR leaders, including Bill Johnson and Randy Clark, have redefined prophecy to include a form of prophecy that *creates* or alters *reality* through spoken "declarations." (This is accomplished, for example, when declarations produce healing from disease.) This type of prophecy is promoted in Randy Clark's book, *Stories of Divine Healing: Supernatural Testimonies That Ignite Faith for Your Healing*. In the introduction, Bill Johnson states that "prophecy either foretells the future *or changes the present*."[54] In another book, Johnson states that prophets "both 'foretell' and 'cause.'" He also says: "In part, the prophetic ministry 'causes' change by declaring such change. That is why the Scriptures state, 'Death and life are in the power of the tongue' (Prov. 18:21)." He also strongly implies that prophets who prophesy judgment on a society, rather than "reformation," actually "cause" the judgments to occur because "the prophetic ministry 'causes' change by declaring such change."[55]

In line with this innovative view of prophecy, Vallotton shares a story about a time when he delivered a declaration as a form of prophecy. He said he was having dinner with a married couple named Gene and Lisa. They had been married for thirteen years and were unable to have a baby. But to Vallotton's surprise, during the dinner, the Lord spoke to him and said, "Tell Lisa that at this time next year she is going to have a child!" Vallotton said he knew of their struggles conceiving and he didn't have faith for this miracle. So he told the Lord that he would not tell Lisa that. But he writes:

53. See, e.g., Mattera, "Analyzing David Wilkerson's Prophecy." We cite Mattera here because he is one of the two initiators of the "Prophetic Standards" statement.

54. Clark, *Stories*, introduction (emphasis ours).

55. Johnson, *God Is Good*, ch. 10.

arrogance! [handwritten margin note]

Then Jesus made a statement that changed my life. He said, "If you don't tell her, she won't get pregnant!" My head was spinning. How could this be true? Was I supposed to believe that my words would determine whether or not a child would come into this world? I decided to whisper the prophecy in Lisa's ear. . . . But a couple of months later, Lisa called and left a message on our answering machine: "Kris, this is Lisa. I thought you might want to know that I am pregnant!"[56]

The idea that a woman would conceive only if Vallotton told her she would is astounding. But this understanding of prophecy is summed up by Johnson: "True prophetic decrees are catalytic. They must be spoken to bring about the change they speak of."[57]

agree — t who will know? [handwritten margin note]

This notion of *prophecy as declaration* has no biblical support or acceptance in the history of Christian thought. And many declarations made by NAR leaders have failed, as we showed in the first chapter. Even high-profile NAR apostles have made declarations that failed. Consider Che Ahn's declaration—made together with Johnson, Ed Silvoso, and other NAR leaders, in 2020, at a conference held at Bethel Church—that racism would be ended in the *ekklesia*, from that night forward.[58] What reasonable person would think that declaration was fulfilled? Even so, making prayer declarations as a form of prophecy remains popular in NAR, and the practice is common among many signers of the "Prophetic Standards" statement. Unaccountably, this practice is not acknowledged in the statement. But we wonder, why not? What do the document's drafters think about this type of prophetic activity?[59] Surely, the document would better serve the church if it included guidance about this increasingly popular understanding of "prophecy," especially since the practice is common among many of the signatories.

56. Vallotton, *Developing a Supernatural Lifestyle*, ch. 10.

57. Johnson, *God Is Good*, ch. 10.

58. *Ekklēsia*, the Greek word used in the New Testament for church, is a specific term used by NAR leaders to refer to their peculiar vision of the church as the governmental instrument God designed to transform society and establish his physical kingdom on earth. See Silvoso, *Ekklesia*. Silvoso was one of the NAR leaders who took part in making the declaration to end racism. To watch a video of that declaration to end racism (including the bizarre antics that took place, i.e., a reenactment from the scene in the movie *Lord of the Rings*, in which the wizard Gandalf confronts the demonic monster Balrog), see Johnson and Ahn, "Gandalf Staff."

59. We already noted that one of the document's drafters has, at least on one occasion, issued public declarations. (See chapter 3, note 53.) Does he view them as a type of prophecy? Are they causally efficacious?

The Statement Does Not Address Prophets Who Claim to Be Giving New or Restored Truths to the Broader Church

The document states that public apologies should be made by prophets if their specific and public predictions about future events don't happen. But unlike prophets in the Bible, who gave prophecies that were specific and could be evaluated (2 Kings 7), most NAR prophecies are vague and untestable. Among these are their revelations of new or restored truths. Such NAR "truths" concern matters of belief and practice, and they therefore have serious implications. How are these prophetic claims to be tested?

Consider Vallotton's claim that Jesus spoke to him one morning in 1998 and told him about a megashift occurring in the church government, from being pastor-led to being apostle-led.[60] This revelation is untestable in the sense that it is not tied to any specific prediction of a future event. So, how is it to be assessed?

If wrong, this prophetic word is no less damaging than his erroneous prophecy about Trump's reelection; it may be even more damaging. Church leaders who believe Vallotton to be a genuine prophet will feel compelled to respond to this prophecy by transitioning their own church government to apostles. And the scope of this revelation is immense: it is given to the global church. Yet the "Prophetic Standards" statement offers no guidance for assessing revelations of this type (other than to declare that they cannot contradict Scripture).

The fact remains that contemporary apostles and prophets claim to reveal critical new truth to the broader church. Thus, the document's silence about these prophets' claims—whether such claims are authentic revelations from God—is a serious omission. It leaves the door open for unbiblical and unhealthy teachings and practices to enter churches through self-described prophets—as, indeed, has already occurred.

A Corner on the Truth

Of all the types of revelation Bethel and NAR prophets claim to give, their "new truths" and "restored truths" are among the most concerning because of their impact on the teachings and practices of churches throughout the world. Recall Johnson's teaching that this generation of the church

60. See chapter 2.

must embrace all these new revelations; their floor should be the previous generation's ceiling for God's plans and purposes to unfold on earth.[61] In other words, each generation must build on the truths restored by the previous generation. Elsewhere, he refers to the accumulation of that new revelation as a spiritual "jump start" for the next generation.[62]

What is the list of new revelations that the church must believe? Is it the same as the lists given by other NAR leaders?[63] What exactly do Christians need to embrace? The new/restored truths we identified in the last chapter would likely be included: teachings about churches transitioning from pastors to apostles in their governance, heaven on earth/the Lord's Prayer, the billion-soul harvest, the goodness of God (as it relates to physical healing), victorious eschatology, and Jesus emptying himself of his divine powers. But Johnson implies there are more. If these truths are so critical to God's plans and to fulfilling the church's mission in the world, he should spell them out clearly and not merely allude to their existence. Otherwise, how are Christians to know which new revelations they are responsible to believe and to act on?

Since Johnson has not done this—so far as we can tell—one might reasonably wonder, why not? By not providing such a list, he certainly has allowed himself the convenience of deniability—even if that is not his intention. One might not feel adequately informed anywhere except at Bethel—or a Bethel-friendly church—where they are purportedly operating with special access to all the relevant new truth.

In the next three chapters, we examine some of the new/restored truths taught by Bethel leaders, starting with Bill Johnson's novel take on the Lord's Prayer.

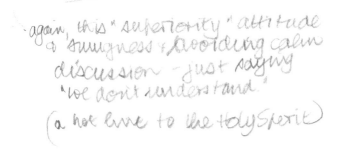

again, this "superiority" attitude & smugness & avoiding calm discussion — just saying "we don't understand." (a hot line to the Holy Spirit)

61. Johnson, *The Supernatural Power*, ch. 11. (We cited this teaching in chapter 4.)

62. Franklin and Davis, *The Physics of Heaven*, ch. 4.

63. See, e.g., Hamon, *Prophetic Scriptures*, 127–28.

—6—

Bringing Heaven to Earth

Our Father in heaven,
hallowed be your name.
Your kingdom come,
your will be done,
on earth as it is in heaven.
Give us this day our daily bread,
and forgive us our debts,
as we also have forgiven our debtors.
And lead us not into temptation,
but deliver us from evil.

—The Lord's Prayer (Matt 6:9–13)[1]

Is it possible that Christians have misunderstood one of Jesus's most important teachings and, as a result, have floundered for centuries in completing their most important assignment?

The answer, astonishingly, is yes—that is, if the apostle Bill Johnson is correct.

The Lord's Prayer—taught by Jesus to his disciples—is the most precious and well-known prayer of Christians from all traditions. During

1. A slightly different version of this prayer appears in Luke 11:1–4.

the early centuries of Christianity, the prayer played an essential role in its worship, teaching, and practice.[2] Today, it's recited during church services, funerals, and before family meals. Children memorize it in Sunday School classes.

Yet despite its special place of honor, most Christians have failed to grasp its true meaning and significance. They know the prayer by heart, but their hearts have missed its meaning. That's what Bill Johnson claims. The prayer conveys God's marching orders for God's people to bring God's kingdom to earth through their spoken words. It's a battle plan, but Christians have blown it.

So how have Christians gotten it so wrong for so long? Historically, they've seen it as a model of petitionary prayer, a guide for how believers should approach God (i.e., intimately and respectfully) and for the types of requests they are free to make of him while they await the coming of his kingdom in its fullness.[3] This understanding of the Lord's Prayer differs radically from Johnson's. For him, Jesus does not commend a pattern for petitionary prayer; the Lord's Prayer has nothing to do with humbly requesting divine favor. Rather, it models a type of prayer known as "binding and loosing" prayer. We explain the significance of binding and loosing prayer more fully later in this chapter. But the basic idea is that Christians wield their God-given authority to bind (or halt) all forms of evil in their tracks and to loose (or release) the blessings of heaven. In addition, the Lord's Prayer teaches believers to use binding and loosing prayer to establish God's earthly kingdom, here and now.[4]

---

2. Hammerling, *The Lord's Prayer in the Early Church: The Pearl of Great Price*. (Note that we list two books written, or edited, by Hammerling—both with similar titles—in our bibliography.)

3. Several interpretations have been advanced, but the standard view is that this is a model for petitionary prayer. In addition to its petitionary character, Christians have seen in the prayer an inducement to godly living, for the petitions reveal God's priorities for our desires and actions. Christians pray for God's will to be done on earth, but they also seek to fulfill God's will on earth through obedience to him. Such obedience has been pursued through various means, including social action. For a history of interpretation of the Lord's Prayer, see Hammerling, *The Lord's Prayer in the Early Church: The Pearl of Great Price*. Also, we assume that this prayer pattern is intended for use by Christians of all generations. But some hold that this prayer was meant as a pattern for the people of Israel and not for the church. They therefore discourage its use by Christians.

4. Bill Johnson's teaching aligns with dominion theology—the view that the church is to take dominion over society and establish God's earthly kingdom before Christ returns. Johnson and other leaders within the New Apostolic Reformation promote a version of dominion theology known as "kingdom now" theology. This theology

Confusion about the Lord's Prayer explains why Christians have failed to complete their God-given assignment. There is an urgent need to recover the true meaning of the Lord's Prayer and to understand the key it holds to establishing God's kingdom. Johnson writes:

> The Lord's Model Prayer provides the clearest instruction on how we bring the reality of His world into this one. . . . Jesus' model reveals the only two real priorities of prayer: First, intimacy with God that is expressed in worship—holy is Your name. And second, to bring His Kingdom to earth, establishing His dominion over the needs of mankind—Your Kingdom come."[5]

But what does Johnson mean when he speaks of establishing God's dominion or kingdom? And, how, specifically, will binding and loosing prayer accomplish this?

Bringing Heaven to Earth

Based on his understanding of the Lord's Prayer, Johnson calls the Christian's assignment "bringing heaven to earth."[6] He teaches that bringing heaven to earth, under the leadership of apostles and prophets, is the believer's "greatest commission," greater than all other commissions given by Jesus.[7] It's greater even than the commission recorded in Matthew 28:16–20, at least as this commission has been understood by generations

---

describes the way the church is to establish God's kingdom, namely, by implementing divine strategies that have been revealed by present-day apostles and prophets for this purpose. Thus, the church must yield to the authority of these present-day apostles and prophets. Another version of dominion theology is known as reconstructionism. Unlike their "kingdom now" counterparts, reconstructionists do not stress the need for apostles, prophets, and miraculous powers to accomplish this dominion mandate. They focus their efforts on education and politics. For more information about dominion theology, see Barron, *Heaven on Earth?*

5. Johnson, *When Heaven Invades Earth*, ch. 5.

6. Johnson uses this phrase throughout his books and other teaching materials. See, e.g., this declaration: "My job is to bring Heaven to earth through my prayers and obedience." See Johnson, *Hosting the Presence*, ch. 5.

7. Johnson refers to this task as the "greatest commission" in the title to the first chapter of his book *The Way of Life*. And he refers to it as "this greatest of all commissions" in chapter 1 of the same book. He also makes it clear that apostles are the ones God has tasked with leading the church in its fulfillment of that commission. He writes: "Understanding the purpose and nature of the apostle, and their assignment in society, will help us to appreciate with much greater insight and conviction the reason behind this [the Lord's] prayer." See *The Way of Life*, ch. 9 (updated 2019 edition).

of Christians. On the standard interpretation of the "Great Commission," recounted in Matthew 28, Jesus called his original disciples to go out into the world to make disciples of him in all nations, baptizing and teaching those who believe. This was to be their greatest assignment.[8] But John-son doesn't see the Great Commission in this way at all. Like others, he speaks of Jesus's assignment in Matthew 28:16–20 as the Great Commis-sion. But, in contrast to the traditional—and most natural understand-ing—of Jesus's admonition, he views it through the same lens he uses on the Lord's Prayer: it is a commission to "disciple" entire nations—not just individuals within those nations—and take dominion of the earth.[9] This is the greatest commission. It's also a restoration of the original "com-mission" God gave Adam and Eve to rule the earth.[10] Anything less than taking dominion is a mere "sub-point" to the greatest commission. The essential task is not to spread the teachings of Jesus to the ends of the earth and make disciples. Johnson writes:

> There is one assignment given that is so large, so all encompass-ing, that every other commission aligns its purpose to the fulfill-ment of that one. Perhaps we could call the other assignments

8. To be precise, Jesus here commissioned eleven of his original disciples. Judas Iscariot, who had taken his life after experiencing horror and remorse following his betrayal of Jesus, was yet to be replaced by Matthias (see Acts 1:12–26). The same Great Commission is repeated in Acts 1:8.

9. Johnson, *God Is Good*, chs. 1, 6. Johnson's interpretation of the Great Commis-sion, found in Matthew 28:16–20, aligns with dominion theology. For his description of the Great Commission as a dominion mandate in his own books and books he has edited, see Johnson, *When Heaven Invades Earth*, ch. 2; Wallnau and Johnson, *Invading Babylon*, introduction and chs. 1, 4. Many other NAR leaders who teach this dominion mandate, like Johnson, frequently interpret the command in Matthew 28:19—"Go therefore and make disciples of all nations"—as a command to "disciple nations," not to make disciples of individuals within all nations. (See, e.g., Wagner, *Dominion!*, 72–73). But, as Barron points out, "they are on dubious ground" with this interpretation: "The New Testament uses 'nations' (Greek *ethnē*) to refer to political entities (cf. Mk 13:8, Ac, 2:5) but also, more generally, to people-groups, especially Gentiles (e.g., Mt 6:32; Gal 2:9; Eph 2:11). The latter meaning seems to have been intended in Matthew 28:19–20, which commands the believers to baptize and teach *the ethnē*; after all, one baptizes individual persons, not civil institutions. Therefore, to find a mandate for national discipleship in this passage seems unwarranted." See Barron, *Heaven on Earth?*, 154.

10. Wallnau and Johnson, *Invading Babylon*, ch. 1. Johnson cites Genesis 1:28–29. The command God gave to Adam and Eve to "have dominion" is often referred to as the "dominion mandate." But historically it has been seen as a mandate to take dominion "over the environment, not over fellow human beings" (Barron, *Heaven on Earth?*, 154).

sub-points to one major point. . . . The assignments to evangelize, to work miracles, to care for the poor, the widow, the orphan, and the like are all practical expressions of this one major task—God's will fully manifest here, with Heaven as its source, model, and inspiration.[11]

This claim that the church's greatest commission is to bring heaven to earth is disputable. In fact, it is revisionist. Johnson revises tradition to suit his purposes. The phrase "bringing heaven to earth" has become a sort of tagline for Bethel and is often used in advertisements for its events and teaching materials. The concept of bringing heaven to earth is also captured in other phrases used by Bethel, including the "invasion" of earth (captured in the title *When Heaven Invades Earth*, one of Johnson's bestselling books), Heaven Come (the name of an annual Bethel conference and a Bethel Music song), and "on earth as it is in heaven" (language borrowed from the Lord's Prayer and emblazoned on the home page of the Bethel Redding website).[12]

Let us consider what it would look like for the church to "bring heaven to earth." Johnson explains:

> When we pray, "Thy kingdom come, Thy will be done," we're praying for the King's dominion and will to be realized right here, right now. . . . What is free to operate in Heaven—joy, peace, wisdom, health, wholeness, and all the other good promises we read about in the Bible—should be free to operate here on this planet, in your home, your church, your business, and your school. What is not free to operate there—sickness, disease, spiritual bondage, and sin—should not be free to operate here, period. . . . We are out to destroy the works of the devil.[13]

In other words, there's no sin, or sickness, or disease, or depression, or poverty in heaven. So, for heaven to come to earth means that none of those things should be found on earth either. And it isn't merely that sin and suffering should not, *ideally*, exist in the world today. Rather, Christians have been tasked to make earth's reality an unqualified reflection of heaven. As Johnson has said, "My assignment isn't to go to heaven; my assignment is to bring heaven. . . . We've been given a

---

11. *The Way of Life*, chs. 1, 9 (updated 2019 edition; his emphasis).

12. Bethel Redding.

13. Johnson, *The Supernatural Power*, ch. 1.

mission and that mission is to pull on the reality of that world until it manifests in this one."[14]

Just how much of heaven can be pulled to earth? Johnson himself contemplates this question. "No one knows for sure," he says, "but we do know through Church history that it's more than we have now. And we know through the Scripture that it's even more than has ever entered our minds."[15] This is telling. For it implies that there may be a limit to what God intends to do through his authority-bearing apostles and prophets. This, in turn, implies a limit to that authority, for the apostle and the prophet cannot say in advance how far this realization of heaven on earth will extend. Such a limit also implies that the apostle and the prophet cannot, simply as a direct consequence of their "binding and loosing" (see below), fully realize the divine goal to bring God's kingdom to earth. In fact, it remains a conveniently open question how far short of fulfillment is permitted.

According to Johnson, the church accomplishes this mission of pulling heaven to earth through prayer: "Our prayer assignment reveals God's overall commission and purpose for our lives. Through prayer, 'on earth as it is in heaven' is to become an increasing reality."[16] But recall that the type of prayer Johnson speaks of here is not petition. Rather, it refers to a type of prayer known as binding and loosing.[17]

---

14. Johnson spoke these words at the Onething conference hosted by the International House of Prayer of Kansas City, Missouri, in 2016. See Johnson, "Session 8." To be clear, Johnson teaches that there are limits to how much of heaven can be pulled to earth through prayer. He writes, "The critics of this view sarcastically say, 'So I guess we're supposed to pray for streets of gold.' No! But our streets should be known for the same purity and blessing as heaven." (See Johnson, *When Heaven Invades Earth*, ch. 5.) Here Johnson resorts to a less than literal, but still very real, comparison between heaven as it is and earth as it should be. His critics may be confused rather than sarcastic, for it is Johnson who insists on such a close correspondence between heaven and earth. But on this point he settles for metaphor. And it's fair to wonder why.

15. Johnson, *When Heaven Invades Earth*, ch. 5.

16. Johnson, *The Way of Life*, ch. 1 (updated 2019 edition).

17. We note that sometimes Johnson uses the language of petition when writing about binding and loosing prayer. For example, in his book *When Heaven Invades Earth* (chap. 5), in a discussion of the Lord's Prayer he writes, "'Give us this day our daily bread.' Is anyone starving in heaven? Of course not. This request is a practical application of how His dominion should be seen here on earth—abundant supply." His use of the word "request" sounds like he is referring to petitionary prayer. But he makes it clear in his teachings about binding and loosing prayer that such prayer is not petitionary but is the issuing of authoritative commands.

Binding and Loosing Prayer

What is binding and loosing prayer? It is based on teachings that originated with leaders in the prosperity gospel/Word of Faith movement, and that are embraced by leaders in the New Apostolic Reformation.[18] According to these teachings, believers have been given spiritual authority to bind (or forbid) the works of Satan, including sickness, addictions, fear, troubled family relationships, and poverty. Likewise, they've been given authority to loose (or permit) God's blessings, including health, peace of mind, strong marriages, successful businesses, and abundant finances. This authority to bind and loose was conferred upon Christians by Jesus when he gave Peter, one of his twelve disciples, the "keys" of the kingdom of heaven.

> And I tell you, you are Peter, and on this rock I will build my church, and the gates of hell shall not prevail against it. I will give you the keys of the kingdom of heaven, and whatever you *bind* on earth shall be bound in heaven, and whatever you *loose* on earth shall be loosed in heaven. (Matt 16:18–19)[19]

Johnson appeals to this passage in support of his doctrine of binding and loosing prayer. He also claims that this type of prayer is "the primary focus for *all* prayer."[20]

> This is the primary focus for all prayer—if it exists in heaven, it is to be loosed on earth. It's the praying Christian who looses heaven's expression here. When the believer prays according to the revealed will of God, faith is specific and focused. Faith grabs hold of that reality. . . . Such an invasion causes the circumstances here to line up with heaven. . . . Again, through prayer we are to exercise the authority given to us. "I will give you the keys of the kingdom of heaven; and whatever you bind on earth shall have been bound in heaven, and whatever you loose on earth shall have been loosed in heaven." Notice the phrase shall have been. The implication is that we can only bind or loose here what has already been bound or loosed there.[21]

18. Kate Bowler describes Word of Faith theology as a variety of the prosperity gospel. See her carefully researched study of the prosperity gospel (Bowler, *Blessed*, ch. 2).

19. Our emphasis.

20. What Johnson says casually and matter-of-factly we draw attention to with italics.

21. Johnson, *When Heaven Invades Earth*, ch. 5. Johnson recounts the time when he first learned about binding and loosing prayer. (See *The Supernatural Power*, ch. 2.)

Believers exercise their authority to bind and loose through their spoken words. In faith, they make verbal affirmations that are believed to be in line with God's will and that release his power to create their desired reality.[22] In much the way God spoke and brought the world into existence, believers today—who are created in the image of God—also have the power to bring things into existence through their spoken affirmations.[23] These affirmations are known as "prophetic declarations," "faith declarations," "prayer declarations," or just "declarations." They're also referred to as "confessions," "proclamations," and "decrees."[24] Johnson uses many of these terms. But whatever term is used, it's crucial that the affirmations are expressed aloud. As he writes, "The decree itself is important because some things don't manifest until they are spoken."[25] Why must they be spoken? For one thing, if they're not spoken they can't be heard by angels who "enforce" the words—or carry them out as their assignments.[26] In fact, angels get "bored" when they don't have any

22. Bowler, *Blessed*, ch. 2. In her book, Bowler describes in detail how teachings about the power of verbal affirmation were promoted by some early Pentecostal leaders, including John G. Lake, and became integral to the teachings of the prosperity gospel/Word of Faith movement. Lake's theology has greatly influenced Johnson's teachings, as evidenced by Johnson's frequent references to Lake in his books. Johnson also co-authored a book celebrating the influence of Lake, among other individuals. (See Johnson and Miskov, *Defining Moments*.) The Lake connection is unmistakable.

23. Johnson teaches that, since God made man in his image, and God "spoke the worlds into being," then human beings have a similar ability, through their speech, to change problematic situations. Listen to his sermon: Johnson, "Power of Confession" (8:00). The logic here is baffling. Johnson needs to make explicit an assumption that is essential to his argument: If a human person is made in God's image, then a human person can do what God can do, without qualification. This is shocking, for more than one reason. Whatever power humans have is derivative and limited, infinitely so in comparison with God's power. And we must ask, has Johnson forgotten that even the unregenerate are made in God's image?

24. Other prominent NAR leaders also promote making declarations and decrees, including Mike Bickle, who writes, "We make decrees to the elements of nature and to inanimate objects (wind, fig tree, mountains, etc.). We make decrees over geographic regions. . . . We make decrees to demon spirits that dwell in people. . . . We may make decrees to angels because they obey the word of the Lord even from our lips (Ps 103:20; 91:11)." See "The Authority of the Believer."

25. Johnson, *God Is Good*, ch. 12.

26. Johnson, "Pastor Bill Johnson Sermons" (18:00). See also Johnson, *When Heaven Invades Earth*, ch. 12. And, in another message, Johnson interprets Psalm 103:20 as teaching that angels carry out spoken prophetic decrees as their assignments. (Note that he referenced the COVID-19 outbreak in this message and insinuated that his followers could avoid the virus through their spoken decrees.) He also said, "Our

declarations to enforce, according to Johnson (which explains why Beni Johnson felt the need to wake them).[27]

Bill Johnson finds scriptural support for making spoken declarations in these words of Jesus to his disciples, "Truly, I say to you, whoever says to this mountain, 'Be taken up and thrown into the sea,' and does not doubt in his heart, but believes that what he says will come to pass, it will be done for him" (Mark 11:23).[28] Johnson gives an example of declarations he made while walking through a carnival held in his community. A fortune-teller had set up a booth there and displayed psychic paraphernalia, including tarot cards and a crystal ball. He writes of this occasion: "As I walked around her tent I began to declare, *You don't exist in heaven; you are not to exist here. . . . I bind you to the word of God that declares that I have authority over you. Be gone!*"[29] The next day, the fortune-teller packed up her things and left town. Johnson confidently announces that his declarations were the reason for her departure.

Johnson's declarations, in that instance, were directed to evil spiritual forces that he believed exerted influence on the fortune teller. But declarations can also be directed to any problematic situations or circumstances, such as sickness, money concerns, or even weather patterns. Recall Bethel leaders' declarations to the wind during the devastating Carr Fire. In chapter 1, we also mentioned declarations they made to raise two-year-old Olive from the dead, heal Nabeel Qureshi of cancer, and for Bethel's churchgoers to experience "perfect health" during the COVID-19 pandemic. All these declarations failed. But proponents of this doctrine believe that declarations are more effective than traditional prayer because it is not necessary to petition God for something he has

decrees let the angelic realm know what their assignment is." (Johnson, "March 15, 2020" [1:40:00].) For another example of Bethel leaders' teaching about angels enforcing declarations, see Vallotton, "Life of a Disciple," and Vallotton, *Developing a Supernatural Lifestyle*, ch. 10. According to Vallotton, there are two ways declarations "*cause the future*": one is when angels carry them out, as we have already described, and the other is "through the grace of God" (which he also refers to as "the operational power of God") and occurs when a prophet's declaration is received in faith. See Vallotton, *Developing a Supernatural Lifestyle*, ch. 10.

27. Johnson, *When Heaven Invades Earth*, ch. 12. (Note that the prayers angels respond to, in Johnson's teaching, are "prayer declarations.") We mentioned Beni Johnson's practice of waking angels in chapter 1, note 138.

28. Johnson, *God Is Good*, ch. 12. Vallotton also appeals to this verse in support of "proclamation" (another term that refers to spoken affirmations that release God's power). See Vallotton, "Life of a Disciple" (31:00).

29. Johnson, *When Heaven Invades Earth*, ch. 5.

(falling power *ourselves* but should not?)

already authorized believers to do themselves.[30] Did Jesus not rebuke his disciples for seeking his assistance, rather than exercising their own authority to bind and loose? This is Johnson's reasoning and method of Scripture interpretation. To support his view, he recalls the occasion when Jesus calmed a storm on the Sea of Galilee.[31]

> Jesus was sleeping in the middle of a life-threatening storm. The disciples woke Him because they were afraid of dying. He exercised authority and released peace over the storm. . . . Even after the disciples got their answer to prayer, a stilled storm, Jesus asked them about their unbelief. . . . He expected them to exercise the authority He had given them to quiet the seas themselves. Instead they asked Him to do it.[32]

?? ,, Indeed, making declarations is a critical practice for the church, according to Johnson. It is critical because God has limited himself to acting in response to declarations. Johnson writes, with stunning dogmatism, "Nothing happens in the Kingdom until first there is a declaration."[33] And when Johnson says "nothing," he really means *nothing*. Consider his statement about the role of declarations in the first and second comings of Christ:

> Intimacy is the main purpose of prayer. And it's through relationship that God entrusts to us the secrets of His heart, that we might express them in [declaration] prayer. That's what He did with Simeon and Anna as He stirred their hearts to pray for the coming of the Messiah long before He was born. Even the return of the Lord will be preceded by the declaration of the bride: "The Spirit and the bride say, 'Come.'" If these things were going to happen anyway, what would be the purpose of prayer? God has

(prayer is petition, thankfulness, intercession — but " not my will but THINE "

— see p13?

30. See Johnson's words about how his prayers became more effective when his view of prayer changed, writing that now, "Instead of asking God to invade my circumstances, I begin to command the *mountains to be removed* in his name" (the emphasis is his, but we wish to draw attention to his use of the word "command"); see Johnson, *When Heaven Invades Earth*, ch. 5.

31. For accounts of this incident, see Matt 8:23–27; Mark 4:35–41; Luke 8:22–25.

32. Johnson, *When Heaven Invades Earth*, ch. 5. Vallotton gives a similar interpretation of this gospel story—that is, Jesus did not want his disciples to pray and ask for his help; rather, he expected them to exercise their own authority to bind the storm. See Vallotton, "Life of a Disciple" (34:00).

33. Johnson, *Hosting the Presence*, ch. 6. He makes a similar statement in Johnson, *God Is Good*, ch. 5.

apparently given Himself a self-imposed restriction—to act in the affairs of man in response to prayer.[34]

Did you catch what Johnson teaches about Christ's first and second comings? Apparently, the occurrence of these two pivotal events was (in the case of Christ's first coming) and is (in the case of his second coming) dependent on the issuing of declarations made by human beings. Jesus's first coming to earth, at the incarnation, was dependent on declarations made by Simeon and Anna. Likewise, his second coming will not occur until the church (or the "Bride") first makes a declaration to that effect. For anyone who understands the significance of these two events within Christianity, these are stunning claims. And if even Christ cannot return until a declaration is made, then declarations are clearly critical to the establishment of God's kingdom.[35]

Other Bethel leaders echo Johnson's teaching that, for even the most momentous purposes, God cannot act until a declaration is made. In a sermon given at Bethel Church, Kris Vallotton said, "Prayer [i.e., making

34. Johnson, *When Heaven Invades Earth*, ch. 5. We note that nowhere in Luke 2, the passage about Anna and Simeon, does it say that Simeon or Anna even prayed for the coming of the Messiah—to say nothing of making declarations. It does say that Simeon was looking for the consolation of Israel. And it says that Anna habitually prayed. But it does not say what she prayed for. Johnson reads his doctrine of declaration prayer into this passage, and then appeals to the passage to demonstrate the authority of this doctrine. This does not even qualify as excusable speculative theology. It is an egregious imposition of freewheeling bias on a text of Scripture.

35. This notion conflicts with Jesus's own teaching that no one knows the day or the hour when Christ shall return (Matt 24:36; cf. Mark 13:32). According to Bethel leaders' teachings, the Old Testament prophecies were themselves declarations made by the Old Testament prophets. See Vallotton, *Heavy Rain*, ch. 15. (Notice that, in this chapter, Vallotton appears to promote a version of the doctrine known as "Manifest Sons of God"—promoted by leaders of the post-World II Latter Rain movement and by some of today's NAR leaders—which is based on a faulty interpretation of Romans 8:19–23. In its most extreme and heretical form, this doctrine maintains that end-time believers, either individually or corporately, will attain deity. Vallotton's language in these pages is ambiguous and vague, so we do not know if his teaching embraces the more extreme elements of this doctrine. But notice his curious statements: "When the Word of the Lord is released into our hearts, we become impregnated with the Father's DNA and give birth to His nature in our lives" and "He [the apostle Paul] preached the Word of God, and as he spoke they [the Galatians] were impregnated with the seeds of the Kingdom, which literally caused Christ to be formed in them." What does he mean when he writes that we "give birth to His [the Father's] nature in our lives" and that Christ was "literally" formed in the Galatians? Does he mean to imply that believers can attain deity? It would be helpful for him to clarify these statements. For more information about the Manifest Sons of God doctrine, see Geivett and Pivec, *A New Apostolic Reformation?*, chs. 1, 18, 19.)

prophetic declarations] is an act of leadership as it *authorizes* God to do his will on our planet."[36]

The converse is also true: that a failure to make declarations means that God is not authorized to do his will. This is because declarations or "prophetic decrees" are "catalytic" for societal transformation.[37] For example, Johnson has suggested that Christians' failure to make declarations for societal transformation in the United States has resulted in the nation's moral decline. This decline includes the legalization of abortion.[38]

Sadly, many Christians have neglected the critical practices of making declarations and binding and loosing prayer. Johnson believes their failure to understand the purpose and effect of prayer is due to a satanic strategy to deceive the church.[39]

An Evaluation of Johnson's Teachings about the Lord's Prayer

Johnson's claim that the Lord's Prayer is a model of binding and loosing prayer is certainly provocative. But there simply are no good reasons for accepting it.

First, nothing in the words of the prayer itself lends to such an interpretation. Prayer, in the Bible, is always directed *to God*, never to demonic beings, angels, or situations.[40] The Lord's Prayer is no exception.

36. Vallotton, "Life of a Disciple" (starting at the beginning of the video). The emphasis is ours.

37. Johnson, *God Is Good*, ch. 10.

38. Johnson, *God Is Good*, ch. 10. Johnson and Vallotton blame this failure to make declarations on an eschatology that expects the world to end soon and for things to get worse (not better) prior to Christ's return. But, in contrast to this allegedly errant eschatology, Vallotton claims the Lord told him that He was going to give the church at large an "apostolic eschatology" with a vision of the end time that expects Christians to effect societal transformation and bring heaven to earth. Vallotton also recommends the book by Eberle and Trench, *Victorious Eschatology*. (See *Heavy Rain*, ch. 15.)

39. See Johnson, *When Heaven Invades Earth*, ch. 5. In the context of the chapter, Johnson is addressing binding and loosing prayer, not more traditional understandings of prayer.

40. We acknowledge that some might object to the claim that prayer never addresses demonic beings or situations. To see our explanation of teachings about "warfare prayer" (i.e., prayer directed to demonic beings), along with our refutation of those teachings, see our book *A New Apostolic Reformation?*, chs. 15, 16. Later in this chapter, we refute Johnson's interpretation of Mark 11:23—which he points to in support of prayer addressing impersonal situations (or "mountains").

It begins with an address to the Father ("Our Father in heaven"). It would not make sense for it to begin by addressing the Father and then abruptly switch to addressing demonic beings or impersonal situations—such as storms or sicknesses—through the making of declarations.[41] Johnson asserts his interpretation without making a case for it. Instead, he smuggles in prosperity/Word of Faith teachings about binding and loosing that were developed nearly two thousand years after Jesus first taught the prayer to his disciples.[42]

The practice of binding and loosing prayer would have been foreign to the Jews and early Christians of the Second Temple period. Prayer in the Jewish and early Christian traditions included praise, thanksgiving, confession, and petition—not making authoritative declarations that tap into God's power to create a desired reality.[43] No doubt, such declarations would have appeared as mechanistic attempts to manipulate God. Jesus expressly warned against such attempts in his teaching leading up to the Lord's Prayer (Matt 6:7–8), when he criticized the pagan gentiles for believing they could employ formulas that would place God under obligation to answer their prayers.[44]

Indeed, prayers directed to the Greek gods reflected their worldview, which did not view the gods as invisible and sovereign—as Jews and Christians viewed their God. Rather, the Greeks conceived of the gods in human form and viewed them as their helpers.[45] They expected them to do their bidding. Yet no pious Jew or Christian would have presumed

41. This observation is made in a critique of teachings about declarations and decrees in a position paper adopted by the College of Prayer International. See Hyer, "Prayer, Declaration."

42. An innovation of the New Apostolic Reformation movement is a broadening of the application of Word of Faith teachings. Historically, these teachings have focused on delivering health and prosperity to individuals. But the New Apostolic Reformation's application of Word of Faith teachings has broadened the focus to bringing health and prosperity not only to individuals, but to cities and the entire world (which is seen as necessary to bringing God's physical kingdom to earth).

43. Jewish and Christian prayer, of course, included statements that declared truth, such as truth about God. But a declaration of truth is something very different from the practice of making a declaration as promoted by Johnson—i.e., the making of a verbal statement that somehow releases God's power.

44. Keener, *Matthew*, 139–40.

45. Aune, "Prayer."

to command or direct God—something binding and loosing prayer certainly appears to do.[46]

When Jesus taught his disciples to pray, he taught them to prioritize the Father's will above their own. This prioritization is expressed in the Lord's Prayer with the words "your will be done" (Matt 6:10).[47] In an older work on the Lord's Prayer, the scholar Sir Robert Anderson focuses on the call for believers (a) to be obedient to the Father's will, and (b) to accept the outworking of God's will in their lives. Note the emphasis on whole and humble obedience to God's will. This is a far cry from what Johnson teaches. If true, then what he says about this passage is very likely false, and horribly misleading. It's not good news for a "declarations" mindset or for a prosperity gospel, which cannot tolerate divine wisdom that does not seem always to conform to *our wills*!

As for himself, Jesus came to earth to do the will of his Father (Heb 10:7), and he prioritized the Father's will in his own prayer life. This can be seen in the moment of his greatest trial, when he prayed at Gethsemane, prior to arrest and crucifixion. He did not make declarations commanding his circumstances to change. Rather, he petitioned his heavenly Father, "if you are willing, remove this cup [of future suffering]

---

46. See also Finkel, "Prayer in Jewish Life." Finkel writes, "In polytheistic worship one seeks to placate or coerce the gods of nature so that they will do one's own bidding, which relates to magic. Biblical faith, however, rejects this approach as useless. It rests its worship on the purity of one's heart or intention and on one's deep sense of creatureliness. The biblically oriented person can only approach the Creator by permission in praise and gratefulness, not with a demand but in hope of being granted a gift." Why do we say that declarations seem to command God? Since declarations purportedly release God's power, and they seek effects that only God can bring about, they may be seen as giving commands to God (despite Johnson's statement that God is "not a cosmic bellhop" [Johnson, *Supernatural Power*, ch. 10]). This understanding of declarations as commands is strengthened by Johnson's teaching, shown earlier in this chapter, that God has limited himself to acting in the affairs of men in response to declarations. This understanding is also strengthened by the teaching of Johnson and other Bethel leaders that, in response to declarations, angels are sent by God to "enforce" the declarations (i.e., make the declarations into realities). Viewed in light of these teachings, declarations appear to give God directions—something that is foreign to the biblical concept of prayer. Worse yet, it violates the principle of submission to God's will in all petition, which always assumes that God knows better than the one who prays, and that God's intentions do not align with beloved petitioners. And we cannot stress enough that God's goodness and power do not in the least depend on the activating, or leveraging, prayers of God's people.

47. See Anderson, *The Lord's Prayer*, 35–50.

from me." But he was quick to add, "Nevertheless, not my will, but yours, be done" (Luke 22:42, cf. Matt 26:39; Mark 14:36).

Notice that Jesus acknowledged and accepted that the Father's will for him, at that time, might involve suffering. This point is important. It undermines Johnson's teaching that we are to look to heaven—where there is no pain or suffering—as a model of God's will for all people today. As the Father's will included suffering for Jesus, so it may also include suffering for Jesus's followers. The apostle Peter was clear on this point (1 Pet 2:18–21).[48] Suffering will be a present reality until the day when God "will wipe every tear from their eyes, and death shall be no more, neither shall there be mourning, nor crying, nor pain anymore, for the former things have passed away" (Rev 21:4).

Following Jesus's submissive posture at Gethsemane, his apostles are never seen making declarations in the book of Acts. They did work miracles, but they were quick to attribute the power for working them to Jesus (Acts 3:16). There is not the least hint that they viewed their spoken words as vehicles of inherent power. And the apostle Paul did not make declarations or teach others to do so. The early church fathers also never promoted anything resembling declarations, even in their numerous commentaries on the Lord's Prayer.[49] They, too, viewed the Lord's Prayer, as petitionary.[50] What's more, it was the common conviction of these writers that God *wants* our prayers, but he does not *need* them.[51] They agreed that God's will is always done on earth, period—whether or

---

48. Like many prosperity/Word of Faith leaders, Johnson teaches that the blood of Jesus set Christians free not only from the power of sin, but also from sickness, poverty, and other suffering in this life. In other words, Jesus experienced suffering so his followers won't have to. See this teaching, for example, in Johnson's sermon titled "Power of Confession." But 1 Peter 2:18–21 clearly teaches that Jesus's followers are not immune from the suffering he experienced but are expected to follow his example of suffering.

49. A summary of these commentaries can be found in Hammerling, *The Lord's Prayer in the Early Church: The Pearl of Great Price*.

50. It wasn't until late—beginning in the sixth century—that some lay Christians in the Western Church began to use the Lord's Prayer as a type of magical incantation. There is also mention that the Lord's Prayer was used as a magical incantation in the East as early as the fourth century. See Hammerling, "The Lord's Prayer in Early Christian Polemics," 223–41. The use of prayer as an incantation is perhaps one of the closest precedents to making declarations that can be found in church history. Outside of this late development, there is no historical precedent for using the Lord's Prayer in this way.

51. Froehlich, "The Lord's Prayer," 77.

not his followers pray for it to be done.[52] Surely they would have been shocked and scandalized by Kris Vallotton's statement that "prayer authorizes God to do his will on our planet"—as if God's hands are tied and he needs his creatures' permission to do what he desires.[53]

In his defense of Bethel teaching, Johnson stresses Jesus's bestowal of authority to bind and loose. Those who act on Bethel teaching are merely using the authority that Jesus has bestowed. This would please God, not dishonor him. However, nothing in Matthew 16:19—a key verse for Johnson's argument—permits the idea that the authority to "bind" and "loose" consists in the authority to bind sickness or loose finances. Notice, this verse does not speak of prayer at all. No interpreters—apart from leaders in the prosperity/Word of Faith movement and the New Apostolic Reformation—have understood Matthew 16:19 this way. The

---

52. Hammerling, "Introduction," 15. Bethel leaders would likely object, since they claim that God never wills suffering or evil.

53. Vallotton, "Life of a Disciple" (starting at the beginning of the video). Many other statements by Bethel leaders also undermine God's sovereignty. For example, see Johnson and Farrelly, "The Sovereignty." In the video we cite here, Johnson maintains that, despite his teaching, he also believes that God is "absolutely sovereign." But we agree with his critics that his statements raise questions about his views on God's sovereignty. We cannot address these complexities here. But, in addition to his statements cited in this chapter, he writes: "[God] has made Himself vulnerable to the desires of His people. History unfolds according to what we do, what we pray, what we don't do and what we don't pray" (Johnson, *The Supernatural Power*, ch. 10). He writes, "He [God] is in charge, but He is not in control." (See Johnson, *God Is Good*, ch. 9; Johnson, *The Way of Life*, ch. 4 [updated 2019 edition].) In other words, God has given us free will, and he has given us the authority to work miracles, but we must exercise that authority. He also writes: "He [Jesus] longs for places on the earth that remind Him of Heaven, places in which He feels at home. Prayer and radical obedience make such places possible" (Johnson, *The Way of Life*, ch. 9 [updated 2019 edition]). And he's written: "The Lord is looking for His Word, declared with courage, so that He *has* to show up to confirm it" (Johnson, *God Is Good*, ch. 10 [his emphasis]). Thus, in his teaching, it seems clear that God needs humankind to accomplish his plans on the earth (even though he has denied that God "needs" our involvement). See Johnson, *God Is Good*, ch. 5. Nevertheless, since God doesn't have complete control, he relies on people, whom Johnson calls God's "co-laborers," to cooperate with him to bring his plans to fulfillment. Let us pause here to make an important clarification. It's certainly true that God graciously *lets* people participate in the working out of his plan. In that sense, they do have important roles to play in the fulfillment of his plan. But he does not *need* them to accomplish his will, absolutely speaking (Acts 17:25), as if his hands, ultimately, are tied without the help of willing men and women ready to get behind his cause. Any such notion—which renders God powerless or lacking in some way—must be soundly rejected as unbiblical. (For an example of another statement by Bethel leaders that undermines God's sovereignty, see chapter 7, note 60.)

importation of meaning that is so convenient to the Bethel cause is an imposition on the text and a poor example to believers who look to their leaders for guidance in responsible Bible study.

Jesus here confirms the authority of church leaders to administer church discipline. This includes the authority to include or to exclude individuals in or from the Christian community. Church leaders have the power to regulate the internal affairs of the church.[54] This understanding aligns with how binding and loosing was understood by the Jews of Jesus's day. The Jewish leaders exercised their authority to bind and loose when interpreting Jewish law and settling disputes regarding it.[55] They did not understand binding and loosing as the authority to bind demons (or loose angels) to do their bidding. A Bethel leader may complain that the practice of Jewish leaders is irrelevant. But we point out that Jesus assumes as background to his statement what his Jewish apostles understood of the practice. He did not correct their understanding or explicitly invest new meaning in the concept of binding and loosing. He adopted familiar language to describe a parallel situation, which probably astonished the disciples. They would, despite their humble station in the world, exercise the very authority normally reserved for sophisticated Jewish leaders. The astounding significance of Jesus's words is seen in this parallel with Jewish understanding and practice.

Craig Keener has this to say about such a confused interpretation of Matthew 16:19:

> The more popular use of "binding" today in many circles (exercising authority over the devil) resembles instead an ancient practice in the magical papyri—also called binding—of manipulating demons to carry out a magician's will. (The Bible does support Christians' authority to cast out real demons . . . but the only "devils" in *this* passage are fully human ones, and they are being cast out of the church!)[56]

Given the meaning of the term "binding and loosing" in its historical and cultural context, Johnson's interpretation of Matthew 16:19—as teaching binding and loosing prayer—comes out of left field.

---

54. Keener, *Matthew*, 289. See also Leon Morris, *The Gospel*, 427. We see this type of authority exercised by Christ's apostles and other early church leaders in Acts 15 during the Council at Jerusalem.

55. Keener, *Matthew*, 273.

56. Keener, *Matthew*, 273 (his emphasis).

But now we must address Johnson's interpretation of Mark 11:23: "Truly, I say to you, whoever says to this mountain, 'Be taken up and thrown into the sea,' and does not doubt in his heart, but believes that what he says will come to pass, it will be done for him." Recall that Johnson turns to this verse for evidence that Jesus instructed his disciples to make verbal declarations. Where does Johnson's interpretation go wrong? It is true that "moving mountains" was a common Jewish metaphor for the removal of seemingly impossible situations. But there's more to say on this point. Johnson's interpretation falls apart in light of Jesus's fuller teaching.

The whole teaching here is that key to seeing answers to prayer is having faith in God to answer those prayers. It's a teaching, then, about the role of faith in effective prayer. And the type of prayer in view here is clearly petitionary. Why do we say it's clear? Because "clear" is a good word for what's obvious. See the verse that immediately follows: "Therefore I tell you, whatever you *ask* in prayer, believe that you have received it, and it will be yours" (v. 24).[57] To ask is to petition. And whom would they petition, but God? That this is petition explains why, if the disciples expect answers when they pray, they must "have faith in God" (v. 22) and "believe" that God will answer the prayer (v. 24).[58] Of course, the theological backdrop of the rest of Scripture shows that, for God to answer prayer requests, the requests must align with his will (1 John 5:14). But note that here the emphasis is on the role of faith in effective, petitionary prayer—not the practice of "declarations." Like other passages of Scripture we have examined in this chapter, Johnson takes isolated statements of Jesus and promotes novel teachings about them, with complete disregard for their context.

KEY POINT The Scriptures have been misinterpreted and misapplied. They have been used to guide believers into practices that have no place in the Christian life. It is a serious matter when Jesus's own words have been misconstrued. And it is ironic to find misguided leaders presume to have authority on the basis of what Jesus taught, when that authority is undermined by their interpretation of Jesus's words.

57. Our emphasis.

58. The fact that Jesus's teaching about moving mountains is a lesson about faith, and not about declarations, is reinforced when we examine a very similar statement made in Matthew 17:19, though under different circumstances. The disciples have asked Jesus why they were unable to cast a demon out of a boy. His answer: "Because of the littleness of your faith." He then adds, "For truly, I say to you, if you have faith like a grain of mustard seed, you will say to this mountain, 'Move from here to there,' and it will move, and nothing will be impossible for you" (v. 20).

The Assemblies of God—the Pentecostal denomination that Johnson's church withdrew from—has strong words for those who promote such "positive confession" teachings—calling them "extreme positions" that "are in conflict with the Word of God" and "bring reproach upon . . . the work of the Lord."[59]

Since Johnson's interpretation of the Lord's Prayer has no scriptural basis or historical precedent, then certainly the burden of proof is on him to show why anyone should accept it—or his claim that it holds the key to establishing God's kingdom on earth.[60] And if it does not hold the key to establishing God's kingdom, then one of his—and Bethel Church's—foundational teachings crumbles, along with many of the church's supporting teachings.

Next, we will explain another new truth God has allegedly given the church known as the "billion-soul harvest."

59. See "The Believer and Positive Confession." Making declarations is a form of "positive confession," though the Assemblies of God paper does not use the term "declarations." This paper was written in 1980 before teachings about making "declarations" were popularized by Bethel and other NAR churches.

60. Hammerling notes an observation made by academics that "anyone seeking an in-depth grasp of the nature of particular spiritual traditions must at some point look at how that tradition observes prayer, because prayer is at the heart of all religious practice and belief." This is insightful. Examining the way Johnson and other Bethel Church leaders view prayer raises serious concerns about their theology. (Hammerling, "Introduction.")

−7−

The "Greater Works" and the "Billion-Soul Harvest"

(= miracles)

I have a promise from God. I am a part of a company of people destined to do greater works than Jesus did in His earthly ministry.

(What conceit !)

("superior Christians" again)

—Bill Johnson[1]

JESUS'S PROMISE IN JOHN 14:12 is astounding: "Truly, truly, I say to you, whoever believes in me will also do the works that I do; and greater works than these will he do, because I am going to the Father." Even more incredible is that his promise wasn't given only to his inner circle of disciples; it is open, potentially, to all—"*whoever* believes."

But what, exactly, are the greater works?

Jesus is the man who turned water to wine, gave sight to the blind, multiplied food, walked on water, and even raised the dead. Did he really promise that all believers would work the same *miracles* that he did—indeed, even greater miracles?

That's what Bill Johnson says: "Jesus' prophecy of us doing greater works than He did has stirred the Church to look for some abstract meaning to this very simple statement. . . . Jesus' statement is not that

(≠ literal interpretation)

1. Johnson, *When Heaven Invades Earth*, ch. 16.

144

(a leap of logic)

hard to understand. Greater means 'greater.' And the works He referred to are signs and wonders."[2]

Johnson asserts that theologians have tried to explain away this astonishing promise, or have watered it down, so that it means something different than what Jesus intended. In this way they excuse the absence of miraculous power in their own lives and churches. But Johnson insists that miraculous signs and wonders are key to transforming cities, converting nations, and extending God's rule. In other words, they're integrally linked to the Great Commission and the church's evangelistic task. By shifting the meaning of Jesus's promise, misguided theologians have allegedly set aside the primary means of fulfilling the church's mission to "bring heaven to earth."[3]

To date, no generation of Christians has believed fully in Jesus's promise, according to Johnson. He teaches that a single, last-days generation—an "Elijah generation"—will finally rise up, take Jesus at his word, and do the "greater works."[4] This generation is at the beginning of the fulfillment of a well-known prophecy, in the New Apostolic Reformation, known as the "billion-soul harvest"—an unprecedented, worldwide revival during which a billion people will be saved and come into God's kingdom.[5]

Johnson boldly declares that the promise is fulfilled in the present generation. Before an audience of thousands of young adults, he proclaimed: "We've been summoned by the Lord to explore and to discover what actually could happen on earth in our lifetime if we actually believed

---

2. Johnson, *When Heaven Invades Earth*, ch. 17.

3. We describe Johnson's revisionist understanding of the church's mission in chapter 6.

4. Johnson, *When Heaven Invades Earth*, chs. 13, 17; *Manifesto*, ch. 5. Similarly, a biography for Kris Vallotton on the Wagner University website states that Vallotton has "a vision for equipping an 'Elijah generation' for the end-time harvest." See Wagner University, "Meet." Johnson has stated that the "greater works" will be performed by an entire generation, not just by certain individuals; and Vallotton said he asked the Lord to give the "mantle" to work miracles that had belonged to the deceased prophet William Branham to an entire generation, and the Lord agreed to grant his request. See "The Real Jesus." (Note that, in addition to Vallotton, Johnson also refers to Branham as a prophet in this video. For a description of Branham's aberrant and heretical teachings, see Geivett and Pivec, *A New Apostolic Reformation?*, ch. 14. See also chapter 3 of this present book.)

5. Johnson, *When Heaven Invades Earth*, introduction, ch. 17. Many other NAR leaders have prophesied and taught about the billion-soul harvest, as we will explain later in this chapter.

what was in this book. I believe that this generation that I'm speaking to now is the signs and wonders generation. I don't take that lightly."[6]

Of this present generation he says that "not even the early Church fulfilled God's full intention for His people. That privilege was reserved for those in the *last leg* of the race. It is *our* destiny."[7]

(again, superiority)

And so, "We have the ball. The alumni from the ages past watch with excitement as the *two-minute offense* has been put on the field. The superior potential of this generation has nothing to do with our goodness, but it does have everything to do with the Master's plan of placing us at this point in history. We are to be the devil's worst nightmare."[8]

Make no mistake, Johnson believes that the church today is on the cusp of fulfilling Jesus's promise. But how did he come to think of the "greater works" in this way? And what are the miracles that he imagines for our time?

The Greater Works

Bill Johnson is emphatic—the greater works are miracles:

> Jesus said, "If I do not do the works of My Father, do not be-lieve Me." The works of the Father are miracles. Even the Son of God stated it was the miraculous that validated His ministry on earth. In that context He said, ". . . he who believes in Me . . . greater works than these he will do, because I go to My Father." The miraculous is a large part of the plan of God for this world. And it is to come through the Church.[9]

Johnson is not alone in his understanding of the verse as a promise about miracles. Many NAR leaders share that understanding. And in a book Johnson coauthored with the "apostle" Randy Clark, Clark intimates that this understanding of the verse is backed by scholarship: "Many New Testament scholars have pointed out that the Greek term *erga* used in John 14:12 to mean 'works' denotes *miraculous works*. So Jesus is saying that anyone who has faith in Him will do the *same miraculous works that He did*. (I want to thank Dr. Gary Greig for providing me with this insight.)"[10]

6. Johnson, "Session 8" (6:00).

7. Johnson, *When Heaven Invades Earth*, ch. 17 (our emphasis).

8. Johnson, *When Heaven Invades Earth*, ch. 14 (Johnson's emphasis).

9. Johnson, *When Heaven Invades Earth*, ch. 12.

10. Johnson and Clark, *The Essential Guide*, ch. 3 (Clark's emphasis). We note the tension between Johnson's claim that theologians have watered down John

And Johnson maintains that the NAR understanding of the word "greater" is supported by the Greek:

> This verse is often explained away by saying it refers to *quantity* of works, not *quality*. As you can see, millions of people should be able to surpass the sheer number of works that Jesus did simply because we are so many. But that waters down the intent of His statement. The word greater is *mizon* in the Greek. It is found 45 times in the New Testament. It is always used to describe "quality," not quantity.[11]

By quality, Johnson means that the miracles must be, in some way, more spectacular or awe-inspiring than the miracles worked by Jesus. But, notice, he never provides a definitive description of what those spectacular miracles might be. He does, however, drop hints about them. For example, in the following Facebook post, he implies that they will include miraculous healings.

> Jesus prophesied that we would do greater works than He did! We can't do greater until we've done the same. #acts10v38 #pentecost #HolySpirit #healing #JesusChrist #john14v12 #ephesians5v18 #healing101[12]

These miracles also will include raising the dead. Writing of the greater works, he relays the following story.

> Give God a chance to do what only He can do. He looks for those who are willing to be *smeared* with Him, allowing His presence to affect others for good. A visiting minister recently told us, "The difference between you and me is this: if I pray for a dead person and they are not raised from the dead, I pray for the next dead person too. I don't quit!"[13]

Clearly, Johnson intends for his readers to follow this minister's example.

The belief that the greater works will include miracles of healing and raising the dead is common in NAR. Writing about the last-days generation of Christians, the apostle Rick Joyner has said: "There will be no plague, disease, or physical condition, including lost limbs, AIDS, poison gas, or radiation, which will resist the healing and miracle gifts working in

14:12—making it about something other than miracles—and Clark's statement that many scholars believe that John 14:12 is a promise about miracles.

11. Johnson, *When Heaven Invades Earth*, ch. 17 (Johnson's emphasis).

12. Johnson, "Jesus prophesied that."

13. Johnson, *When Heaven Invades Earth*, ch. 12 (his emphasis).

the saints during this time."[14] And the notion that the greater works would include miraculous healings was central to the ministry of the British healing evangelist Smith Wigglesworth (1859–1947). Wigglesworth is reported to have healed many people of sicknesses and even raised the dead. He is esteemed today by many NAR leaders, including Johnson.[15]

Healing the sick. Raising the dead. These are among the greater works. Yet there's more.[16] There must be more since Jesus healed the sick and raised the dead, and the promise is that his followers would do *even greater* miracles than he did. But what could the more possibly be?

One answer to this question is that the "more" will include supernatural revelation. Johnson teaches that the last-days generation of the church will receive divine revelation that will disclose supernatural solutions to the world's most perplexing problems.

> It will be miracles of healing for sure but it will also be ideas, favour, and deliverances. Do you know there are even plans in Heaven that can help to fix traffic problems? There is no problem that he has not thought of. There's not one problem. The ozone layer, the conflict in the Middle East, there is not one thing that anybody is facing that he has not already thought through and come up with the perfect solution for. He is just waiting for his sons and his daughters to realise who they are and say, "Papa, how about the answer?"[17]

The greater works, then, will include divine strategies to eliminate pollution and resolve international conflicts. They will even include strategies to end a global pandemic. In 2020, soon after COVID-19 became a crisis in the United States, several influential apostles and prophets—Bill Johnson, Ché Ahn, Ed Silvoso, Kris Vallotton, and Shawn Bolz—gathered for a Facebook Live event on March 20, 2020. These leaders made

---

14. Joyner, *The Harvest*, 167–68.

15. Johnson, *Defining Moments*, 123–44.

16. Delivering people from demonic affliction is also included in the greater works. See Johnson, *When Heaven Invades Earth*, ch. 17, and the foreword written by Randy Clark in Johnson's book *The Supernatural Power*. And Mike Bickle, who has spoken at Bethel Church and has had Bill Johnson speak at his church, teaches that the greater works Christians will perform include the loosing of God's end-time judgments on the earth as described in the book of Revelation. These include hail, falling stars, and an army riding fire-breathing horses; these will destroy one-third of the earth's population. For more about Bickle's distinctive view of the greater works, see Geivett and Pivec, *A New Apostolic Reformation?*, ch. 18.

17. Johnson, *Manifesto*, ch. 5.

prayer decrees that God was "moving strategy from heaven and wisdom" to defeat the virus and that he "will move in the hearts of scientists, and hopefully Christian scientists, that will find a cure for this."[18]

Elsewhere, Johnson speaks of "vast resources of revelation in heaven for the areas of education and business, the arts and music" that "have yet to be tapped anywhere near to their fullness." He writes of yet-to-be composed melodies and music lyrics that would "stir the world to conversion." He notes that we already "see acceleration" in the development of technology, science, and medicine. And he's "convinced that the pace of revelation will increase very rapidly in these last hours of history."[19]

In sum, Christians have been given an amazing promise of miraculous revelation and power capable of transforming the world. It's inconceivable to Johnson that they would not avail themselves of that power.

> I cannot stand by and say, "Oh, that's for somebody else." Not if God says it is possible to step into greater works. Not if it is possible to see nations discipled. Not if it is possible to have words become reality, and to raise the dead and see things transformed that are absolute impossibilities. I cannot stand by and realise that it is possible but decide it's just not for me.[20]

Unfortunately, many Christians are doing just that, according to Johnson.

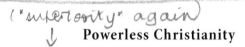

Powerless Christianity

The corollary of Johnson's interpretation of "greater works" is that all other Christians—at least all those who do not accept his interpretation—are dropping the ball. In his view, "powerless Christianity" is an epidemic infecting much of the church.[21] He writes of "countless millions who confess salvation in Jesus, but never *pursue the gifts* as commanded"—which is to say that they do not seek to prophesy, heal the sick, or practice the other miraculous gifts described in 1 Corinthians 12. As a result, these Christians "accomplish little or nothing for the Kingdom."[22]

18. Silvoso and Johnson, "Acts 19" (51:00). See our explanation of NAR teachings about decrees and declarations in chapter 6.

19. Johnson, *The Supernatural Power*, ch. 3.

20. Johnson, *Manifesto*, ch. 2.

21. Johnson uses the term "powerless Christianity" in *When Heaven Invades Earth*, ch. 11.

22. Johnson, *When Heaven Invades Earth*, ch. 10.

This is pretty stern stuff. And the problem is long-standing. No generation in the history of the church has attained to the standard set by Jesus.

> For two thousand years, we've been comparing ourselves to the previous generation, noticing only slight differences. And to console ourselves with the task at hand—the Great Commission to disciple nations, displaying the greater works—many create watered-down doctrines that dismantle the example and commandments that Jesus gave us.[23] Instead of comparing ourselves with ourselves, we should have been using the original standard found in the life of Jesus so that the measure of God's goodness revealed in Christ would have remained the same through the past two thousand years. God is bringing us back to the original measurement so that He might be revealed more accurately as the Father who loves well.[24]

Did you catch what he said about Christians *creating* watered-down doctrines? The allegation that the church actually has created new doctrines for the sole purpose of justifying its own lack of supernatural power is repeated by Johnson throughout his books and sermons.[25] But what are these watered-down doctrines? He blames cessationism—the view that the miraculous gifts listed in 1 Corinthians 12 are no longer active in the church. He appears to have cessationism in mind when he states that a "lie . . . has given rise to an entire branch of theology that has infected the Body of Christ with a fear of the Holy Spirit."[26] He dismisses the doctrine for having zero basis in Scripture. And he maligns its defenders for having an ulterior motive.

> If you assign ten new believers the task of studying the Bible to find God's heart for this generation, not one of them would conclude that spiritual gifts are not for today. You have to be taught that stuff! The doctrine stating *signs and wonders are no longer needed because we have the Bible* was created by people

(but god + the Holy Spirit are the source of power + interpreting scripture)

23. Note that Jesus's promise, in John 14:12, has become a command, in Johnson's teaching.

24. Johnson, *God Is Good*, ch. 1. Johnson's statement aligns with the restorationist theology of the New Apostolic Reformation. We explain the NAR teaching that the church has lost truths that need restoring by present-day prophets in chapter 4 of this book and in Geivett and Pivec, *A New Apostolic Reformation?*, ch. 11.

25. See also Johnson, *God Is Good*, ch. 1; *When Heaven Invades Earth*, chs. 7, 10.

26. Johnson, *When Heaven Invades Earth*, ch. 10.

who hadn't seen God's power and needed an explanation to justify their own powerless churches.[27]

Johnson takes direct aim at theologians who promote cessationism; they're motivated by fear and a desire to defend the status quo.

> Can you imagine what would have happened if our fear-oriented theologians had been there [after God delivered the Israelites from Egypt]? They would have created new doctrines explaining why the supernatural ministry that brought them out of Egypt was no longer necessary to bring them into the Promised Land. After all, now they had the tablets of stone.[28]

—but look at the record of all that went wrong till they arrived

Johnson charges cessationists with preaching an inauthentic gospel. This accusation is implicit in his contrast between an "authentic gospel" with one that "isn't backed with signs and wonders": "It's been my pursuit of Him [God] that has led me to this passion for an authentic gospel. Something happened in me that won't let me accept a gospel that isn't backed with signs and wonders."[29]

"Belief" kept the leaders going

It may seem overly harsh for Johnson to charge cessationists with preaching an inauthentic gospel simply because they do not believe in present-day miraculous gifts. Such a statement could be construed as needlessly divisive. Christians should be able to express disagreement over non-essential doctrines of the Christian faith without being accused of preaching an inauthentic gospel. But Johnson's charge reveals that he considers his teachings about signs and wonders to be *central* to the gospel. *NB*

This point is so important to understanding Johnson's teachings that we wish to highlight it. For Johnson, his signs and wonders teachings are not peripheral, but are central to the gospel. Signs and wonders are so integral to the gospel that he refers to this "authentic gospel" as the "gospel of the kingdom."[30] He also states that many Christians misunderstand the gospel of the kingdom.

---

27. Johnson, *When Heaven Invades Earth*, ch. 8 (his emphasis).

28. Johnson, *When Heaven Invades Earth*, ch. 7. Cessationists argue that, since the church has the completed Scriptures, the miraculous gifts of the Holy Spirit are no longer needed. So, Johnson's tongue-in-cheek reference to the completed "tablets of stone" indicates that Johnson has cessationists in view when he chastises "fear-oriented theologians."

29. Johnson, *When Heaven Invades Earth*, ch. 12.

30. Johnson, *When Heaven Invades Earth*, ch. 1.

The present day understanding of *preaching the gospel of the Kingdom* means to preach a message that will bring as many people to conversion as possible. But what did preaching the gospel of the Kingdom mean to Jesus? Every instance in which He either did it, or commanded it, miracles followed. The message was to be a declaration of His lordship and dominion over all things, followed by demonstrations of power, illustrating that His world is invading ours through signs and wonders.[31]

(lowers Jesus to the status of a magician)

In effect, Johnson charges anyone who denies his view with preaching a false gospel (though he has denied that is his intention).[32] This has three implications: (1) it applies to non-cessationists, as well as cessationists; (2) it entails that *if* theirs is the true gospel, then his own gospel is a false gospel; and, (3) and this is true of evangelists and teachers through church history. *u, they've all got it wrong*

Other than cessationism, another doctrine has contributed to a powerless church, according to Johnson: the teaching about the supreme importance of character. He believes that many Christians have mistakenly emphasized a pursuit of Christlike character over miraculous power because they believe character is the more important of the two. Yet both are indispensable:

NB

(miraculous power is more exciting to the masses)

("entertainment" again)

> While character must be at the heart of our ministries, power revolutionizes the world around us. Until the Church returns to Jesus's model for true revolutionaries, we will continue to be recognized by the world merely as nice people—while it is overcome with disease and torment, on its way to hell.[33]

(not exciting enough)

no! nice people get things done + change lives.

For Johnson, the choice to pursue miraculous power is a matter of obedience. Jesus's teachings included "specific training on how to live and

~ where ??

---

31. Johnson, *When Heaven Invades Earth*, ch. 17 (Johnson's emphasis). Some theologians who are not NAR also refer to the gospel of the kingdom as including more than just the gospel of forgiveness of sins. These include N. T. Wright and Tim Mackie (cofounder of the Bible Project). But their teachings about the gospel of the kingdom do not emphasize the necessity of present-day signs and wonders and taking dominion.

32. We note that in the *Rediscover Bethel* series, Dann Farrelly asks Bill Johnson if he believes that people who don't believe in present-day signs and wonders are "heretics" or "don't have the gospel." Johnson replies, "Oh goodness, no. No. Not at all. I just think the miracle lifestyle is for everybody." See Johnson and Farrelly, "Episode 6." But we have difficulty reconciling this statement with those cited above.

33. Johnson, *When Heaven Invades Earth*, ch. 10.

operate in the miraculous"—including instructions to heal the sick, cleanse lepers, and raise the dead.[34] What other choice have we but to obey?

Notice that he claims Jesus provided "training" for working miracles. When did Jesus do that? We can't think of any such instances in the Gospels.[35] But it seems Johnson may be seeking to establish precedent for the Bethel School of Supernatural Ministry and other NAR training centers for working miracles.[36]

Yet Johnson holds that an erroneous emphasis on character over power explains why fewer miracles are reported in North America than other parts of the world. He asks, "Is it possible the reason there are so few miracles in North America is because too many before us thought they had to become better Christians before God could use them? Yes! That single lie has kept us in perpetual immaturity because it protects us from the power-encounter that transforms us."[37]

Johnson links power-encounters—that is, personal experiences of God's miraculous power—with personal transformation. There is a reason for this. In Johnson's view, character growth in individuals actually depends on their obeying Jesus's commands to heal the sick and raise the dead and operating in the miraculous gifts. To prove his point, he shares the story of a close friend who, for a time in his life, had a deep character flaw. Johnson doesn't name the flaw, but says it was spiritually crippling for this man and his family. Yet this man also had a "very strong prophetic anointing," according to Johnson.[38] When Johnson confronted the man with his secret sin, the man wept with deep sorrow.

Part of Johnson's spiritual discipline of this man included a temporary restriction on the use of his prophetic gift. Yet, after several months of this restriction, Johnson began to feel troubled. He recalled the words in 1 Samuel 10:6 where the prophet Samuel addresses King Saul: "Then

34. Johnson, *When Heaven Invades Earth*, ch. 10. He cites Matt 10:1, 5–8, 17 and Luke 9:1–6.

35. NAR leaders may point to Jesus's words in Mark 9:29, where he tells his disciples—who asked him why they were unable to cast out a demon—that "this kind cannot be driven out by anything but prayer." Some manuscripts add "and fasting." But his words, which encouraged his disciples to greater faith through the means of prayer and dependence on God, are very different from the training provided in the Bethel School of Supernatural Ministry.

36. To learn more about how Bethel School of Supernatural Ministry seeks to "activate" miraculous gifts in individuals, see Pivec and Geivett, *Counterfeit Kingdom*, ch. 3.

37. Johnson, *When Heaven Invades Earth*, ch. 10.

38. Johnson, *When Heaven Invades Earth*, ch. 10.

the Spirit of the LORD will rush upon you, and you will prophesy with them *and be turned into another man*."[39] Johnson believes the verse teaches an important principle: "The anointing transforms the vessel it flows through."[40] When he allowed his friend to resume the use of his prophetic gift, there was "a new purity and power in his voice." Johnson says, "It was his personal encounter with the anointing in ministry that 'turned him into another man.'"[41]

In short, Johnson's position is that power creates character, not the other way around. But does this bear out in Scripture? In the case of Saul, the transformation didn't last (1 Sam 15).[42] Also consider Samson. God granted him terrific supernatural power, but Samson struck out on character right to the bitter end (Judg 13–16). In the New Testament, we learn that Christians at Corinth exhibited an impressive array of miraculous gifts. Yet the apostle Paul rebuked them for their division, their sexual immorality, their elitism, and their self-centeredness (1 Cor 1:10; 5:1–13; 6:12–20; 8:9; 9:23; 11:17–34). Their experiences of miraculous power did nothing to transform their character for the better.

For Johnson, prioritizing character over power is more than just misguided. It promotes spiritual immaturity. He believes that, together with cessationism, these two doctrines have prevented many Christians from pursuing the greater works that Jesus promised. These doctrines were created by today's church leaders who, like the Pharisees of Jesus's day, see a threat to their positions of power and influence. Johnson writes: "In a similar way, many leaders today feel threatened over a possible shift in theological positions that implies we've not been as successful in ministry as we could have been."[43]

But the time for excuses is over. Rather than manufacturing self-serving doctrines "that explain away our weakness and anemic faith," Christians should consider why the greater works have not been

---

39. Our emphasis.

40. Johnson, *When Heaven Invades Earth*, ch. 10.

41. Johnson, *When Heaven Invades Earth*, ch. 10.

42. Johnson acknowledges that Saul's transformation did not last: "I realize that in the scripture above, Saul did not remain devoted to the Lord. But that is not the fault of the experience. He didn't steward the grace that God gave him in that moment and forfeited the momentum that God created for his personal victory. The truth remains—the anointing of God upon us makes personal transformation much more available." See *The Way of Life*, ch. 12 (updated 2019 edition).

43. Johnson, *God Is Good*, ch. 1.

happening.[44] The good news is that things are about to change. Power-less Christianity is coming to an end because many Christians have had enough. Johnson writes:

> The company of people who have joined this quest for an au-thentic gospel—*the gospel of the Kingdom*—is increasing. . . . We will no longer make up excuses for powerlessness because powerlessness is inexcusable. Our mandate is simple: raise up a generation that can openly display the raw power of God.[45]

— but what about teaching + preaching the whole Bible? Head + heart.

Normal Christianity

Members of this rising generation will have radically different expecta-tions of what the Christian life should look like. The "normal Christian life," as Johnson calls it, demands vigorous pursuit of miracles.[46] In *The Supernatural Power of a Transformed Mind*, he writes that "signs, won-ders, and miracles are as normal to the gospel as it is normal for you to get up in the morning and breathe."[47] Bethel prophet Kris Vallotton echoes Johnson's teaching:

> The truth is, every believer can be a miracle worker or a healer. These aspects of the Christian life are not relegated to leaders in the church, or apostles or prophets! . . . And I believe if we want to start stepping into being world changers, then demonstrating the kingdom on earth as it is in heaven should become "normal Christianity"![48]

but what does the kingdom of heaven look like?

Johnson goes further when he announces that it is abnormal for a Christian to have no appetite for miracles. "It has been written into our spiritual DNA," he says, "to hunger for the impossibilities around us to bow at the name of Jesus."[49] If that natural appetite isn't there, then "it has been taught and reasoned away," or has "not been exercised," or has "been buried under disappointment."[50]

or maybe it's not part of what being a christian is about.

44. Johnson, *God Is Good*, ch. 1.

45. Johnson, *When Heaven Invades Earth*, ch. 1 (our emphasis).

46. Johnson, *When Heaven Invades Earth*, ch. 1.

47. Johnson, *The Supernatural Power*, ch. 11.

48. Vallotton, "Why Miracles."

49. Johnson, *When Heaven Invades Earth*, ch. 1.

50. Johnson, *When Heaven Invades Earth*, ch. 7.

To recover a proper appetite for miracles, Christians must "shift their perspective on reality." They must acknowledge that this material world is not the ultimate reality and affirm the greater reality of God's invisible kingdom. This shift Johnson calls "repentance."[51] Repentance is a prerequisite for gaining access to that kingdom's supernatural power. Access to supernatural power is possible only to those whose repentance leads to a "renewed mind."[52] Repentant Christians also acquire an "ability to see into the spiritual realm" (a.k.a. "God's kingdom" or "heaven")—a characteristic of "faith."[53] Seeing into the spiritual realm is crucial, for "faith actualizes what it realizes."[54] In other words, when you see what is happening in that invisible realm, through prayer declarations, you are "able to pull" from that realm into this one.[55] This ability to see into the spiritual realm is paramount. "Herein lies the secret to the supernatural realm that we want restored to the Church."[56]

Notice, when Johnson deploys familiar theological terms— "repentance," "renewed mind," and "faith"—he imbues them with meanings that are foreign to Scripture.[57] Johnson's notions reflect a kind of mind-over-matter activity similar to that found in the nineteenth-century metaphysical New Thought movement or in today's New Age movement. New Thought thinkers saw the material world as "contingent upon the mind." They also believed that "people shared in God's power to create by means of thought" and that God made "the spoken word the

51. Johnson, *When Heaven Invades Earth*, ch. 11; *The Supernatural Power*, ch. 1. Johnson cites Matthew 4:17 in support of this teaching: "Repent, for the kingdom of heaven is at hand."

52. Developing supernatural power through a "renewed mind" is the focus of Johnson's book *The Supernatural Power of a Transformed Mind*, esp. ch 1.

53. Johnson, *When Heaven Invades Earth*, ch. 4. (Notice that Johnson often uses the terms "God's kingdom" and "heaven" interchangeably. See, e.g., *When Invades Earth*, ch. 2.)

54. Johnson, *When Heaven Invades Earth*, ch. 4.

55. Johnson, *When Heaven Invades Earth*, ch. 4. In chapter 6, we explain Johnson's teaching that prayers pulling heaven to earth are "prayer declarations."

56. Johnson, *When Heaven Invades Earth*, ch. 4.

57. Repentance in the Bible is generally repentance from sin (Luke 5:32; 15:7, 10; 24:47, Acts 2:38; 3:19); a "renewed mind" is able to discern God's will and behave Christianly (Rom 12:2); and, "faith" is trust in God. In Exodus 4:1–9 and 29–31, the act of faith [belief] is linked to Moses' miracles. And, in the New Testament, Jesus associates healings with faith. So, faith was evidence of trust in the supernatural power of God.

template for activating power."[58] This "spoken word" talk sounds a lot like Johnson's "prayer declarations."[59] As expected, Johnson denies this.[60] But denials are unconvincing when he sidesteps the need to explain how his doctrines differ from esoteric mentalism.

At any rate, the call for Christians to repent, have faith, and act with a renewed mind to perform miracles is urgent. To "validate the identity of both the Son of God and His church," Christians must aggressively pursue miracles.[61] Johnson cites John 10:37: "Unless I do the works of the Father, do not believe me." Of this verse, Johnson writes with uninhibited forthrightness: "Jesus gave people the right to disbelieve it all if there was no demonstration of power upon His ministry. I hunger for the day when the Church will make the same statement to the world. *If we're not doing the miracles that Jesus did, you don't have to believe us.*"[62]

Eager to accommodate his inventive theology to tradition, Johnson naturally must assimilate the doctrine of the resurrection to his vision of the supernatural for today. To that end, he writes, "It's about him being revealed as alive, raised from the dead, in every act of the miraculous. . . . That's the message, that's the story: he's not dead, he's alive, and it must be

---

58. Bowler, *Blessed*, ch. 1.

59. We explain his teachings about "prayer declarations" in more detail in chapter 6.

60. Johnson, *The Supernatural Mind*, ch. 1. At the same time, Johnson frequently makes statements that suggest the human mind has access to spiritual power that can alter physical reality. For example, he says: "The lack of miracles isn't because it is not in God's will for us. The problem exists between our ears" (Johnson, *When Heaven Invades Earth*, ch. 1), and, "The mind is the essential tool in bringing Kingdom reality. . . . God has made it to be the gatekeeper of the supernatural." He also states that "when a mind goes astray . . . God's freedom to establish His will on earth is limited." (This last statement seems to undermine God's sovereignty.) For Johnson's strange teaching, see ch. 1 in Johnson, *The Supernatural Power*. In her book *Blessed*, Kate Bowler explains how New Thought ideas about the power of the mind influenced the modern prosperity gospel/Word of Faith movement (a movement whose teachings—as we have shown in this book—have been incorporated into NAR and have influenced Johnson's teachings). Robert Bowman argues that the evangelical faith-cure movement—which arose in the same cultural context as the New Thought movement and around the same time—had a greater influence on early Word of Faith teachers than the New Thought movement. (See Bowman, *The Word-Faith Controversy*.) See also Alisa Childers's interview with former New Ager Melissa Dougherty discussing how the "hyper-charismatic movement" and NAR have been infiltrated by New Thought and New Age teachings. (Childers and Dougherty, "The Law.")

61. Johnson, *When Heaven Invades Earth*, ch. 11.

62. Johnson, *When Heaven Invades Earth*, ch. 9 (Johnson's emphasis).

demonstrated."[63] Demonstrated how? By present-day miracles, routinely performed by any and all who repent in faith of a suspicion regarding the possibility of personal miracle-working power. Miracles are the "key" to bringing repentance to our sin-filled cities—"the Sodoms and Gomorrahs of our day,"[64] also the San Franciscos and the Amsterdams, the New Orleanses and the Rio de Janeiros.[65] Reaching beyond the natural sense of Jesus's words in Matthew 11:20–24, Johnson writes:

> Tyre, Sidon, and Sodom would have repented had they been exposed to the same dimension of *outpouring*! Did you hear it? *They would have repented!* It's a prophetic promise for today. Miracles on the streets of the "sin cities" of the world *will cause them to repent!* It is this secret that gives us access to the heart of these great cities! The San Franciscos and the Amsterdams, the New Orleans and the Rio de Janeiros of this world will repent… if there is an army of saints, full of the Holy Ghost, walking their streets, caring for the broken, bringing the God of power into their impossible circumstances. They will repent! That's a promise. They simply await those with the message of the Kingdom to come.[66]

wishful thinking

Miracles of acts of kindness + gospel message

Billion-Soul Harvest

When this army of miracle workers rises, unprecedented worldwide revival will take place. Indeed, Johnson is convinced that the expected great revival is already underway. He announces, with that typical flare for authoritative pronouncement, "This is the moment in history that all the prophets pointed to, all the prophets spoke of."[67] (You'd have to be a prophet to know something like that!) He further declares:

> The exploits of the present and coming revival will surpass all the accomplishments of the Church in all history combined. Over one billion souls will be saved. Stadiums will be filled with people 24 hours a day, for days on end, with miracles beyond

63. Johnson, "Session 8" (27:00).

64. Johnson, "Session 8" (14:00).

65. Johnson, *When Heaven Invades Earth*, ch. 11.

66. Johnson, *When Heaven Invades Earth*, ch. 11 (Johnson's emphasis).

67. Johnson, *The Way of Life*, ch. 17 (updated 2019 edition).

number: healings, conversions, resurrections, and deliverances too many to count.[68]

Johnson's prophetic jubilations concerning a great, end-time revival to be fueled by miracles (which will fill stadiums and usher a billion souls into the kingdom) are shared by many other apostles, prophets, and NAR teachers today, including Ché Ahn, Lou Engle, Randy Clark, Heidi Baker, and Mike Bickle.[69] All chime in with expectant zeal. These teachings are often credited to two influential prophets who foretold an end-time revival accompanied by miracles—Bob Jones (1930–2014) and Paul Cain (1929–2019).[70] These prophets, though dead, still speak.

Jones is still revered by many NAR leaders, including Bill Johnson and Mike Bickle.[71] His "billion-soul harvest" prophecy, as it has come to be known, was first revealed to him August 8, 1975. According to Jones, the Lord brought him back from the dead—the devil having allegedly first killed him (for prophesying about God's judgment on the United States for

---

68. Johnson, *When Heaven Invades Earth*, ch. 17.

69. Ahn, "It's Time"; Engle, "Day 3: Atomic Power"; Strand, "'A Billion-Soul Harvest'"; Ellis, "Heidi Baker"; and Bickle, *Growing in the Prophetic*, 77, 81–82.

70. Mike Bickle says he heard talk of a billion-soul harvest from Leonard Ravenhill (an English evangelist and author who died in 1994) before he ever heard of it from Bob Jones and Paul Cain. According to Bickle, Ravenhill cited E. M. Bounds (an American clergyman who wrote many books about prayer and died in 1913) as his source, claiming Bounds had a prophetic dream about the billion-soul harvest. Bickle also speculates that Ravenhill, with whom he spoke personally, may also have received direct revelation from God about the harvest. We do not know if Bickle's representations of Ravenhill's or Bounds's views can be confirmed (that is, that they actually held to the vision of the billion-soul harvest as it is taught by Bickle and other apostles and prophets). We would be eager to see documentation of those views if it is available. And Bickle also says the "prophet" Bob Jones personally shared his revelation about the billion-soul harvest with him. In addition to these sources of prophetic revelation, Bickle believes there is scriptural support for the billion-soul harvest and cites Revelation 7:9. (See Lewis, Rowntree, and Bickle, "Billion Soul Harvest.") But this verse says nothing about a billion-soul harvest characterized by miraculous signs and wonders, as described by Jones and Cain and taught by NAR leaders. It merely says that there will be a great multitude of people from every nation, tribe, people and language around God's throne, "coming out of the great tribulation" (see verse 14). There are no passages of Scripture that teach the NAR doctrine of the billion-soul harvest.

71. LeClaire, "Mike Bickle, Bill Johnson." Vallotton also confirms that Jones was a prophet. And Vallotton claims that Jones said his prophetic mantle would pass to him and others upon Jones's death; see Vallotton, "Remembering." For a description and documentation of Jones's and Cain's disqualifying moral failures, see Geivett and Pivec, *A New Apostolic Reformation?*, ch. 14.

its abortion and homosexuality). God, it is said, brought him back from the
dead and called him to raise up leaders for this coming revival.

> The Lord said, "I have a very specific assignment for you." . . .
> The Lord said, "I want you to go back, because if you do, this
> movement is going to result in a billion souls being saved." I'm
> talking about the whole end-time move of God.[72]

Paul Cain gave a much-touted prophecy about miracle-workers
who will pack out stadiums during this revival. Here are the words of
his prophecy.

> For they will be the faceless generation of men who will stand on
> a platform with thousands and multitudes and masses all about.
> And the news media—ABC, NBC, CBS, CNN—will be saying,
> "Ladies and gentlemen, we have no news tonight to report but
> good news. The whole world is going mad over Jesus. They're
> falling on their face and saying Jesus is Lord. . . . There is no
> sports news tonight because all the football stadiums, and all
> the ballparks, and all the colosseums are filled to overflowing,
> with thousands gathering." . . . And they're saying, "We have
> a resurrection over here and then twisted, mangled bodies are
> being made straight." And then the news announcers are say-
> ing, "Ladies and gentlemen, we don't know who these people
> are. They're almost faceless. And they're speaking great wisdom.
> And they're speaking things that are bringing about resurrec-
> tions and bringing about healings."[73]

(wishful thinking)

Cain's prophecy has been called the "Stadium Christianity" prophecy. It's
been the driving force behind many of the stadium-sized revival events
organized by today's apostles and prophets.[74]

72. Bickle, "Session 2." This document also shows that Jones prophesied specifically that the revival would result from "a youth movement, a prayer movement of
singers and musicians." This prophecy, along with a number of other prophetic words
given by Jones to Bickle in the 1980s and '90s lay behind Bickle's establishment of the
(IHOP KC) International House of Prayer in Kansas City, Missouri—an organization with emphases on youth, prayer, and music. See also Jones, "Bob Jones August 1975."

73. Cain, "Paul Cain Stadium Christianity Prophecy."

74. Lou Engle directly credited Cain's prophecy about Stadium Christianity for being the impetus behind the stadium events he has organized in cities throughout the
United States, through his two organizations, The Call and The Send. Following Cain's
death, Engle made a video announcement about the influence of Cain's prophecy on
his life, stating, "I think the whole world has wakened this morning to the sad news
that Paul Cain, a great prophet in America and the nations, has passed away. . . . He
shaped my whole life in many ways by the prophetic gift that was upon him. We're

Stadium events are seen as so critical to the coming revival that some NAR leaders have suggested that Satan caused COVID-19 in an effort to put a stop to these upcoming events.[75] But Satan's attacks aside, "the greatest harvest of souls of all time is about to come in," according to Bill Johnson.[76] After all, Jesus's greater works promise remains in effect for a generation of Christians who will actually believe it and act upon it. Johnson writes:

> When he [Jesus] said, "Greater works than these shall you do," he wasn't just throwing out flowery ideas, embellishments, or compliments to make people feel good about themselves. He was prophesying about the destiny of humanity, that there would be a generation that would all rise up with the call and mantle that Jesus was carrying.[77]   *— yes, but is this it?*

These are stunning claims. In the next chapter, we evaluate Johnson's teachings about the "greater works" and the "billion-soul harvest."

---

in Florida doing a Florida tour before The Send, going from city to city, with a vision of Stadium Christianity that Paul thirty, forty, years ago declared that the stadiums of America and the world will be filled with preaching of Jesus, and signs and wonders and miracles. It's a very famous prophecy that has actually dominated my life for twenty-five, thirty years." See Engle, "Paul Cain."

75. One such leader is Mike Bickle, the founder of the International House of Prayer in Kansas City, Missouri (IHOPKC). Bickle hired Engle to his IHOPKC staff. He has promoted Engle's stadium events, including The Send event that was scheduled for October 2020 at Kansas City's Arrowhead Stadium. Organizers expected as many as seventy-five thousand people to attend. But restrictions on large gatherings, due to the COVID-19 pandemic, led to a rescheduling of the event for June 12, 2021. (It was rescheduled again, and ultimately held on May 14, 2022.) Bickle called the virus "a plan in the kingdom of darkness against the body of Christ." He reported, "This year there's twenty stadium events planned in America. Big football stadiums, twenty of them. Never in history have twenty stadium events been planned in one nation in one year. This is remarkable, and the enemy wants to stop that." (See Bickle and Lim, "IHOPKC Leadership Panel Discussion," 11:00.) Engle concurs that stadium events are Satan's target. He wrote: "Amazingly, I believe that 2020 has been marked by the Holy Spirit as the year of Stadium Christianity and explosive advance of the Kingdom. In America alone, I believe, 20 stadiums are being prepared for prayer and evangelistic breakthroughs. Satan has risen up in rage to halt this mighty advance. . . . It has become our conviction that this storm has been stirred up by a high-level demonic principality to hinder the surge of the Church's mighty assault of fasting, prayer, sending, and missions on the global gates of Hades." (See Engle, "A Plague.")

76. Johnson, *God Is Good*, ch. 1.

77. Johnson, *Manifesto*, ch. 5.

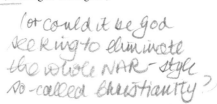

(or could it be god seeking to eliminate the whole NAR-style so-called christianity?)

—8—

Evaluating Bethel Teachings about the "Greater Works" and the "Billion-Soul Harvest"

This is either the Lord or, like, an evil magician.

—Dann Farrelly, lead pastor at Bethel,
speaking about the glory cloud
that appeared at the church[1]

+ how to tell which?

BILL JOHNSON TEACHES THAT one generation of Christians is destined to do greater miracles than Jesus.[2] This is largely based on a single verse in the Gospels—John 14:12.

Johnson's Interpretation of John 14:12

Johnson's interpretation of this verse—an interpretation held by many NAR leaders—is puzzling. Puzzling, also, is Randy Clark's suggestion that this peculiar interpretation has the support of scholarship. Nothing could be further from the truth.

1. Johnson and Farrelly, "Glory Clouds" (8:00).
2. We explained these teachings in the last chapter.

162

Recall, from our last chapter, that Clark confidently says, "Many New Testament scholars have pointed out that the Greek term *erga* used in John 14:12 to mean 'works' denotes *miraculous works*. So Jesus is saying that anyone who has faith in Him will do the *same miraculous works that He did*. (I want to thank Dr. Gary Greig for providing me with this insight.)"[3] Also, Johnson says, "The word *greater* is *mizon* in the Greek. It is found 45 times in the New Testament. It is always used to describe 'quality,' not quantity."[4]

With these two statements, Clark and Johnson have, misleadingly, portrayed scholars as agreeing with them that John 14:12 is a promise of miracle-working power for all Christians, and even greater power than that exercised by Jesus. But who are the "many" scholars who agree with them? The only scholar Clark names—Gary S. Greig—has deep ties with the New Apostolic Reformation movement, having worked over the years with prominent NAR apostles, including Clark and Brian Simmons (translator for the so-called Passion Translation), and having taught at the Wagner Leadership Institute—a non-accredited school for training leaders in the New Apostolic Reformation.[5] Greig is named as a professional reviewer for the Passion Translation, which, notably, is endorsed by Johnson, despite the controversy surrounding it.[6] The translator, Simmons, claims to have literally been visited by Christ and commissioned to make this translation, and to have been given "secrets of the Hebrew language" and divine "downloads," enabling him to translate.[7] Yet it has

3. Johnson and Clark, *The Essential Guide to Healing*, ch. 3 (Clark's emphasis).

4. Johnson, *When Heaven Invades Earth*, ch. 17 (his emphasis).

5. According to an author biography found on the website of *The Pneuma Review* journal, "Gary S. Greig, Ph.D. (University of Chicago), is Vice President for Content, Bible and Theology for Gospel Light Publications and Regal Books and an adjunct faculty mentor of United Theological Seminary (Dayton, Ohio) and of Dr. Randy Clark's Global Awakening Ministries. He was an associate professor of Hebrew and Old Testament at Regent University, School of Divinity from 1995–1998, and before that an adjunct professor of Hebrew for Fuller Theological Seminary." (See "Author Archive.") He is also named as a "faculty mentor" for Clark's doctor of ministry thesis for United Theological Seminary. See Clark, "A Study." Among the adjunct and associate professor roles Greig has held, he taught controversial courses in healing ministry and spiritual warfare at Fuller Theological Seminary in the 1990s, during the tenure of the NAR apostle C. Peter Wagner.

6. Johnson also has preached from this translation in the pulpit and he wrote the foreword for a special 2020 Bethel edition of the Passion Translation.

7. Simmons is the founder of Passion and Fire Ministries in Madison, Connecticut. To see his claims about how his translation was produced, see Roth and Simmons, *It's Supernatural!*

been shown by numerous other scholars—including some on Bible translation committees—to be unreliable and informed by theological bias.[8] That theological bias can be found throughout the Passion Translation, including its rendering of John 14:12.

> I tell you this timeless truth: The person who follows me in faith, believing in me, will do the same mighty miracles that I do—even greater miracles than these because I go to be with my Father!

In a conspicuous departure from English Bible translation: where all other major Bible translations have rendered the word *erga* as "works," the Passion Translation renders this word as "miracles." And, what's more, these are not just any miracles; they are "mighty miracles."[9]

8. A prominent critic of the translation—Mike Winger, an associate pastor and the founder of BibleThinker—commissioned leading Bible scholars, including Douglas Moo, Darrell Bock, Nijay Gupta, and Tremper Longman, to review this translation. Interviews with these scholars about the translation, along with links to their written reviews, can be found on Winger's YouTube channel. See Winger, *The Passion Project*. For overviews of this translation and the problems with it, see Pivec, "Important Facts"; Childers, "Here's Why." For other scholarly reviews, see Shead, "Burning Scripture"; Wilson, "What's Wrong." See also the entire chapter we wrote about the many problems with the Passion Translation in Pivec and Geivett, *Counterfeit Kingdom*, ch. 7.

9. Following are the renderings of John 14:12 by several major Bible translations:

NIV: "Very truly I tell you, whoever believes in me will do the works I have been doing, and they will do even greater things than these, because I am going to the Father."

ESV: "Truly, truly, I say to you, whoever believes in me will also do the works that I do; and greater works than these will he do, because I am going to the Father."

NASB: "Truly, truly, I say to you, he who believes in Me, the works that I do, he will do also; and greater *works* than these he will do; because I am going to the Father."

NRSV: "Very truly, I tell you, the one who believes in me will also do the works that I do and, in fact, will do greater works than these, because I am going to the Father."

KJV: "Verily, verily, I say unto you, He that believeth on me, the works that I do shall he do also; and greater *works* than these shall he do; because I go unto my Father."

CSB: "Truly I tell you, the one who believes in me will also do the works that I do. And he will do even greater works than these, because I am going to the Father."

Brian Simmons has not *translated* this passage, in the proper sense of the term. Rather, he has *interpreted erga*, the Greek word for "works," as "miracles." Jesus's works, though they included miracles, were by no means limited to miracles. Nor were his miracles his greatest works, relative to his primary mission in the world. His miracles played a critical role in attesting to the authority of Jesus as the Son of God to call men and women to repentance, to interpret Scripture with total accuracy, to exercise superior power over evil forces, and to set forth conditions for life in God's kingdom (John 10:24–25, 38; Luke 7:22; Acts 2:22; cf. Mark 2). The larger work of Jesus Christ was redemptive, aimed at reconciling men and women to God (Mark 10:45; 2 Cor 5:18–21; 1 Tim 2:5–6). Greig's role in producing the Passion Translation, and his sympathetic theological outlook, might explain his support for Simmons's NAR-friendly interpretation of John 14:12.

The consensus among scholars addressing this passage is that the "works" Jesus promised his followers—while not necessarily excluding miracles—were not referring *primarily* to them either. Had Jesus wanted to refer specifically to miracles, he could have used other words. Andreas Köstenberger, who writes with particular expertise on the book of John—observes:

> In the light of John's avoidance of "signs" terminology with reference to the disciples, and in the light of the fact that the emphasis of "works" terminology likewise is not necessarily, nor even primarily, on the miraculous (as in "signs and wonders"), one should caution against using John 14:12 in support for a

HCSB: "I assure you: The one who believes in Me will also do the works that I do. And he will do even greater works than these, because I am going to the Father."

Even the popular paraphrase *The Message* follows the major translations in this matter: "The person who trusts me will not only do what I'm doing but even greater things, because I, on my way to the Father, am giving you the same work to do that I've been doing. You can count on it." The Living Bible (1971), an older paraphrase, does, however, use "miracles" in place of "works." But this has always been advertised as a paraphrase. Of the sixty-one versions cited in Bible Gateway for this verse, The Living Bible is the *only* one that renders *erga* as "miracles." See Bible Gateway. Curiously, the NET Bible breaks ranks with the others, with this rendering of John 14:12: "I tell you the solemn truth, the person who believes in me will perform the miraculous deeds that I am doing, and will perform greater deeds than these, because I am going to the Father." We do not know the reason for the NET Bible's unusual rendering of *erga* as miraculous deeds. Yet the editors' notes make it clear that they do not see this verse as supporting the notion that Jesus's disciples would work more amazing miracles than Jesus did. (See NET Bible.)

theology that advocates the expectation of a believer's working of miracles today. The issue is not so much that is it possible to exclude this notion entirely from the Johannine reference as to demonstrate that such a theology was clearly not central in John's intention.[10]

In brief, miracles aren't the focus of John 14:12. To equate the "works" of this passage with miracles—as Clark and Johnson have done—is to go beyond what the text permits.

Scholars are also virtually unanimous in holding that any miracles worked by Jesus's followers could not possibly exceed the grandeur of his own miracles. The following observation by D. A. Carson is representative: "Nor can *greater works* mean 'more spectacular' or 'more supernatural' works: it is hard to imagine works that are more spectacular or supernatural than the raising of Lazarus from the dead, the multiplication of bread, and the turning of water into wine."[11] So, while Johnson may be correct to note that "greater" likely refers to quality, not quantity, he then makes an incorrect leap. The works of Jesus's followers would not be greater in the sense that they would be more amazing, but in the sense that they would belong to a more advanced eschatological era following Christ's glorification. In other words, following Jesus's completed work on the cross, the deeds of his disciples would be enlarged because they now had the full gospel to proclaim and new spiritual resources to help them proclaim it, including the partnership of the Holy Spirit (Acts 1:8). Jesus uttered a spectacular promise to those who were present and to all who believe. We should therefore look to the early history of the Christian church for evidence of the "greater works" that Jesus envisioned. That is, we should first *look for the facts in the book of Acts*.

Moreover, no Johannine scholars that we know of believe that Jesus's promise would be realized only by a single, last-days generation of the church. Where is it foretold that the "greater works" are to be specially expected in the last days? And, if they are to be expected in the last days only, why is Bill Johnson critical of all past generations of Christians? Why fault them for failing to attain to the greater works when God had planned those works to be done only by Christians living in the end time? This notion is undermined by the simple fact the testimony was given to "whoever believes." The NAR view is threatened with a dilemma: widen the intended scope of Jesus's promise to include the present generation of

10. Köstenberger, "The 'Greater Works,'" 127.

11. Carson, *The Gospel*, 495. See also Ridderbos, *The Gospel*, 497.

believers, but restrict it so as to exclude countless previous generations of believers. Any insinuation that most Christians through church history have failed to truly believe Jesus beggars belief. It's also elitist—sharply opposed to the egalitarian nature of Jesus's promise.

Simply put, Clark and Johnson do not have scholarly support for their interpretation of John 14:12. They've gone out on a limb with it. Yet, as we'll see, Johnson has made it a cornerstone argument in support of his project of raising up an end-time, miracle-working generation of Christians.

Other Scriptural Problems with Johnson's Teachings about the "Greater Works"

Johnson's teachings about an end-time generation of miracle-workers fall apart for at least three other reasons.

First, he claims that Christians' performance of miracles is required *ie, compulsory* if their message is to have any credibility. Indeed, he claims that the unbelieving world has the right to disbelieve their message if they are not working miracles. Contrary to Johnson's teaching, Jesus's statement in John 10:37—"Unless I do the works of the Father, do not believe me"— *KEY POINT* is not transferable to the church. Jesus was not calling others to do the works of the Father; he was speaking uniquely of himself. In this way he presented his own works as evidence of his identity, including his deity. And notice that he was not speaking here of his *miraculous* works, but rather *all* of his "works," in very broad terms. This verse says nothing about a requirement that all of Jesus's followers must work miracles to validate the Christian message.

Second, should God choose to work miraculous signs today, it's not certain that they will lead to large-scale conversions—*pace* Johnson's teaching about Matthew 11:20–24, which we explained in the last chapter. This passage does not contain a "prophetic promise" that today's sin-filled cities will repent if only they witness signs and wonders. The only promise in this passage is a promise of judgment. For him to read it the way he has, Johnson apparently must believe that he has received prophetic illumination, for there is no other explanation for this irregular understanding of it.[12] Quite differently from being a promise about the irresistible power of miracles, the passage shows that even the mightiest miracles will not produce repentance among the hard-hearted.

---

12. We explain the NAR doctrine of "prophetic illumination" in chapter 4.

† unrepentant cities in Israel/Judea, ie contemporary with Christ.

In fact, this theme runs through the Gospels and all of Scripture. For example, we see it again in John's Gospel. In 12:37 we read, "Though [Jesus] had done so many signs before them, they still did not believe in him." And in the Pentateuch, the miracles performed by Moses did not get Pharaoh to repent; rather, his heart grew more recalcitrant (Exod 7–11). And in the book of Revelation, it is said that spectacular miracles will be performed by "two witnesses"—they will stop the rain from falling and turn bodies of water to blood—yet this will fail to convince many people (Rev 11).

Human wickedness is a great obstacle to belief, even when confronted with miracles. The reason these miracles fail to persuade is on account of the wickedness of the people. In response to Jesus's ministry, the Jewish leaders demanded one miraculous sign after another, and it was never enough to produce repentance.

> And the Pharisees and Sadducees came, and to test him they asked him to show them a sign from heaven. He answered them, ". . . An evil and adulterous generation seeks for a sign, but no sign will be given to it except the sign of Jonah." (Matt 16:1–4)

It was not merely the fact that a sign had been asked for that leads Jesus to call them "an evil and adulterous generation," but because their motives when asking were impure. They were relentlessly putting Jesus to the test. He had already performed many signs, yet they demanded another, proving their obstinacy and refusal to believe. And so he refused to accommodate their vile interests and perform additional signs on demand.[13] Instead, he told them that the only sign he would give them was "the sign of Jonah," forecasting his resurrection. His resurrection would furnish all the support they could reasonably demand (see Rom 1:4). Yet even that sign would fail to convince most of them. And if his resurrection would not convince them, then no other miraculous sign could (see Luke 16:31).

This brings us to our third point. The greatest miraculous sign has already been given. We don't need a continuous stream of miracles to

---

13. Johnson says that, whenever he teaches about the "absolute need for miracles," someone sends him Matthew 16:4—"An evil and adulterous generation seeks for a sign"—to argue that it is wrong to seek miracles. But what was evil, according to Johnson, was not that the Pharisees asked for a sign; it was that they asked for *another* sign (after having seen many signs) because their hearts were hard. (See Johnson, "Session 8" [17:00].) We agree. And this supports our point: that miraculous signs are not the key to getting wicked people to repent (as Johnson teaches).

sustain confidence about the truth of Christianity's core propositions. The well-attested miracle of the resurrection of Jesus is good enough. It is both sufficient and necessary. If Christ has not been raised, then we're in a heap of trouble. NAR miracles do nothing to confirm the historicity of the resurrection and no expectation of miracles, as described today, is inherent in the pivotal event of the resurrection.

This should take undue burden off any Christians who, following Johnson's teaching, think they must perform miraculous signs to prove Jesus's identity.[14] They should recall that Jesus and his apostles consistently presented the resurrection as the ultimate proof of his identity and the truth of their message (Matt 16:1–4; John 2:18–21; Acts 2:22–36; 17:30–31; 1 Cor 15:1–8; Rom 1:4). And today, his resurrection—a historically documented event—remains the ultimate proof. Any other miraculous sign performed today would pale in comparison. (Do NAR leaders really think they can improve upon the actual work of Jesus and his apostles? That's pretty impressive competition.)

This quashes Johnson's characterization of a Christianity in which signs and wonders are not normative as "powerless." Has he forgotten about the huge display of power by Jesus on a Roman cross? According to the apostle Paul, the gospel about Jesus and his resurrection from the dead is the "power of God" making salvation available to all those who believe (Rom 1:1–16). Paul says nothing about the gospel requiring ongoing miracles as a demonstration of its veracity. And that's a very good thing when, despite the fervent prayer declarations of hundreds of people at Bethel, someone like Nabeel Qureshi is not healed. Or when the church's claims of thousands of healings a year remain largely unsubstantiated.[15]

14. We explained Johnson's teaching about this in chapter 7.

15. We mention Nabeel Qureshi's story in chapter 1. To be sure, Bethel has released testimonies of healing that appear to provide medical documentation. For example, see Conant, "Healed from MS." But that documentation would be difficult to verify independently. Also, the testimonies accompanied by medical documentation are few in number and do not come anywhere near substantiating the "hundreds of healings, miracles, salvations and divine interventions" Vallotton claims the Bethel movement sees "every month." (See Vallotton, *Heavy Rain*, ch. 16.) Johnson also claims that thousands of healings have occurred at the church (Johnson, *God Is Good*, ch. 11). We are not the only ones who doubt the veracity of all these healing claims. In private conversation with the authors, one prominent NAR leader from outside Bethel Church told us he was skeptical of Bethel's claims about the high number of miracles occurring regularly at the church. Even scholars who have set out to document evidence for contemporary miracles acknowledge that "miracles are still the exception rather than the rule." (See Keener, *Miracles Today*, 221; see also Moreland, *A Simple Guide*, 111,

Let us be clear. We're not skeptical about the supernatural. We're skeptical about Bethel's claims. There could, in principle, be evidence that some past event was a miracle. But what evidence is required? More than what is offered. Nothing in Scripture or in Christian history makes it at all antecedently likely that a particular miracle of the recent past was going to happen. Each miracle claim must therefore be evaluated on the evidence of its actual occurrence. Calling for evidence is a credit to Christian conviction, for otherwise that conviction is baseless. Let us not confuse credulity with faith. And let us not scorn the faith of those who seek reasons to believe.

There is ample evidence that many people are prepared to believe miracle reports without adequate evidence. It is no credit to biblical faith for its defenders to accept a low bar for reasonable acceptance. To be sure, many people have a desire for NAR miracles to be authentic.

Lackluster Miracles: "Glory" Clouds or "Glitter" Clouds?

Recall that Bethel leaders teach that the church has entered an end-time age of supernaturalism. What an affront to the Holy Spirit, first, because he works on his own timetable and in his own way, and second, because you would think that the Holy Spirit would be able to produce more impressive results if that was his intention. You would expect that if their doctrine of the greater works was true, we would see miracles on a truly magnificent scale. Yet most Bethel "miracles" take place within the safe confines of their gatherings, with little exposure on a grand, public level. If all the healings that they allege were actually occurring, that would surely be front-page news. Jesus's opponents did not dispute the occurrence of his miraculous works (though some did falsely attribute his ministry of casting out demons to demonic sources). In fact, some of his accusers took advantage of opportunities to catch Jesus performing miraculous works on the Sabbath, and thereby convict him of violating the Sabbath (see Mark 3:1–6, for example). But today what we often get are snickers from the media when they cover Bethel and its miracle claims.[16]

where Moreland, talking about the percentage of people who are healed as a result of his own practice of what he calls "healing prayer," states: "Still, in my experience and that of others I've spoken with, the percentage of people who get completely well, or at least experience some improvement, is somewhere between 5 percent and 25 percent, the latter figure being rare." See also our concluding chapter.)

16. For one example, see Hitt, "The Mystical Megachurch." Notice the cynical tone of this article.

Rather than grand miracles of truly biblical proportions, more often we see zany claims of angel feathers, indoor gusts of wind, and glory clouds manifesting in meetings. Even some Bethel leaders have questioned the validity of some of these miracles. Notably, Dann Farrelly, lead pastor at Bethel, said that when he first saw the glory cloud he was "taken aback" that it was not necessarily impressive. He said, "Somehow I thought when the Lord would show up so dramatically, everybody would know it—you know, everybody would be on their face before the Lord."[17] Instead, people were pulling out their phones to film the cloud.

Though the cloud was "undeniable" and "shocking," Farrelly said, he had expected the presence of God to be more compelling than a mere "glitter cloud." While observing it, he even entertained the thought that it could be the work of a "trickster" or an "illusionist" or an "evil magician." Ultimately, he concluded it was of the Lord.[18] But the fact that even a Bethel leader was underwhelmed by the cloud—and that he contemplated the possibility that its source was deceptive—is telling. It didn't seem to him, initially at least, to be worthy of a work of God.

NAR theology of the miraculous generates the expectation that miracles are spectacular, God-honoring, and plentiful. When stood up against the record of the Old and New Testaments, the Bethel track record is embarrassing. What passes for divine action at Bethel is sub-standard, the effect of frenetic human doings: activation exercises, fire tunnels, and the making of prayer declarations, with little evidence of the Spirit's direct agency. Human stratagems, with no biblical precedent, are the order of the day. Some may regret that miracles are not as plentiful as they may have been at various times in biblical history. But let us at least insist on a respectable biblical standard for a true work of God when it happens.

In all this frenzy, there are disproportionately few warnings about the danger of "false" and deceiving signs and wonders—something that Jesus and the apostles warned about with sobering emphasis (Matt 7:21–23; 2 Thess 2:9–12; Rev 13:13–14). The very real possibility of being deceived is, astonishingly, downplayed by Johnson, who assures his followers: "We must trust God's ability to keep us more than we trust the

17. Johnson and Farrelly, "Glory Clouds" (6:00).

18. He indicated that he accepted it as a genuine miracle after Bethel investigated and ruled out all other possibilities (such as something coming from the air conditioners in the ceiling). But Johnson said he knew it was of God because he had previously experienced the same presence of the "Spirit of God" filling his room when he was spending time alone with God. See Johnson and Farrelly, "Glory Clouds" (13:00).

devil's ability to deceive."[19] You might expect the leader of a movement dealing in legitimate miracles to urge greater caution, not less.

In short, Scripture does not support Johnson's teaching that Christians today *must* be performing greater works, as in greater or more spectacular, miracles. Neither does experience, observation, and close inspection of the evidence support this doctrine.

Where Are the "Greater Works"?

Tellingly, Johnson concedes that most Christians today haven't even done the same works as Jesus when he says, "We can't do greater until we've done the same."[20]

(ie, sign up to his supernatural lives courses & pay money to Bethel).

A Theology That Can't Be Demonstrated

This is a painful acknowledgment. It should be a clue that there's a problem with his theology.

Indeed, he inadvertently admitted his theology isn't working when speaking to a group of young people at the International House of Prayer in Kansas City. He said:

> I'd like to suggest to you that if everyone who believed miracles were for today actually could demonstrate them, there would no longer be a group of people that didn't believe they were for today. It's the living witness of *having a theology that we can't demonstrate* that speaks against us.[21]

His words, not ours.

Notice—in the above quotation—how he suggests that those who disagree with NAR teachings don't believe that miracles happen today. Because Johnson routinely misrepresents his critics, we want to be very clear on this point. We are not arguing that God doesn't work miracles today. Nor are we arguing for a cessationist position against the existence of present-day miraculous gifts, such as gifts of healing and prophesying.[22]

19. Vallotton and Johnson, *The Supernatural Ways*, foreword.

20. Johnson, "Jesus prophesied that."

21. Johnson, "Session 8" (19:00) (our emphasis).

22. Recall from our preface that we have set this question aside in this book, as it does not have direct bearing on our argumentation against NAR.

As we showed in the last chapter, Johnson places the blame for opposition to NAR teaching primarily on cessationists, which is not accurate. Many continuationists, who believe God still gives miraculous gifts, oppose Johnson's teachings. This is an important point.

But the debate, when it comes to Johnson's teachings, is not between cessationists and continuationists. The miraculous gifts are not the issue at all—despite Johnson's efforts to frame it as a debate between cessationists and continuationists. The issue here is Johnson's peculiar teachings about the greater works—teachings that both cessationists and many continuationists find themselves at odds with. For example, the Assemblies of God has issued a position paper describing as "erroneous" the beliefs of those who "locate the Kingdom primarily on earth" and "claim that most of the supernatural power of the Kingdom is currently available to a militant Church and that the fulfillment of the Kingdom will occur during the Church Age." Instead, the Assemblies of God church holds that "the next major fulfillment of Bible prophecy will be the Rapture, at which time the dead in Christ will be resurrected and the Church will be caught up from the earth, forever to be with the Lord (1 Cor 15:51,52; 1 Thess 4:14–17)."[23] There is no space in Assemblies of God doctrine for miracles so spectacular that they will succeed in Christianizing much of the world, eradicating wars, poverty, and sickness, and setting up God's kingdom on earth prior to the rapture and Christ's return.

Lowered Expectations

Another clue that Johnson's greater works theology isn't working comes from apparent adjustments in his position. We explained at the start of the last chapter that, in many of Johnson's writings and speaking engagements over the years, he expresses a belief that the present generation is the generation that will rise up and do the "greater works" and see the billion-soul harvest—indeed, that the beginnings of the harvest are here.[24] Yet, in his 2018 book *The Way of Life: Experiencing the Culture of Heaven on Earth*, he makes multiple statements indicating that the fulfillment of

---

23. "Kingdom of God," General Presbytery.

24. However, even his earlier statements sometimes left wiggle room as to the timing of fulfillment of Jesus's promise. For example, in 2010 he told his audience that he believed the present generation "could" experience the greater works, not that they would for certain. See "The Real Jesus."

the promise may be further off than he has previously suggested—and, in fact, will not be realized until future generations come upon the scene. For example, he writes: "This knowledge enables us to help design a godly culture and create a momentum for the future generations to enjoy."[25] He says, "We live to make the world better for generations that we will never see,"[26] and, "We work to leave a legacy and an inheritance for future generations, just as previous generations have done for us. While anticipating Christ's glorious return, we simply do not know when He will come, which should inspire us to have a long-term earthly vision."[27]

that ✓
at least
is
true

Once calling the present generation the "signs and wonders generation" and declaring it to be "in the last leg of the race," he has taken to saying that the present generation must "work to leave a legacy and an inheritance for future generations." Why the change in expectations? Is it possible that Johnson, who is aging and has yet to see the fulfillment he anticipated, has backed off his earlier predictions?

Only a year later, Johnson appeared to backtrack on his backtracking. In 2019 he released an updated edition of his book *The Way of Life* and added a chapter titled "Designed for Glory," which includes statements that were not made in the original edition of the book. While retaining relevant statements from the earlier edition of his book, he added statements hinting that the fulfillment of the prophecy will at least *begin* with the present generation—seeming to move back toward his earlier position. He writes, "We are in the beginning of a one-billion-soul harvest. And that's just counting the young people. We are going to see masses of people come into the Kingdom." He also writes, "We are facing an opportunity to reap the greatest harvest of all time. There are more people that are about to be saved than have been saved in all of human history."[28]

Why did he feel the need to update his book and add a chapter including these more optimistic statements? Were readers confused, by the original edition of this book, with his suddenly subdued expectations? Did he feel the need to defend his earlier claims about the present generation?[29]

---

25. Johnson, *The Way of Life*, ch. 15 (2018 edition).

26. Johnson, *The Way of Life*, ch. 18 (2018 edition).

27. Johnson, *The Way of Life*, ch. 18 (2018 edition).

28. Johnson, *The Way of Life*, ch. 17 (updated 2019 edition).

29. We thank Godfrey Higgins for pointing out to us the very different, more optimistic, tone found in the additional chapter included in Johnson's updated 2019 edition of *The Way of Life*. He made this point in an unpublished paper. (Higgins, "The Pure Theology of Jesus," appendix III.)

We don't know the answer to these questions. But whatever the reason, Johnson initially seemed to lower expectations for his readers, indicating they may not necessarily see the complete fulfillment of Jesus's greater works promise in their lifetimes; and then he reversed course. Even suggesting such a thing—after years of making such bold pronouncements about the present generation—suggests that Johnson has not seen his greater works teachings pan out.

A Faulty Foundation

Upon the faulty foundation of his greater works teaching, Johnson has staked the reputation of the Christian faith for this generation. But thank God that the veracity of Christianity is based on a more secure footing than an ever-shifting, evolving theology that—even according to one of its main proponents, Bill Johnson—has not been adequately demonstrated. No generation, up through the present generation, has collectively performed the same miracles as Jesus, to say nothing of greater miracles. Blessed be God, the historical evidence for the resurrection, as documented by the apostles in Scripture, does not ebb and flow with the pronouncements of present-day prophets and apostles or the abilities of their followers to drum up more and bigger miracles.

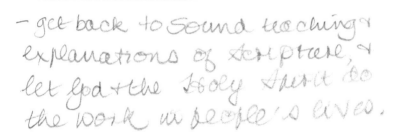

—9—

Reckless Christianity

Behold, I am against those who prophesy lying dreams,
declares the LORD, and who tell them and lead my
people astray by their lies and their recklessness.

—God speaking to Jeremiah in Jeremiah 23:32

WE BEGAN THIS BOOK with the story of how Bill Johnson resolved to "have more" of God "*at any cost*."[1] He wanted God's miraculous power to operate in his life and ministry, even if it meant losing the respectability of others. He's kept true to his word. While he has a worldwide following and the support of a few prominent Christians, he has persisted in making Bethel Church his laboratory for spiritual "experimentation"— despite being the target of strenuous criticism.[2]

1. Our emphasis.

2. Christian radio host Michael Brown has defended Bill Johnson and Bethel Church. Francis Chan and Mike Bickle are advocates, as well. In a panel discussion with these leaders, Chan said that, when he agreed to speak at Mike Bickle's church for the Onething conference in 2013, he received a "barrage of criticism" and pleadings from fellow Christians to rescind his agreement because of Bickle's controversial teachings. He wondered, at first, if he had made a mistake. But he went anyway, and he now believes the criticisms about Bickle and other NAR leaders were slanderous. He told Johnson, "Bill, you blow me away with your words and your heart behind them. You need to know that it's that heart that changed me, it's that type of character and

A Risk-Taking Culture

In line with Johnson's pursuit of having more of God at any cost, Bethel Church has adopted a "risk-taking culture." As they have said, "you must be willing to fail to succeed."[3] So, they accept that "messes" will be made from time to time, and have admitted that the words and practices of people at the church have sometimes "crossed a line."[4] But that's OK because any messes that are created can be cleaned up (so they say). And they're more than worth the risk. But we disagree. The reckless way Bethel has gone about things is not God's way, and it has left a wake of confusion and destruction. In this chapter we spotlight some of the reckless teachings and practices that Bethel has promoted in their relentless quest for "more" of God, what they've promised, and what they've actually delivered.

A Reckless Narrative  *(summary)*

Bethel leaders (together with other NAR leaders) are rewriting the Christian narrative. They claim that Jesus always intended that apostles and prophets in each generation must govern the church so they can give their new revelations that will equip Christians to work greater miracles than Jesus worked, trigger a worldwide revival (the "billion-soul harvest"), and bring God's kingdom to earth. They want their narrative to become normative. They tell the story of Christianity differently than it has been told going back to the first generation of Christians. They use every device at their disposal, including the revisioning of the church's greatest task, the Great Commission as a commission to "bring heaven to earth".[5] They've also redefined the historic Christian practice of prayer to include making "prayer declarations." They view declarations as the most powerful type of prayer. (Since declarations are not prayer at all, a life patterned along these lines is, in effect, a prayerless life.)[6] Even more

---

kindness that can only come from the Spirit to love like that in the midst of slander." See Johnson and Chan, "The Unveiling."

3. See chapter 1.

4. See chapter 1.

5. We showed this in chapter 6.

6. We have to get prayer right, which those in NAR do not. Whatever serves as a substitute for prayer, even when it is called prayer, is not prayer at all. (Of course, people in NAR may still pray petitionary prayers in addition to making prayer

significant is their whole scheme of bringing heaven to earth based on
their teachings about declarations and the "greater works."

With their revisionist teachings, they promise their followers that
they can play a pivotal part in God's end-time plan to bring his kingdom
to earth. In reality, they've diminished God's sovereignty. What has our
God, the sovereign Lord of the universe, been up to all this time when
Christians, allegedly, lost their way—forgetting the true governors of the
church (apostles and prophets) and the true meaning of Jesus's promise in John 14:12? Somehow, the church lost this thread, so critical to
the fabric of Christianity, and neglected its task for nearly two thousand
years. It would appear that, contrary to the words of Jesus, the gates of
hell have indeed prevailed against the church—at least until the NAR
movement came along and set things right in recent decades.[7] Presently,
God is restoring centuries of neglected truths. But we find in the Scriptures no indicators that there would be such an interruption, no hint that
neglected truths would be restored, and no criteria for confirming the
alleged authenticity of this new movement of the Spirit.

They've also created confusion about the nature of the gospel, con-
flating it with the manifestation of the miraculous. Indeed, all this other
business that will supposedly bring heaven to earth—the declarations,
activation exercises, prophecies, healing, and miracle-working—is what
defines the Bethel movement and qualifies it as seriously errant on some
very important issues. Those things are their message.[8] This can be seen
by studying their books and other teaching materials. For those who have
defended Bethel by saying its leaders *do* teach the gospel of salvation, we
ask them to show us where this gospel emerges as a major emphasis. It's
generally on the back shelf. It seems the only time it moves to the fore-
front is when Bethel leaders are challenged.[9] They add layers and layers
of extrabiblical teachings and practices and make them central.[10]

declarations. But if making declarations is the only sort of "prayer" they do, they are
not truly praying.)

7. Jesus's words can be found in Matthew 16:18.

8. During an interview, a former Bethel elder, Mark Mack, said one thing that frus-
trated him at Bethel was how Bill Johnson's message during every Sunday service was
about healing and miraculous signs and wonders "to the exclusion of everything else."
See Mack and Kozar, "Behind the Scenes."

9. Johnson and Farrelly, "Episode 1" (1:21:00).

10. And they exert psychological pressure on their followers. People see in this
evidence of cult-like tendencies. We explain, at length, the control tactics NAR leaders
employ in Pivec and Geivett, *Counterfeit Kingdom*, ch. 5.

The simple gospel of Jesus as a message comes to us without all the frills of a raging fever for spectacular miracles and prophecy. But it does begin and end with the miraculous: it begins with the miracle of Jesus's resurrection from the dead; it ends in miraculous reconciliation with God. Sadly, this true gospel is blurred in Bethel's revisionist scheme. The Bethel movement cannot be allowed a free pass. A proper response calls for nothing less than recovery of the gospel of salvation.

A Reckless Authority

Bethel teaches that apostles and prophets, with their new revelations, are "first" and "second" in God's "order of priority" in church government. Pastors and elders, who merely expound the Scriptures, must submit to their direction. In return for coming under apostles' "spiritual covering," they (and those who attend their churches) are promised miraculous powers, prosperity, and prayers that will be answered by angels they can commission. These are tantalizing promises.

But Bethel's apostles and prophets are usurpers—claiming authority in the church (and beyond the church) that they do not have. A concerning aspect of their spurious claims to authority is that their followers become dependent on them for their revelations and miraculous powers. These so-called apostles also place extrabiblical demands on people. They teach that obedience to God requires obeying commands that they speciously claim are taught in Scripture—such as the supposed command for all believers to heal the sick and prophesy in their everyday lives. Scripture does not teach that all Christians must work miracles—to say nothing of "greater miracles" than those that Jesus worked. Like the scribes and the Pharisees Jesus condemned in Matthew 23:4, they place heavy burdens on their followers—burdens they cannot lift themselves. Which Bethel apostle or prophet is consistently working miracles or getting vital prophecies consistently right?[11] At best, the new truths and practices they've revealed are dispensable; at worst, they are deceptive abuses of power. Note that Bethel leaders believe the authority of apostles is far greater than the authority of pastors, for apostles have special authority from God to give new revelation and work miracles, and their

/ almost worshipping their leader)

11. By miracles, we mean miracles of a caliber that inspires awe and can be verified by non-partial outsiders, since that is the caliber of miracles projected by NAR leaders. See Pivec and Geivett, *Counterfeit Kingdom*, Special Appendix.

authority is recognized as influential even in the angelic realm. Clearly, the potential for spiritual abuse by a supposed apostle is much greater than the potential for abuse by a pastor or other church leader.[12]

To make matters worse, they have never demonstrated that they have the authority they so audaciously seek to wield in the lives of their followers. They assume confirmation of their prophetic/apostolic authority when their prophecies "come true." But when their prophecies fail and their authority falters, they plead that they are not false prophets. We are expected to take their word for it that they are true prophets, and yet they deny one straightforward biblical norm for testing their authority, which is perfect prophetic accuracy—a norm, when violated, that is fully sufficient for identifying false prophets. But even if their prophecies were to "come true," this would not be enough to confirm their prophetic authority. How are we to know that a successful "prediction" was not a lucky guess? The burden of proof is on them to first demonstrate that they are, in fact, genuine prophets of God.[13] A true prophet of God speaks with knowledge of what God has revealed, and does not speculate or qualify with hedges, as is the norm in NAR.[14]

By demanding that *they* direct the church and that their followers receive their dubious revelations, they have endangered their followers with spiritual abuse and deception.

A Reckless Way to Interpret Scripture

Johnson claims to receive special prophetic illumination into the Scripture. Thus, his followers are promised the freshest, most relevant, most applicable insights into God's Word.

Yet, he also admits that he could get it wrong sometimes. Thus, he redirects people's attention away from Scripture (which is infallible) to his divinely channeled words (which he admits are fallible).[15] It's egregious for one preaching to others the basic truths of God to assume that God is speaking through them, though they may be hearing unreliably

---

12. For examples of spiritual abuse at the hands of an apostle, see Pivec and Geivett, *Counterfeit Kingdom*, ch. 5. Of course, pastors also have been guilty of spiritual abuse.

13. We show how they could do this in Pivec and Geivett, *Counterfeit Kingdom*, ch. 4.

14. See chapters 4 and 5, and Pivec and Geivett, *Counterfeit Kingdom*, ch. 4.

15. See chapter 4.

(as if God is unreliably channeling his message to the sheep through Bill Johnson). His words, he allows, are not equal to Scripture. But he implies that they are superior to the fruit of careful Bible study and line-by-line expository preaching from the biblical text. Johnson is saying, in effect, that the standard hermeneutic—where interpretative practice is governed by reasonable rules and criteria—is not adequate for discerning these truths that are somehow contained in Scripture.

A troubling feature of the broader NAR movement is the way leaders promote idiosyncratic interpretations that are not corroborated by standard commentaries written by recognized scholars. They begin with a handful of concepts and assumptions about prophecy, healing, miracles, divine guidance, etc., and they view nearly *every* passage of Scripture through the resulting lens. Any biblical language that could possibly be construed as a fit with those assumptions is nuanced accordingly. This is a seat-of-the-pants hermeneutic of interpretive opportunism.

In addition to receiving prophetic illumination, Johnson also dogmatically interprets passages of Scripture that the more studious must later correct. And he does not exhibit a receptiveness to their correction. Indeed, when prominent scholars have pointed out problems, say, with The Passion Translation of the Bible, he has shown disregard for their evaluations and plowed ahead in his authoritative endorsement of it, though he has no expertise in the field of Bible translation.

Some individuals we've spoken with—including scholars who identify as "charismatic" in their theology—defend Johnson with a reminder that he's not a theologian or scholar, that he's not formally trained. "So he doesn't always get every interpretation and teaching correct? That doesn't make him a heretic." That may be so. But we also remind people that Johnson leads a congregation of more than eleven thousand people. Moreover, he claims to be an authoritative apostle and thousands of people worldwide believe he receives revelation for the church at large. Surely he must be held to a higher standard than that of "not a heretic" (Jas 3:1). Also, you would think that if Johnson does receive revelation directly from God, then his liabilities, due to a lack of formal training, are compensated. Should his defenders really be making excuses for him when he muffs his interpretation of Scripture—if indeed Johnson has special insight, as an apostle-prophet, into the meaning of Scripture? As an apostle/prophet, should we not suppose that Johnson has access to knowledge that does not depend on formal training? And is Johnson thereby protected from criticism? We think not. His errors are evidence that he lacks the prophetic gift and the apostolic authority that have been ascribed to him and that he ascribes to himself.

The sad result of Johnson's reckless approach to Scripture is that his followers are not equipped to interpret the Bible for themselves (because they must rely on his special insights that are available only to him) and they are led astray by his errant interpretations.

A Reckless Mandate

Many NAR leaders, including Johnson, have promoted the so-called Seven Mountain Mandate. This divine strategy holds the keys to establishing God's kingdom on earth, they say. But it is a strained theological construct that rests on poor exegesis of Scripture and, like Bethel's revisionist narrative, produces confusion about the message of the gospel. It subsumes the gospel message under a politically activist and triumphalist agenda that aims to "take over" all sectors of society. It demands submission to prophets and apostles who set the agenda and employ suspicious tactics. This will seem alarmingly subversive to many who think religious freedom is protected by the US Constitution. And it paints a negative, gravely mistaken, and embarrassing picture of the church that compromises Christian witness among thoughtful nonbelievers.

Reckless Apologetics

Bethel leaders also have their own apologetics, consisting mostly in the activation of miraculous powers, fulfilled prophecies for today, and prayer declarations. They promise that believers can demonstrate that Jesus rose from the dead by working miracles.[16] Indeed, such a demonstration of modern miracles is critical to the church's apologetic, they claim. But this is a deeply flawed basis for Christian belief.

If ever God were going to do a miracle to validate his special presence at Bethel Church, it seems he would have done so when the eyes of the world were on the church's attempts to raise Olive Heiligenthal. But that's not what happened.[17] For the first several days, optimism about an imminent resurrection fueled the hopes of many and inspired

16. See chapter 7.

17. This is counterevidence that needs to be considered as people weigh the total evidence for the alleged miraculous character of the community.

countless declarations. But eventually, the harsh finality of her passing had to be acknowledged. And before Olive's passing, God missed another opportunity to show up in a big way when Bethel made declarations for Nabeel Qureshi's healing from cancer.

Following failed expectations like these, belief persists only in the face of powerful counterevidence, and such belief is not a credit to biblical faith. When faith is grounded in modern miracles, it is likely to fail. How long can the faith of NAR participants survive when the track record is so appalling?

Reckless Teachings about Miracles

Despite their very public failures to work miracles, Bethel leaders still claim that miracles, such as healings of sickness and disease, are happening at their church regularly. Holding out hope for a healing, thousands of people have flocked to the church.

But again, their promises do not deliver. Upon closer inspection, the "miracles" occurring at Bethel don't seem like miracles at all. Their leaders speak of partial, incremental, and non-lasting healings, and focus on percentages of people who they claim have been healed.[18] This track record doesn't come close to replicating the record of miracles in the New Testament, and that is especially significant, since their own premise is that God is at work in the same way (and in an even greater way) today as in the New Testament.[19] And, of course, their declarations haven't worked either (regarding COVID-19, the Carr Fire, and Nabeel Qureshi, for example).

The question, when it comes to Bethel teaching about miracles, is not whether God is able to act supernaturally in today's world. The real problems lie elsewhere: the false hope of healing held out to all who are sick, the presumption of being able to teach anyone to work miracles (through the technology of "activation"), and the fact that there are fewer documented cases of healings than is to be expected given NAR leaders' own teachings.[20]

18. Johnson and Clark, *The Essential Guide*, ch. 11; Clark, "A Study"; Johnson; "Why Does Some Healing Not Last?"

19. For more discussion of this point, see Pivec and Geivett, *Counterfeit Kingdom*, Special Appendix.

20. Certainly, there has been a recent effort by some associated with these leaders to furnish medical documentation to validate individual miracle claims. The *Send*

God always wills to heal, and my experience must rise to that reality, not the other way around—or so Johnson teaches. This teaching is confusing, circular, poorly developed, and overly simplistic. To save God's goodness, he diminishes God's power—which is the very power we need to deliver us from our trials.[21] And, tragically, his teachings place a great burden on people who are already suffering and grieving and who can't figure out why they have not been healed—compounding their pain.[22] Indeed, Johnson acknowledges that self-condemnation is a major problem among those who embrace Bethel teachings about miracles.[23]

Proof documentary is one example. (See chapter 3, note 54.) But their efforts are disappointing in comparison with expectations generated. Those evaluating NAR and the Bethel movement shouldn't focus on their evidence for individual miracles but the big picture of their miracles (that is, what they teach about the high frequency and type of miracles that should be expected). By their own admission, miracles are not always happening. (See Vallotton's comments in Yoars, "The Radical Revivalists.") And Johnson admits that not every sick person he has prayed for has been healed, including his own father. (See Johnson and Clark, *The Essential Guide*, ch. 7, and Johnson, *God Is Good*, ch. 11.) We note that respected Christian apologists who are not part of NAR took part in the *Send Proof* documentary. These scholars argued for the plausibility of miracles. We do not disagree with them on that point, but we do have concerns that their participation in a documentary produced by a Bethel teacher and featuring the "healing ministries" of NAR "miracle-workers" (including Bill Johnson, Randy Clark, Ché Ahn, Heidi and Rolland Baker, and Shawn Bolz) lends their credibility to NAR and its aberrant and damaging teachings about miracles. One can believe that God performs miracles without believing that there are present-day miracle workers or, if there are present-day miracle workers, that these specific leaders are miracle workers. We also note that the documentary, though it features Bill Johnson and others from Bethel Church, in fact offers no specific medical evidence for any of the Bethel miracles of healing.

21. Beisner, *Psalms of Promise*, 62.

22. See Pivec and Geivett, *Counterfeit Kingdom*, ch. 9.

23. Johnson, *The Way of Life*, ch. 2 (updated 2019 edition). Rather than attend closely to these substantive concerns about Bethel's theology about miracles delineated by Christian supernaturalists like ourselves, the church's leaders tend to mischaracterize their critics as anti-supernatural. Many Christians would like to know, do miracles happen today, and on what basis should we accept contemporary miracle reports? They are not inherently skeptical about the miraculous; they simply want to be responsible believers. Bethel teachers certainly affirm the miraculous. But they make other, more controversial, claims: (1) Christians who do not perform miracles are disobedient, (2) all *can* perform miracles if they develop the right mindset and if they take part in "prophetic activation exercises," (3) working miracles is the chief means of validating the truth of Christianity, and (4) miracles can and will lead to the repentance of sinful cities. One may believe that God is indeed working miracles today, often through select human agents, without endorsing these several additional points about present-day miracles.

Bethel Responds to Their Critics

A dominant theme of the *Rediscover Bethel* video series, as we discussed in chapter 1, is that Bethel Church has been misunderstood and unfairly maligned.[24] Speakers claim they have never demanded that Bethel attendees accept any Bethel beliefs other than the core Christian doctrines affirmed by the church, such as the doctrine of the deity of Christ.[25] In truth, however, they push their novel teachings rather emphatically and authoritatively—by proclaiming them to be new revelations God has given to the church and suggesting that acceptance of them is pivotal to fulfilling your destiny and being part of what God is doing in the world today. The Rediscover Bethel videos are an admission that Bethel Church has a public relations problem. What other church has had to address so many accusations regarding their bizarre teachings and practices?

In these videos, the speakers deny that they portray other Christians as inferior or that they stoke division among believers.[26] So, if your acquaintance with Bethel teaching was limited to what is presented in

---

24. Bethel leaders are not the only NAR leaders that have recently responded to the mounting criticism against their teachings. In an effort to refute our characterization of NAR, Randy Clark released the results of a survey he conducted of present-day apostles and other Christian leaders. Those results are included in an academic paper he published containing his written critique of our work on NAR (along with critiques written by several students in his Global Awakening Theological Seminary). See Clark, "A Response." He claims the answers to his survey show that our description of those leaders' beliefs is inaccurate. His strategy was to poll these individuals with questions based on statements in our book *A New Apostolic Reformation?* While we appreciate the effort he has made, we have to say that a survey is an inadequate instrument for refuting our claims. We acknowledge in our book that NAR is not a monolithic movement where everyone agrees in all details. So any effective refutation must interact directly with our specific arguments and the sources we cite in our books, about the specific individuals we name (and in the context that we name them). An anonymous survey with only twenty-two respondents (including individuals who do not view themselves as apostles, as well as individuals we did not name in our book, let alone name as being part of NAR), that paints with an overly broad brush, cannot truly be called a refutation of our claims. And the questions his survey asked, in our opinion, were leading and were not the questions *we* would have asked to determine those leaders' beliefs.

25. Johnson and Farrelly, "Episode 6" (1:00:00).

26. "We're not, like . . . if you want to be a real Christian, you stay here at Bethel," Vallotton says. (See Vallotton and Farrelly, "Episode 4" [48:00].) And Farrelly, after acknowledging that there are thousands of Christian denominations in the world, says that Bethel leaders don't see their movement as "*the* way, but just as part of the Lord's team." (See Johnson and Farrelly, "Episode 6.")

these videos, you might think that Bethel leaders have always been gracious toward those who disagree with them. But as we've shown, they have a track record of chastising and vilifying those who question their beliefs. If you disagree with Johnson's teachings about miracles, you have committed a "theological crime"—one that "should nauseate all of us."[27] And people who teach the Scriptures, "but don't burn with passion" to work miracles, are "not in love" with God.[28] This persistent needling by Bethel leaders betrays a judgmental spirit that presumes to know the hearts of individual Christians and the depth of their relationship with God.[29] It is distinctly ungracious to castigate the objects of God's grace as somehow spiritually destitute. And it seems insincere when these leaders play the victims. Yet we welcome the more temperate tone exemplified in the recent videos, and we hope this shift marks a permanent move away from divisive rhetoric.

How to Respond?

People concerned about the "Bethel effect" on their churches and other organizations often ask for guidance. We offer the following suggestions.[30]

1. Avoid Any Alignment with Bethel

We urge pastors to be wary of aligning with the church, whether formally (through the Bethel Leaders Network) or informally (by inviting Bethel speakers, using Bethel resources, performing or otherwise incorporating Bethel music, etc.). Bill Johnson has stated explicitly that he seeks to export Bethel's teachings and practices to churches through

27. Johnson, *God Is Good*, ch. 10.

28. Johnson, "Onething 2016" (starting at 2:14:00).

29. In a recent video responding to critics of NAR, Daniel Kolenda, the president and CEO of Christ for All Nations, assumes a mocking tone toward NAR critics, describing them pejoratively as "heresy-hunting evangelicals." He chides them for criticizing today's apostles and says they "have always hated charismatics" and are "jealous" of them because they have the largest churches in the world and the most popular Christian music. "Meanwhile," he says, "the critics sit there in their boring, depressing, dying churches." See Kolenda, "What is the N.A.R.?" In all of this, he completely ignores the weighty arguments critics have raised. But critics may see in this reactionary response encouraging evidence that NAR leaders are feeling the burn.

30. See our detailed advice for parents in Pivec and Geivett, *Counterfeit Kingdom*, ch. 10.

its music.[31] As we've noted elsewhere, the use of Bethel music furthers the cause of this movement and educates believers in the theology of the movement, a theology that is intentionally incorporated into the songs' lyrics.[32] Since the music is deliberately used to promote NAR theology, we urge musicians to suspend collaboration with Bethel Music and other NAR music groups.

The leaders in any ministry should be reluctant to promote speakers, conferences, or books that have close associations with Bethel or ones that promote NAR teachings generally. Churches should vet potential pastoral hires for signs of NAR leanings. Because Bethel Church is so intentional and energetic about exporting its doctrine to churches globally, people must be vigilant and watch for encroachment of Bethel teachings and practices in their congregations. Often, an initial, and seemingly harmless, indicator of encroachment is the use of Bethel songs in congregational worship.

Also, church missions boards should vet (for Bethel/NAR influence) any missionaries who receive financial support from their congregations. We've learned of missionaries who serve with large missions organizations and, to complete the organization's education requirements, choose to go to Bethel and attend BSSM (or a conference at the church) rather than attend a traditional Bible college or seminary. Many of these missionaries have adopted Bethel's beliefs—all the while working under the auspices of respected agencies and receiving funding from more theologically conservative churches that have no idea what these missionaries are teaching on the field. We encourage missions agencies to establish parameters for the type of education and training they consider acceptable for their candidates.

Naturally, we would discourage Christian leaders from endorsing Bill Johnson's books (or those of other Bethel leaders), supporting

---

31. A video clip of Bill Johnson's statement is shown in Winger, "Bill Johnson's Theology" (10:00).

32. We note that author and pastor Sam Storms, a self-described charismatic Christian, has defended Bethel Music by citing Bethel's statement of faith and declaring it to be "profoundly evangelical and orthodox and consistent with the historic creeds of Christianity." He argues that concerns about Bethel are about secondary theological issues or ministry-style preferences and therefore should not prevent someone from using Bethel Music. (See "A Defense.") While Bethel's theology may not rise to the level of heresy, we have shown that its theology and practices do give cause for serious concern. (See our analysis of specific Bethel Music lyrics in Pivec and Geivett, *Counterfeit Kingdom*, ch. 8.)

Bethel's work, or referring people to its ministry. Bethel teachings are a serious threat to the church. Any manifestation of them is dangerous, though in different ways and to different degrees, depending on specific circumstances. It would be unwise to accommodate certain defining features of Bethel teaching within a group for the sake of embracing what is "good."

Instead of partnering with Bethel and other NAR organizations and using their theologically tainted resources, churches and other ministries should partner with organizations and Christian leaders who promote biblically sound teaching. They should strive to use only music that is sound and theologically rich and will contribute to the spiritual health of their people. And they should be sure not only to tell people what Scripture says, but also to teach them how to read and properly interpret it for themselves.

We want to stress that churches do need to be evaluated individually. You cannot simply assume that a church that is part of a denomination or association abides by the official documents or the official position of that larger group. So, for example, we cited several official documents of the Assemblies of God denomination demonstrating clear separation from NAR. But this does not mean that individual Assemblies churches all abide by these standards. A noteworthy example is James River Church in Springfield, Missouri, pastored by John Lindell. This was dramatically illustrated by the Week of Power conference hosted in March 2023 by James River Church and featuring Bill Johnson and Randy Clark as the primary guest speakers, giving them a significant platform and influence in the church. We encourage all who attend Assemblies of God churches to read for themselves the "Apostles and Prophets" statement available on the Assemblies website and hold their pastors accountable to these standards. So many have thought that because the denomination has adopted these standards every Assemblies church follows them. But that's just not the case.

2   Be Alert to NAR Tactics and Propaganda

Be aware that many NAR leaders deny that they are part of the New Apostolic Reformation. For example, the International House of Prayer in Kansas City, Missouri, has a statement on their website downplaying their extreme teachings and claiming they are not part of the New Apostolic Reformation. It's titled "What Is IHOPKC's Stance on the New

Apostolic Reformation?" Also, many of the individuals we have identified as being NAR leaders have signed another statement titled "NAR and Christian Nationalism"—drafted by Joseph Mattera and Michael Brown and published in 2022—denying any affiliation with NAR. But in our public response to this statement,[33] we show that multiple signatories of the statement have taught NAR teachings over the years, and that they are indeed NAR. We also document how NAR leaders have removed language from their websites, where they once candidly described themselves as part of the New Apostolic Reformation and parroted C. Peter Wagner's controversial teachings and descriptions of the NAR movement. Some, including Mattera and Brown, have accused critics of NAR of being conspiracy theorists who have either made up the existence of NAR or exaggerated the size and dangers of this movement. Be on the lookout for these tactics.

NAR leaders also are skilled at employing language for subterfuge—using jargon, equivocation, and euphemisms to hide what's really going on. Watch out for these word games. For example, NAR leaders often describe certain churches as "apostolic" without saying exactly what they mean by that. This jargon term refers to churches that defer to the authority of NAR apostles, and "apostolic people" are those who attend such churches. Equivocation occurs in their use of the word "prayer," when often what they really mean is "declaration" (which, we have shown, is not prayer at all). We've shown how they've redefined the Great Commission, investing it with novel meaning. They also commonly employ euphemisms. For example, NAR leaders have lately begun referring to apostleship as a "grace gift" or "function" in the church, moving somewhat away from the language of governing "office." This is concerning because some non-NAR groups, including the Assemblies of God, also refer to a contemporary spiritual "gift" of apostleship and apostolic "function."[34] NAR leaders' intentional use of this euphemism creates confusion and results in NAR further penetrating other groups that might be averse to talk of governing offices.[35]

NAR leaders are also great propagandists. Their messaging and marketing convey the idea that miracles are the norm at Bethel and other NAR churches. Somehow people in those churches are able to ignore or dismiss

33. Geivett and Pivec, "Response." (brainwashed; influenced by [illegible])

34. "Apostles and Prophets."

35. To learn more about other euphemisms employed by NAR leaders, see Pivec and Geivett, *Counterfeit Kingdom*, ch. 5.

the gap between reality and the propaganda. There are reasons for their inability to confront the gap: the constant repetition of the message, the desirability of the message, the feeling that others are experiencing what's promised, even if they aren't. And then there's the fact that any admission of a gap is unbelief, which, in the NAR worldview, nixes the possibility for a miracle to occur. So they have to rid themselves of that unbelief.

3   Know What Draws People to Bethel

It's critical for Christians to understand what draws people to Bethel. Many seek healing, whether physical or emotional. People who are sick or have experienced trauma are especially vulnerable. We all have psychological vulnerabilities, and these can be exploited. Every person wishes to experience hope and joy. We all want lives that matter and we desire to do important things. NAR harnesses that desire with the promise of power to make a difference by working signs and wonders and prophesying.

If this is right, it could explain why some people do find their way out of the irrational and false beliefs found at Bethel. The psychological effects begin to wane. The beliefs and practices fail them. They stop ignoring the sense they had—a sense many former NAR participants have told us about—that "something was not quite right" (even though they couldn't put their finger on it at the time).[36] And they begin to think harder about what is taught. Notably, many people who have shared their stories of deconversion from NAR express deep remorse and repentance for ever having embraced NAR beliefs. They acknowledge that those beliefs appealed to their ego and insecurities. They confess their naivete, their ignorance of Scripture, and their disposition to let emotion and "crowd psychology" substitute for a true work of God.[37] Knowing *how*

36. Longtime Bethel attender of thirty-four years and former elder Mark Mack said he was initially drawn to Bethel by a "desire to belong to something that you think is greater than you." Yet he also often had the sense "something's not right here." See Mack and Kozar, "Behind the Scenes" (1:00). When he questioned unusual things being promoted by church leaders (phenomena such as people falling to the ground, shaking, and making animal noises during times of worship), he said he was assured that those things were of God. He was also told "our minds are at war with God," meaning that he should not trust his critical reasoning process when assessing these things (19:00). This is what we call a "brainstopper." In another work, we have identified several other brain stopping catchphrases used by NAR leaders to discourage critical thinking by their followers. See Pivec and Geivett, *Counterfeit Kingdom*, ch. 5.

37. We've been struck by how often these good-hearted people, initially disposed

Bethel/NAR teachings hook people may help provide a springboard for helping those in "recovery."[38]

An Alternative: Careful Christianity

Bethel leaders acknowledge that their "risky" teachings and practices are the source of their "messes."[39] So long as they embrace those teachings and practices, new messes will keep appearing. And the practices, likely, will become riskier and venture more outside the box. That's because you "keep them" the way you "catch them." People who, initially, are drawn to the church because of its claims to extraordinary happenings will expect the church to continue providing a steady diet of miracles.

But disciples of Jesus must be cautious. At Bethel, acting recklessly is held up as a virtue, but that is not God's way. We see this in the stern words God gave to the prophet Jeremiah for the false prophets of his day when they prophesied recklessly: "Behold, I am against those who prophesy lying dreams, declares the LORD, and who tell them and lead my people astray by their lies and their *recklessness,* when I did not send them or charge them. So they do not profit this people at all, declares the LORD" (Jer 23:32).[40] And Jesus's warning about false prophets who will work miracles puts us on notice to be appropriately critical (Matt 7:15; 24:24). We are admonished to exercise caution in our acceptance of any new teachings and revelations and are given the example of the Bereans as a model (Acts 17:11; see also 1 Thess 5:21; 1 John 4:1). Surely, it is honorable if you choose to risk your personal comfort and safety for the sake of the gospel. But that is very different from conducting "risky" spiritual "experiments" to generate supernatural power. Bethel is intentionally playing with fire. And many people have been burned (Prov 6:27).

to accept and buy into the message, get to a point on their own where they get a bad feeling in their spirit. That isn't typical in Christian ministry. How do NAR leaders explain this? How could they fault such sensitive, often very humble, people for their alarm? What would account for it? Since discernment skills within the movement are, essentially, emotional, NAR leaders can't really object that doubters are acting emotionally.

 38. NAR recovery groups have been created to provide support and encouragement for those who have left the NAR movement. Some of those groups can be found on Facebook, such as the page "NAR Recovery Group (Non-Denominational)."

39. See chapter 1.

40. The emphasis is ours. Other Scriptures that are critical of "reckless" behavior are Judg 9:4; Prov 14:16; Luke 15:13 and 2 Tim 3:4.

Bethel leaders say any messes in their "risk-taking culture" can easily be cleaned up. They are worth the hassle—so long as their church can achieve its desired outcome. But what of the people around the world who were troubled by the fact that Olive did not wake up and also that Nabeel Qureshi, a prominent leader, was not healed of cancer? What of those individuals who have sought, to no avail, to be "activated" in a prophetic gift? What happens when prophecies of "success" and "greatness" do not come to fruition? What of the scores of believers who have been disillusioned in their Christian faith because of false expectations stoked by Bethel's various teachings?[41] How many of these have left the faith altogether? And what of the disrepute brought to the way of Christianity because of outlandish antics like grave soaking and the failed predictions by NAR prophets?

Some risks are not worth taking.

---

41. Recall the stories we shared in our opening chapter. We share other testimonials in Pivec and Geivett, *Counterfeit Kingdom.*

Bibliography

Ahn, Ché. "It's Time for Bob Jones' Prophesied Billion-Soul Harvest." *Charisma News*. February 16, 2016. Accessed August 11, 2021. https://www.charismanews.com/opinion/55184-che-ahn-it-s-time-for-bob-jones-prophesied-billion-soul-harvest.

————. *Modern-Day Apostles: Operating in Your Apostolic Office and Anointing*. Shippensburg, PA: Destiny Image, 2019. Kindle.

Alisa Childers Podcast. "NAR: Movement or Myth? With Holly Pivec, Doug Geivett and Michael Brown." YouTube video, 1:47:34. Uploaded by Alisa Childers. March 21, 2020. Accessed March 21, 2023. https://www.youtube.com/watch?v=mOYFfVtgsuI.

Anderson, Robert. *The Lord's Prayer, a Manual of Religious Knowledge*. Vol. 3. 3rd ed. The Englishman's Library. London: James Burns, 1841.

"Apostles and Prophets." General Presbytery of the Assemblies of God. August 6, 2001. Accessed August 8, 2021. https://ag.org/Beliefs/Position-Papers/Apostles-and-Prophets.

Arnold, Clinton E. *Ephesians*. Zondervan Exegetical Commentary on the New Testament. Grand Rapids: Zondervan, 2010.

Associated Press. "'Come Out of That Grave in Jesus' Name': California Church Prays to Resurrect Girl." NBC News. December 19, 2019. Accessed August 1, 2021. https://www.nbcnews.com/news/us-news/come-out-grave-jesus-name-california-church-prays-resurrect-girl-n1105246.

Aune, David E. "Prayer in the Greco-Roman World." In *Into God's Presence: Prayer in the New Testament*, edited by Richard N. Longenecker, 23–42. Grand Rapids: Eerdmans, 2002. Kindle.

"Author Archive for Gary Greig." *Pneuma Review*. Archived at Wayback Machine July 12, 2022. Accessed July 12, 2022. http://pneumareview.com/author/garysgreig.

Backlund, Steve, and Wendy Backlund. "Contagious Hope—Steve and Wendy Backlund (Pt 2) 5.29.15." YouTube video, 52:53. Uploaded by Hope

Church. June 7, 2015. Accessed August 9, 2021. https://www.youtube.com/watch?v=9AUuJI7AtoU&t=1892s.

Badash, David. "'How Theocracies Are Born': Experts Warn of 'Trump's Jesus Fascists' after Report on Christian GOP Churches." New Civil Rights Movement. July 12, 2021. Accessed August 7, 2021. https://www.thenewcivilrightsmovement.com/2021/07/how-theocracies-are-born-experts-warn-of-trumps-jesus-fascists-after-report-on-christian-gop-churches.

Barna Group. "Americans Divided on the Importance of Church." March 24, 2014. Accessed August 1, 2021. https://www.barna.com/research/americans-divided-on-the-importance-of-church.

———. "Atheism Doubles among Generation Z." January 24, 2018. Accessed August 1, 2021. https://www.barna.com/research/atheism-doubles-among-generation-z.

Barron, Bruce. *Heaven on Earth? The Social and Political Agendas of Dominion Theology.* Grand Rapids: Zondervan, 1992.

Beisner, E. Calvin. *Psalms of Promise: Celebrating the Majesty and Faithfulness of God.* 2nd ed. Phillipsburg, NJ: P&R, 1988.

"The Believer and Positive Confession." General Presbytery of the Assemblies of God. August 19, 1980. Accessed August 10, 2021. https://ag.org/Beliefs/Position-Papers/The-Believer-and-Positive-Confession.

Bethel. "About Bethel." Accessed June 11, 2022. https://www.bethel.com/about.

———. "Bethel Statement on Olive Heiligenthal." December 20, 2019. Accessed August 1, 2021. https://www.bethel.com/press/olive.

———. "Bethel Statement Regarding Christalignment." January 5, 2018. Archived at the Wayback Machine July 26, 2021. Accessed July 26, 2022. https://web.archive.org/web/20210726193434/https://www.bethel.com/about/christalignment.

———. "It's a Different Life: Testimony (Bethel Church)." YouTube video, 2:30. November 3, 2017. Accessed August 6, 2021. https://www.youtube.com/watch?v=g8lOQHRo4hM.

———. "Offering Readings." Accessed April 12, 2022. https://www.bethel.com/offering-readings.

———. "School of the Prophets." Archived at the Wayback Machine June 13, 2022. Accessed June 13, 2022. https://web.archive.org/web/20220613055422/https://www.bethel.com/calendar/school-of-the-prophets.

Bethel Church and Christianity. "Beni Johnson (right) modeling grave sucking. . . ." Facebook. March 20, 2014. Accessed August 8, 2021. https://www.facebook.com/BethelChurchandChristianity/photos/a.354593814577648/650160615020965.

———. "Bethel leaders made a video called Rediscover Bethel. . . ." Facebook. June 9, 2021. Accessed August 1, 2021. https://www.facebook.com/BethelChurchandChristianity/photos/a.604267139610313/3935045753199085.

———. "A few people have asked Bill Johnson. . . ." Facebook. March 20, 2014. Accessed June 13, 2022. https://www.facebook.com/BethelChurchandChristianity/posts/a-few-people-have-asked-bill-johnson-direct-questions-about-his-association-with/10152032816530875.

———. "Here's a conversation I (Bart) had with Beni Johnson from a few years ago." Facebook. May 19, 2015. Accessed August 3, 2021. https://www.facebook.com/BethelChurchandChristianity/photos/a.604267139610313/840220182681673/?type=3&theater.

———. "Senior Pastor Beni Johnson 'grabbing some' at the grave of C. S. Lewis." Facebook. September 4, 2014. Accessed August 8, 2021. https://www.facebook.com/BethelChurchandChristianity/photos/a.354593814577648/726511277385898.

———. "They'll stop at nothing." Facebook. June 25, 2019. Accessed June 13, 2022. https://www.facebook.com/BethelChurchandChristianity/posts/pfbid02heqVGPmZcB0924NuQByz3VHKUDJimicdirAtpcQtTLgCj1hwcpVY5xZZy2Ya19bHl.

Bethel Church, Redding. "Father we thank you for Redding and all who live there." Facebook. July 27, 2018. Accessed August 3, 2021. https://www.facebook.com/permalink.php?story_fbid=10155714781851824&id=156375031823.

Bethel Leaders Network. "What Leaders Are Saying about Bethel Leaders Network." YouTube video, 2:06. Uploaded by Bethel Leaders Network. Accessed August 9, 2021. https://www.youtube.com/watch?v=zCLCz6_I30Q&t=47s.

Bethel Leaders Network Information Packet. PDF. Bethel Leaders Network. Updated November 3, 2021. Accessed June 25, 2022. https://s6avwg5v.pages.infusionsoft.net.

"Bethel Pastor Contradicts Bill Johnson's Narrative on the Now Infamous Practice of 'Grave Sucking.'" *Pulpit and Pen.* April 19, 2018. Accessed August 3, 2021. https://pulpitandpen.org/2018/04/19/bethel-pastor-contradicts-bill-johnsons-narrative-infamous-grave-sucking.

Bethel Redding. Accessed January 3, 2019. http://www.bethelredding.com.

———. "Membership Requirements," PDF. Accessed August 1, 2021. https://bethelredding.com/sites/default/files/2017_membership_application_packet.pdf.

———. "Our Mission." Archived at the Wayback Machine June 22, 2021. Accessed June 24, 2022. https://web.archive.org/web/20210622190910/https://bethelredding.com/about/our-mission.

Bethel School of Supernatural Ministry. "School Structure." Accessed August 12, 2021. https://bssm.net/school/academics.

Bethel Sozo. "What Is Sozo?" Bethel Sozo. Archived at the Wayback Machine, May 10, 2021. Accessed June 16, 2022. https://web.archive.org/web/20210510192358/https://www.bethelsozo.com.

Bethel Statement of Purpose, Statement of Faith, and Bylaws. Bethel Church of Redding. Approved February 13, 2018.

Bible Gateway. Accessed June 6, 2022. https://www.biblegateway.com.

Bickle, Mike. "The Authority of the Believer: Prophetic Decrees." PDF. *MikeBickle.org.* February 8, 2007. Accessed July 17, 2022. https://mikebickle.org/wp-content/uploads/2007/02/Authority-of-the-Believer-Prophetic-Decrees-020807.pdf.

———. *Growing in the Prophetic: A Practical, Biblical Guide to Dreams, Visions, and Spiritual Gifts.* Rev. ed. Lake Mary, FL: Charisma House, 2008. http://mikebickle.org/books. PDF e-book.

———. "Session 2: Explosion of Light, the White Horse, and the Chariots." PDF Transcript. MikeBickle.org. April 25, 2011. Accessed August 15, 2021. https://backup.storage.sardius.media/file/akamaiBackup-ihopkc-103762/IHOP/906/411/20110425_T_Explosion_of_Light_the_White_Horse_and_the_Chariots_IPH02.pdf.

Bickle, Mike, Daniel Lim, Stuart Greaves, Dana Chandler, and Dean Briggs. "IHOPKC Leadership Panel Discussion." Video, 1:01:01. Uploaded to International House of Prayer's Facebook Page. March 19, 2020. Accessed August 11, 2021. https://www.facebook.com/49840698384/videos/2625134174424822.

"Bill." Bill Johnson Ministries. Archived at Wayback Machine December 22, 2019. Accessed August 1, 2021. https://web.archive.org/web/20191222014340/http://bjm.org/bill.

"Bill Johnson False Teacher." YouTube video, 4:54. Uploaded by Raideragent. August 19, 2010. Accessed August 13, 2021. https://www.youtube.com/watch?v=UzAwFYKe3h0&t=3s.

Blair, Leonardo. "Bethel Church Pastor Beni Johnson Says She's Felt 'So Much Peace' Despite Cancer Diagnosis." *Christian Today*. August 17, 2018. Accessed August 13, 2021. https://www.christiantoday.com/article/bethel-church-pastor-beni-johnson-says-shes-felt-so-much-peace-despite-cancer-diagnosis/130230.htm.

———. "God Is Going to End Impeachment, Give Trump Another Term, Bethel's Kris Vallotton Prophesies." *Christian Post*. December 18, 2019. Accessed August 9, 2021. https://www.christianpost.com/news/god-is-going-to-end-impeachment-give-trump-another-term-bethels-kris-vallotton-prophesies.html.

Bolz, Shawn. "Any response please direct to us privately." Facebook. January 8, 2021. Accessed August 9, 2021. https://www.facebook.com/ShawnBolz/posts/10165166390920657.

Boorman, Georgi. "Sorry, Bethel Music, But God's Love Just Isn't 'Reckless.'" *The Federalist*. December 28, 2018. Accessed August 1, 2021. https://thefederalist.com/2018/12/28/sorry-bethel-music-gods-love-just-isnt-reckless.

Boorstein, Michelle. "For Some Christians, the Capitol Riot Doesn't Change the Prophecy: Trump Will Be President." *Washington Post*. January 14, 2021. Accessed August 15, 2021. https://www.washingtonpost.com/religion/2021/01/14/prophets-apostles-christian-prophesy-trump-won-biden-capitol.

Bowler, Kate. *Blessed: A History of the American Prosperity Gospel*. New York: Oxford University Press, 2013. Kindle.

Bowman, Robert M., Jr. *The Word-Faith Controversy: Understanding the Health and Wealth Gospel*. Grand Rapids: Baker, 2001.

Branson-Potts, Hailey, and Anita Chabria. "God, Masks and Trump: What a Coronavirus Outbreak at a California Church Says about the Election." *Los Angeles Times*. November 1, 2020. Accessed August 3, 2021. https://www.latimes.com/california/story/2020-11-01/god-masks-and-trump-what-a-coronavirus-outbreak-at-a-california-church-reveals-about-the-election.

Brown, Michael, and Bill Johnson. "Dr. Brown Interviews Pastor Bill Johnson." *The Line of Fire with Dr. Michael Brown*. YouTube video, 46:31. Uploaded by AskDrBrown. October 12, 2016. Accessed August 8, 2021. https://www.youtube.com/watch?v=Af1hswGOjZg.

Brown, Michael L. "A Unified Call for Accountability on the Heels of the Failed Trump Prophecies." *Tri-State Voice*. April 30, 2021. Accessed February 10, 2023. https://tristatevoice.com/2021/04/30/a-unified-call-for-accountability-on-the-heels-of-failed-trump-prophecies.

"BSSM: Nabeel Qureshi Testimony." Video, 0:15. Uploaded to Bethel Church, Redding's Facebook Page. December 14, 2016. Accessed August 3, 2021. https://fb.watch/eD4RyunTpa.

BSSM School Planting. "10 Ways to Be Activated in the Supernatural." Accessed July 17, 2021. https://bssm.net/schoolplanting/2017/01/10/10-ways-to-be-activated-in-the-supernatural.

———. "Are You More Religious Than Jesus?" Accessed August 1, 2021. http://bssm.net/schoolplanting/2017/11/14/are-you-more-religious-than-jesus.

Cain, Paul. "Paul Cain Stadium Christianity Prophecy." YouTube video, 2:14. Uploaded by Contend Global. May 2, 2016. Accessed August 11, 2021. https://www.youtube.com/watch?v=nCVSXNsodko&t=1s.

Campbell, Murray. "Update on Questions Relating to Bethel and Bill Johnson." *MurrayCampbell.net* (blog). October 8, 2018. Accessed August 3, 2021. https://murraycampbell.net/2018/10/08/update-on-questions-relating-to-bethel-and-bill-johnson.

Cantor, Ron. "What (I Felt) God Told Me about the Election in September." Messiah's Mandate. November 8, 2020. Archived at the Wayback Machine June 14, 2021. Accessed June 10, 2022. https://web.archive.org/web/20210614005029/https://messiahsmandate.org/what-i-felt-god-told-me-about-the-election-in-september.

Carson, D. A. *The Gospel according to John*. Pillar New Testament Commentary. Grand Rapids: Eerdmans, 1991.

Carter, Joe. "9 Things You Should Know about the Bethel Church Movement." *Gospel Coalition* (US edition). September 29, 2018. Accessed June 13, 2022. https://www.thegospelcoalition.org/article/9-things-you-should-know-about-the-bethel-church-movement.

———. "9 Things You Should Know about Jim Jones and the Jonestown Massacre." *Gospel Coalition* (US edition). November 14, 2018. Accessed June 24, 2022. https://www.thegospelcoalition.org/article/9-things-know-jim-jones-jonestown-massacre.

Chandler, Michele, and David Benda. "Ask the Record Searchlight: Latest on New Bethel Campus; Trolleys in Redding?" *Redding Record Searchlight*. June 10, 2021. Accessed August 1, 2021. https://www.redding.com/story/news/2021/06/10/bethel-campus-redding-employee-shortage-ask-r-s-live-chat/7605984002.

Chapman, Mike. "'Olive Hasn't Been Raised': After Praying for Miracle, Girl's Family Now Plans Memorial." *Redding Record Searchlight*. December 21, 2019. Accessed August 1, 2021. https://www.usatoday.com/story/news/nation/2019/12/21/bethel-church-prayer-hasnt-brought-olive-back-life/2724417001.

Chen, Tanya, and Stephanie McNeal. "The Evangelical Parents of a Young Girl Who Died Are Using Social Media to Ask for Her Resurrection." *BuzzFeed News*. December 20, 2019. Accessed August 1, 2021. https:///www.buzzfeednews.com/article/tanyachen/evangelical-parents-of-a-young-girl-who-died-social-media.

Childers, Alisa. "Here's Why Christians Should Be Concerned about the Passion Translation of the Bible." *Alisa Childers*. June 25, 2018. Accessed August 12, 2021. https://www.alisachilders.com/blog/heres-why-christians-should-be-concerned-about-the-passion-translation-of-the-bible.

Childers, Alisa, and Melissa Dougherty. "The Law of Attraction and Hyper-Charismatic Movement with Melissa Dougherty." YouTube video, 8:12. Uploaded by Alisa Childers. April 18, 2021. Accessed July 12, 2022. https://www.youtube.com/watch?v=va9uLggfxWA.

Christerson, Brad. "How Self-Proclaimed 'Prophets' Gave Religious Motivation for the Capitol Hill Attack." *National Interest*. January 13, 2021. Accessed August 6, 2021. https://nationalinterest.org/blog/reboot/how-self-proclaimed-prophets-gave-religious-motivation-capitol-hill-attack-176284.

Christerson, Brad, and Richard Flory. *The Rise of Network Christianity: How Independent Leaders Are Changing the Religious Landscape*. New York: Oxford University Press, 2017. Kindle.

Churchwatcher. "Documenting Benny Hinn's Necromancy and Encounters with the Dead." Church Watch Central. October 25, 2015. Accessed August 8, 2021. https://churchwatchcentral.com/2015/10/15/documenting-benny-hinns-necromancy-and-encounters-with-the-dead.

———. "Watch Dr. Michael Brown as He Reacts to Ché Ahn Publicly Recognizing Him as an 'Apostle.'" Church Watch Central. Video, 4:05. October 19, 2020. Accessed August 9, 2021. https://churchwatchcentral.com/2020/10/19/watch-dr-michael-brown-as-he-reacts-to-che-ahn-publicly-recognizing-him-as-an-apostle.

Clark, Randy. "A Response to New Apostolic Reformation Critics Revised and Expanded." Prepared by Dr. Randy Clark and by Students of Global Awakening Theological Seminary of Family of Faith Christian University Academia. August 24, 2022. Accessed February 13, 2023. https://www.academia.edu/85538549/A_Response_to_New_Apostolic_Reformation_Critics_Revised_and_Expanded.

———. *Stories of Divine Healing: Supernatural Testimonies That Ignite Faith for Your Healing*. Shippensburg, PA: Destiny Image, 2018.

———. "A Study of the Effects of Christian Prayer on Pain or Mobility Restrictions from Surgeries Involving Implanted Materials." Doctor of ministry thesis, United Theological Seminary, 2013. Academia. https://www.academia.edu/43109000/Study_of_the_Effects_of_Christian_Prayer.

Coats, Brenda Renee. "My Take on the 'Reckless Love' Controversy." *Patheos.* April 12, 2018. Accessed August 1, 2021. https://www.patheos.com/blogs/felixculpa/2018/04/my-take-on-the-reckless-love-controversy.html.

Collins, John Andrew. *Jim Jones: The Malachi 4 Elijah Prophecy*. Jeffersonville, IN: Dark Mystery, 2017.

Conant, "Mr." (first name not identified) and "Mrs." (first name not identified). "Healed from MS: Conant's Testimony (Bethel Church)." YouTube video, 5:22. Uploaded by Bethel. October 25, 2017. Accessed August 12, 2021. https://www.youtube.com/watch?v=O3GZTg8cwog.

Cook, Bruce, ed. *Aligning with the Apostolic: An Anthology of Apostleship: Apostles and Apostolic Movement in the Seven Mountains of Culture*. 5 vols. LakeBay, WA: Kingdom House, 2012–13. Kindle.

Crowder, John. "The term 'grave sucking,' . . ." Video, 0:24. Uploaded to Bethel Church and Christianity's Facebook Page. May 19, 2015. Accessed August 8, 2021. https://www.facebook.com/BethelChurchandChristianity/videos/840158736021151.

"Culture of Honor." *BeWatchful.org.* June 18, 2016. Accessed August 7, 2021. https://bewatchful.org/2016/06/18/culture-of-honor.

Dallimore, Arnold A. *Forerunner of the Charismatic Movement: The Life of Edward Irving*. Chicago: Moody, 1983.

Davis, Lindsay, Jeff Durbin, and Jeremiah Roberts. "Defecting from Bethel (Part 2): Exclusive." Cultish. YouTube video, 59:26. Uploaded by Apologia Studios. May 10, 2019. Accessed June 16, 2022. https://www.youtube.com/watch?v=GF2t_VRorXQ&t=3092s.

Davis, Lindsay, Jeff Durbin, and Jeremiah Roberts. "Exclusive: Defecting from Bethel." Cultish. YouTube video, 50:06. Uploaded by Apologia Studios. April 24, 2019. Accessed June 16, 2022. https://www.youtube.com/watch?v=-TlYGF1_kJg.

Dead Raising Team. "Our Director." Dead Raising Team. Accessed December 12, 2021. http://deadraisingteam.com/our-director.

Deckman, Melissa. "Generation Z and Religion: What New Data Show." *Religion in Public* (blog). February 10, 2020. Accessed August 1, 2021. https:/religioninpublic. blog/2020/02/10/generation-z-and-religion-what-new-data-show.

Dedmon, Kevin. *The Ultimate Treasure Hunt: A Guide to Supernatural Evangelism through Supernatural Encounters*. Shippensburg, PA: Destiny Image, 2007. Kindle.

Dedmon, Theresa. "Beauty for Ashes." *Theresa Dedmon*. July 30, 2018. Accessed August 3, 2021. https://www.theresadedmon.com/blog/beauty-for-ashes.

"Divine Healing." General Presbytery of the Assemblies of God. August 9–11, 2010. Accessed August 13, 2021. https://ag.org/Beliefs/Position-Papers/Divine-Healing.

Dreher, Rod. "Eric Metaxes's American Apocalypse." *The American Conservative*. December 10, 2020. Accessed August 9, 2021. https://theamericanconservative. com/dreher/eric-metaxas-trump-bloodshed-american-apocalypse-live-not-by-lies.

Duin, Julia. "The Charismatic Christians Prophesying Trump's Victory (and Not Backing Down)." Religion Unplugged. November 16, 2020. Accessed August 9, 2021. https:// religionunplugged.com/news/2020/11/16/the-charismatic-christians-prophesying-trumps-victory-and-not-backing-down.

Eberle, Harold R., and Martin Trench. *Victorious Eschatology: A Partial Preterist View*. 2nd ed. Yakima, WA: Worldcast, 2007.

"Eight More Women, Including Sisters Accuse Prophet Bushiri of Rape." Sahara Reporters. March 23, 2021. Accessed August 9, 2021. https://saharareporters.com/2021/03/23/ eight-more-women-including-sisters-accuse-prophet-bushiri-rape.

Ellis, Mark. "Heidi Baker: 'This Is 9-1-1 for Christians; God Needs All Hands on Deck.'" God Reports. March 31, 2020. Accessed August 11, 2021. https://www. godreports.com/2020/03/heidi-baker-this-is-9-1-1-for-christians-god-needs-all-hands-on-deck.

Engle, Lou. "Day 3: Atomic Power for the Harvest." The Jesus Fast. March 3, 2019. Accessed August 11, 2021. https://thejesusfast.global/atomic-power-for-the-harvest.

———. "Paul Cain: Celebrating His Life, Words, and Faith, with Lou Engle." YouTube video, 7:02. Uploaded by Lou Engle. February 13, 2019. Accessed July 12, 2022. https://www.youtube.com/watch?v=GUlQypWk6Og&t=81s.

———. "A Plague Has Broken Out." Bethany Church (Weddington, NC). March 18, 2020. Accessed August 11, 2021. https://www.mybethany.com/esther-fast-to-end-corona-virus-day-1.

Erdman, Jonathan. "The Giant Fire Whirl from California's Carr Fire Produced Damage Similar to an EF3 Tornado in Redding, an NWS Survey Found." Weather Channel. August 3, 2018. Accessed August 15, 2021. https://weather.com/safety/wildfires/ news/2018-08-03-fire-whirl-carr-fire-california-damage.

"Excerpts from Bethel Church's Open Heavens Conference 2019." YouTube video, 4:24. Uploaded by Raideragent. July 28, 2022. Accessed July 28, 2022. https://www. youtube.com/watch?v=hsXgoxctINs.

"False Teachers Love False Teachers: William Branham." YouTube video, 4:11. Uploaded by The Messed Up Church. November 6, 2019. Accessed August 9, 2021. https:// www.youtube.com/watch?v=J9GbGKctQuU.

Finkel, Asher. "Prayer in Jewish Life of the First Century as Background to Early Christianity." In *Into God's Presence: Prayer in the New Testament*, edited by Richard N. Longenecker, 43–65. Grand Rapids: Eerdmans, 2002. Kindle.

Fitzgerald, Ben. "Bethel Church Soaking Up the 'Anointing' of Dead Men, or Grave Sucking." YouTube video, 5:44. Uploaded by Raideragent. December 8, 2011. Accessed August 3, 2021. https://www.youtube.com/watch?time_continue=124&v=LrHPTs8cLls.

Flinchbaugh, C. Hope. "Ignite the Fire." *Charisma*. February 28, 2007. Accessed January 5, 2019. https://charismamag.com/charisma-archive/ignite-the-fire.

Franklin, Judy, and Ellyn Davis, eds. *The Physics of Heaven: Exploring God's Mysteries of Sound, Light, Energy, Vibrations, and Quantum Physics*. Shippensburg, PA: Destiny Image, 2012. Kindle.

Froehlich, Karlfried. "The Lord's Prayer in Patristic Literature." In *A History of Prayer: The First to the Fifteenth Century*, edited by Roy Hammerling, 59–77. Leiden: Brill, 2008.

Geivett, R. Douglas, and Holly Pivec. *God's Super-Apostles: Encountering the Worldwide Prophets and Apostles Movement*. Reissue ed. Bellingham, WA: Lexham, 2018. First published 2014, Weaver Book Company.

———. *A New Apostolic Reformation? A Biblical Response to a Worldwide Movement*. Reissue ed. Bellingham, WA: Lexham, 2018. First published 2014, Weaver Book Company.

———. "Response to Joseph Mattera and Michael Brown, Statement on 'NAR and Christian Nationalism.'" *Holly Pivec* (blog). December 31, 2022. Accessed February 13, 2023. https://www.hollypivec.com/blog/narandchristiannationalism.

Graham, Ruth. "Christian Prophets Are on the Rise. What Happens When They're Wrong?" *New York Times*. February 11, 2021. Accessed August 10, 2021. https://www.nytimes.com/2021/02/11/us/christian-prophets-predictions.html.

Grudem, Wayne. *The Gift of Prophecy in the New Testament and Today*. Rev. ed. Wheaton, IL: Crossway, 2000.

Hafner, Josh. "Meet the Evangelicals Who Prophesied a Trump Win." *USA Today*. November 10, 2016. Accessed August 10, 2021. https://www.usatoday.com/story/news/nation-now/2016/11/10/meet-evangelicals-prophesied-trump-win/93575144.

Hammerling, Roy. "Introduction: Prayer—A Simply Complicated Scholarly Problem." In *A History of Prayer: The First to the Fifteenth Century*, edited by Roy Hammerling, 1–27. Leiden: Brill, 2008.

———. "The Lord's Prayer in Early Christian Polemics to the Eighth Century." In *A History of Prayer: The First to the Fifteenth Century*, edited by Roy Hammerling, 223–41. Leiden: Brill, 2008.

———. *The Lord's Prayer in the Early Church: The Pearl of Great Price*. New York: Palgrave MacMillan, 2010.

Hamon, Bill. *Apostles, Prophets, and the Coming Moves of God: God's End-Time Plans for His Church and Planet Earth*. Santa Rosa Beach, FL: Destiny Image, 1997.

———. *Prophetic Scriptures Yet to Be Fulfilled: During the Third and Final Church Reformation*. Shippensburg, PA: Destiny Image, 2010.

Hardy, Elle. "The 'Modern Apostles' Who Want to Reshape America Ahead of the End Times." *The Outline*. March 19, 2020. Accessed August 6, 2021. https://theoutline.com/post/8856/seven-mountain-mandate-trump-paula-white.

Hensley-Clancy, Molly. "Meet the 'Young Saints' of Bethel Who Go to College to Perform Miracles." *BuzzFeed News*. October 12, 2017. Accessed August 1, 2021. https://www.buzzfeednews.com/article/mollyhensleyclancy/meet-the-young-saints-of-bethel-who-go-to-college-to.

Higgins, Godfrey. "The Pure Theology of Jesus and the Teaching of Bill Johnson, Senior Pastor of Bethel Church Redding California: A Comparative Study in the Gospel of John Chapter 5." Draft of a personal paper, 2021.

Hill, Joshua S. "Defending God's 'Reckless Love': Looking at Cory Asbury's 'Reckless Love.'" *JoshuaSHill.me* (blog). July 30, 2019. Accessed August 6, 2021. https://joshuashill.me/defending-gods-reckless-love.

Hinn, Costi W., and Anthony G. Wood. *Defining Deception: Freeing the Church from the Mystical-Miracle Movement*. El Cajon, CA: Southern California Seminary Press, 2018.

Hitt, Tarpley. "The Mystical Megachurch Ruling Over Soccer Star Megan Rapinoe's Hometown." *Daily Beast*. July 20, 2019. Accessed August 12, 2021. https://www.thedailybeast.com/the-mystical-megachurch-ruling-over-world-cup-soccer-star-megan-rapinoes-hometown.

Holy Koolaid. "Evangelicals Freak Out." YouTube video, 10:56. November 19, 2020. Accessed August 9, 2021. https://www.youtube.com/watch?v=9gIAtDxyTaM.

Hyer, William. "Prayer, Declaration, and 'Decreeing Prayer.'" College of Prayer International. Accessed August 21, 2019. http://www.collegeofprayer.org/uploads/3/7/5/9/37593771/praying_declaring_decreeing.pdf.

International Coalition of Apostolic Leaders. "Prophetic Standards Statement." April 30, 2021. Accessed August 15, 2021. https://www.icaleaders.com/news/2021/4/30/prophetic-standards-statement.

International House of Prayer. "What Is IHOPKC's Stance on the New Apostolic Reformation?" Archived at the Wayback Machine February 23, 2023. Accessed May 18, 2023. https://web.archive.org/web/20230223083001/https://www.ihopkc.org/press-center/faq/ihopkc-part-new-apostolic-reformation/.

Jacobs, Cindy. "ACPE [Apostolic Council of Prophetic Elders] Word of the Lord for 2020." Elijah List. January 21, 2020. Accessed August 10, 2021. https://www.elijahlist.com/words/display_word.html?ID=23126.

Jesus Culture. "About Jesus Culture." Accessed August 1, 2021. https://jesusculture.com/about.

Jobe, Kari (@karijobe). "We're still standing in faith for Olive to wake up." Instagram. December 17, 2019. Accessed August 8, 2021. https://www.instagram.com/p/B6MPihMHtO7.

Johnson, Beni. "Wakey, Wakey." *Benij.org*. March 16, 2009. Archived at the Wayback Machine February 15, 2020. Accessed August 7, 2021. https://web.archive.org/web/20200215173044/http://www.benij.org/blog.php?id=1.

Johnson, Beni, and Bill Johnson. *The Power of Communion: Accessing Miracles through the Body and Blood of Jesus*. Shippensburg, PA: Destiny Image, 2019.

Johnson, Bill. "Bill Johnson: Claiming the Power to Heal as Jesus Did." *Charisma Magazine*. November 21, 2014. Accessed July 13, 2022. https://charismamag.com/supernatural/youve-got-the-power.

———. "Bill Johnson's Testimony." YouTube video, 24:27. Uploaded by Catch the Fire Toronto. May 16, 2011. Accessed August 8, 2021. https://www.youtube.com/watch?v=jpYkptDWpzM&t=2s.

———. "Eat Meat, Don't Eat the Bones." YouTube video, 57:17. Uploaded by Live Forever BJ. March 30, 2015. Accessed July 21, 2021. https://www.youtube.com/watch?v=5igclUvzKKI&t=2s.

———. *God Is Good: He's Better Than You Think*. Shippensburg, PA: Destiny Image, 2016. Kindle.

————. *Hosting the Presence: Unveiling Heaven's Agenda.* Shippensburg, PA: Destiny Image, 2012. Kindle.

————. "How Your Miracle Can Release the Spirit of Prophecy." *Charisma Magazine.* October 23, 2014. Accessed July 17, 2022. https://charismamag.com/spiritual-growth-spirit/how-your-miracle-can-release-the-spirit-of-prophecy.

————. "Is It Always God's Will to Heal Someone?" Bill Johnson Ministries. Archived at the Wayback Machine February 24, 2019. Accessed July 13, 2022. https://web.archive.org/web/20190224194911/http://bjm.org/qa/is-it-always-gods-will-to-heal-someone.

————. "Jesus, Full of the Holy Spirit—Bill Johnson (Full Sermon)." YouTube video, 49:53. Uploaded by Bill Johnson Teaching (Official). May 27, 2021. Accessed July 29, 2022. https://www.youtube.com/watch?v=S-vkfpXOnig.

————. "Jesus prophesied that we would do greater works than He did!" Facebook. June 1, 2020. Accessed August 11, 2021. https://www.facebook.com/BillJohnsonMinistries/photos/a.432919458386/10157833665088387.

————. "Jonathan David and Melissa Helser—Bill Johnson: Onething 2016 CET." YouTube video, 2:20:50. Uploaded by MajorChange. January 18, 2017. Accessed August 6, 2021. https://www.youtube.com/watch?v=9sysxooMrio&t=6259s.

————. "July 11, 2021—Sunday Service (Bethel Church)." YouTube video, 2:03:27. Uploaded by Bethel. July 11, 2021. Accessed August 13, 2021. https://www.youtube.com/watch?v=zAHdiuJT2qs.

————. *Manifesto for a Normal Christian Life.* Based on transcripts from the "HTB Talks" (given at Holy Trinity Brompton Church in London, May 2010). Redding, CA: Bill Johnson Ministries, 2012. Kindle.

————. "March 15th, 2020, Sunday AM Service (Bethel Live)." YouTube video, 2:30:21. Uploaded by Bethel. March 15, 2020. Accessed August 10, 2021. https://www.youtube.com/watch?v=GhxuvrTUB2s.

————. *Open Heavens: Positioning Yourself to Encounter the God of Revival.* Shippensburg, PA: Destiny Image, 2021.

————. "Pastor Bill Johnson Sermons: How to Pray and Decree." YouTube video, 1:11:25. Uploaded by Bill Johnson Ministry. June 8, 2016. Accessed July 9, 2022. https://www.youtube.com/watch?v=NdUzAMVnc4Y.

————. "Power of Confession—Sunday AM." Bethel.TV. Video, 40:37. January 20, 2019. Accessed June 17, 2022. https://www.bethel.tv/home.

————. "The Real Jesus (Part 4)—by Bill Johnson." YouTube video, 14:52 Uploaded by ChasingRiver. September 2, 2010. Accessed August 11, 2021. https://www.youtube.com/watch?v=vHcRI6ojoHI.

————. "Recovering Our Spiritual Inheritance." In *The Physics of Heaven: Exploring God's Mysteries of Sound, Light, Energy, Vibrations, and Quantum Physics*, edited by Judy Franklin and Ellyn Davis, 29–38. Shippensburg, PA: Destiny Image, 2012. Kindle.

————. "Response to Glory Cloud at Bethel." YouTube video, 14:17. Uploaded by Pastorkimo4960. October 22, 2011. Accessed August 1, 2021. https://www.youtube.com/watch?v=tcPkOR4Lwjo.

————. "Session 8." Onething Conference at the International House of Prayer in Kansas City, Missouri (December 30, 2016). Video, 01:27:33. December 30, 2016. Accessed August 10, 2021. https://www.ihopkc.org/resources/asset/2016_12_30_1900_ONETHING_MSG_BILLJOHNSON/auto/true.

———. "Stewards of Revival." iBethel.TV video, 52:06. On-line Sermons.org. Uploaded September 7, 2021. https://online-sermons.org/billjohnson/4727-bill-johnson-stewards-of-revival.html.

———. *The Supernatural Power of a Transformed Mind: Access to a Life of Miracles.* Expanded ed. Shippensburg, PA: Destiny Image, 2014. Kindle.

———. *The Way of Life: Experiencing the Culture of Heaven on Earth.* Shippensburg, PA: Destiny Image, 2018. Kindle.

———. *The Way of Life: Experiencing the Culture of Heaven on Earth.* Updated ed. Shippensburg, PA: Destiny Image, 2019. Kindle.

———. *When Heaven Invades Earth: A Practical Guide to a Life of Miracles.* Shippensburg, PA: Destiny Image, 2003. Kindle.

———. "Why Does Some Healing Not Last?" YouTube video, 13:08. Uploaded by Bill Johnson Teaching (Official). March 1, 2021. Accessed July 21, 2022. https://www.youtube.com/watch?v=4EQd5BDqSqo.

Johnson, Bill, Ché Ahn, Ed Silvoso, and Marlyne Barrett. "Gandalf Staff Prophetic Word with Bill Johnson." YouTube video, 5:47. Uploaded by Megan Verdugo. September 2, 2020. Accessed August 7, 2021. https://www.youtube.com/watch?v=O8b3yumhMNU&t=175s.

Johnson, Bill, Francis Chan, Mike Bickle, Asher Intrater, and David Demian. "The Unveiling." YouTube video, 12:43. Uploaded by Popular Gospel. May 15, 2020. Accessed August 1, 2021. https://www.youtube.com/watch?v=pNBGhgUT6JU&t=1s.

Johnson, Bill, and Randy Clark. *The Essential Guide to Healing: Equipping All Christians to Pray for the Sick.* Bloomington, MN: Chosen, 2011. Kindle.

Johnson, Bill, and Dann Farrelly. "Bill Johnson: The Theology of Sickness and Healing." *Rediscover Bethel.* YouTube video, 19:14. Uploaded by Bethel. June 10, 2021. Accessed August 13, 2021. https://www.youtube.com/watch?v=9_7g_0GvJ50.

———. "Does Bethel Church Teach Grave Soaking?" *Rediscover Bethel.* YouTube video, 25:54. Uploaded by Bethel. June 24, 2021. Accessed August 7, 2021. https://www.youtube.com/watch?v=Z8wBGmpOWRo&t=1243s.

———. "Episode 1: Bethel's Beliefs about Jesus, God's Sovereignty, and Bible Translations." *Rediscover Bethel.* YouTube video, 1:39:33. Uploaded by Bethel. June 8, 2021. Accessed August 1, 2021. https://www.youtube.com/watch?v=XZ2xjnXYfm8&t=28s.

———. "Episode 2: Jesus, the Cross, and Preaching." *Rediscover Bethel.* YouTube video, 1:02:54. Uploaded by Bethel. June 15, 2021. Accessed August 2, 2021. https://www.youtube.com/watch?v=w2vRRZwN1Wg&t=1755s.

———. "Episode 3: The Supernatural, Signs and Wonders." *Rediscover Bethel.* YouTube video, 1:26:28. Uploaded by Bethel. June 23, 2021. Accessed August 3, 2021. https://www.youtube.com/watch?v=3c7s-WCKIrQ&t=3492s.

———. "Episode 6: Church Structure, Teaching, Rumors, and Politics." *Rediscover Bethel.* YouTube video, 1:31:41. Uploaded by Bethel. July 13, 2021. Accessed August 1, 2021. https://www.youtube.com/watch?v=a8NIyedUex8&t=3712s.

———. "Glory Clouds and Gold Dust, Signs and Wonders." *Rediscover Bethel.* YouTube video, 14:29. Uploaded by Bethel. June 28, 2021. Accessed August 1, 2021. https://youtube.com/watch?v=fFO9d61ynBI&t=519s.

———. "Holy Laughter: Being Drunk in the Spirit." *Rediscover Bethel.* YouTube video, 14:32. Uploaded by Bethel. June 28, 2021. Accessed August 1, 2021. https://www.youtube.com/watch?v=QKpievvFhMI&t=8s.

———. "Is the Passion Translation Heresy?" *Rediscover Bethel*. YouTube video, 10:12. Uploaded by Bethel. June 11, 2021. Accessed August 1, 2021. https://www.youtube.com/watch?v=2kpL4YhUhYU.

———. "Kenosis and Jesus' Deity: Was Jesus Fully God and Fully Man?" *Rediscover Bethel*. YouTube video, 18:29. Uploaded by Bethel. June 15, 2021. Accessed July 13, 2022. https://www.youtube.com/watch?v=7lRuBrdhAmg&t=15s.

———. "The Sovereignty of God." *Rediscover Bethel*. YouTube video, 8:45. Uploaded by Bethel. June 11, 2021. Accessed August 13, 2021. https://www.youtube.com/watch?v=wVw-r8DNeQw&t=107s.

Johnson, Bill, and the Leadership of Bethel Church, Redding, CA. "Bethel and the Assemblies of God." iBethel. Letter. N.d. (sometime soon after January 17, 2006). Archived at the Wayback Machine July 1, 2011. Accessed August 1, 2021. https://web.archive.org/web/20110701134709/http://www.ibethel.org/bethel-and-the-assemblies-of-god.

Johnson, Bill, and Jennifer A. Miskov. *Defining Moments: God-Encounters with Ordinary People Who Changed the World*. New Kensington, PA: Whitaker House, 2016.

Johnson, Bill, and Kris Vallotton. "5-Fold Live with Bill Johnson." Video, 27:55. Uploaded to Kris Vallotton's Facebook Page. June 11, 2020. Accessed June 23, 2022. https://www.facebook.com/kvministries/videos/312254066444682.

Johnson, Bill, Lance Wallnau, and Dutch Sheets. "The Victory Channel Is Live with Flashpoint!" Video, 58:53. The Victory Channel. Uploaded to Bill Johnson's Facebook Page. December 15, 2020. Accessed August 7, 2021. https://www.facebook.com/54557413386/videos/697082457678460.

Johnson, Jenn. "Black and White." A Talk Given at the Women's Conference at Bethel Church, August 28, 2009, Morning Session. YouTube video, 12:11. Uploaded by Bethel. May 21, 2011. Accessed August 7, 2021. https://www.youtube.com/watch?v=qdeqtJvkE5w.

———. "By the Blood (Healing for Cancer) [Spontaneous Worship]." YouTube video, 8:36. Uploaded by ABBALONGTOYOU. April 24, 2017. Accessed July 15, 2022. https://www.youtube.com/watch?v=kjDJLJwl-fI.

———. "Jenn Johnson—Holy Spirit Is Like a Sneaky Blue Genie." YouTube video, 1:26. Uploaded by Elmoziffle. June 22, 2013. Accessed August 7, 2021. https://www.youtube.com/watch?v=-Wu-WqLjoJo&t=3s.

Johnson, Todd M., and Gina A. Zurlo. *World Christian Encyclopedia*. 3rd ed. Edinburgh: Edinburgh University Press, 2019.

Jones, Bob. "Bob Jones August 1975 Death Experience." YouTube video, 19:11. Uploaded by NCF Media. January 17, 2019. Accessed August 11, 2021. https://www.youtube.com/watch?v=Ta8SL1joYao.

Joyner, Rick. *The Apostolic Ministry*. Wilkesboro, NC: MorningStar, 2004.

———. *The Call*. Wilkesboro, NC: MorningStar, 2006.

———. *The Harvest*. Wilkesboro, NC: MorningStar, 1989.

Justice, Jessilyn, and Taylor Berglund. "Banning Liebscher: Why Bill Johnson Didn't Immediately Shut Down Grave Sucking." *Charisma News*. August 1, 2020. Accessed August 8, 2021. https://www.charismanews.com/culture/82099-bethel-pastor-why-bill-johnson-didn-t-immediately-shut-down-grave-sucking.

Kaya, Kells Anderson. "Apostle Arrested for Rape." *ZiMetro News*. October 3, 2019. Accessed August 9, 2021. https://www.zimetro.co.zw/apostle-arrested-for-rape.

Keener, Craig. "Failed Trump Prophecies Offer a Lesson in Humility." *Christianity Today.* January 20, 2021. Accessed August 9, 2021. https://www.christianitytoday.com/ct/2021/january-web-only/trump-prophets-apologize-election-prophecies-humility.html.

———. *Matthew.* IVP New Testament Commentary Series. Downers Grove, IL: IVP Academic, 1997.

———. *Miracles Today: The Supernatural Work of God in the Modern World.* Grand Rapids: Baker Academic, 2021.

"Kingdom of God." General Presbytery of the Assemblies of God. August 9–11, 2010. Accessed August 12, 2021. https://ag.org/Beliefs/Position-Papers/Kingdom-of-God.

Kolenda, Daniel. "Are There Apostles in the Church Today?" YouTube video, 2:14:25. Uploaded by Daniel Kolenda: Off the Record. July 11, 2022. Accessed July 28, 2022. https://www.youtube.com/watch?v=XOrssO8QEzw&t=4s.

———. "What Is the N.A.R. and Am I Part of It?" YouTube video, 1:40:50. Uploaded by Daniel Kolenda: Off the Record Podcast. May 10, 2021. Accessed July 28, 2022. https://www.youtube.com/watch?v=BzcBsvnErkc&t=5s.

Köstenberger, Andreas J. "The 'Greater Works' of the Believer according to John 14:12." *Didaskalia: Journal of Providence College and Seminary* 6.2 (1995) 36–45.

"Kundalini at Bethel Church in Redding." YouTube video, 6:08. Uploaded by Raideragent. September 12, 2010. Accessed August 6, 2021. https://www.youtube.com/watch?v=cipO2JpXXWw&t=112s.

Law, Jeannie Ortega. "Sozo Prayer Spreading Worldwide, but What Is It?" *Christian Post.* May 19, 2019. Accessed August 1, 2021. https://www.christianpost.com/news/sozo-prayer-spreading-worldwide-but-what-is-it.html.

Lea, Jessica. "Ministry Leaders Apologize for Prophesying Trump Win." *Church Leaders.* January 12, 2021. Accessed August 10, 2021. https://churchleaders.com/news/388444-jeremiah-johnson-prophesying-trump.html/2.

LeClaire, Jennifer. "Mike Bickle, Bill Johnson Join Spiritual Leaders in Honoring the Late Prophet Bob Jones." *Charisma News.* February 14, 2014. Accessed August 11, 2021. https://www.charismanews.com/us/42799-mike-bickle-bill-johnson-join-spiritual-leaders-in-honoring-the-late-prophet-bob-jones.

Lemon, Jason. "Christian 'Prophet' Claims God Didn't Restore Trump Yet to Make People Doubt Prophecies." *Newsweek.* June 11, 2021. Accessed August 10, 2021. https://www.newsweek.com/christian-prophet-claims-god-didnt-restore-trump-yet-make-people-doubt-prophecies-1599922.

Lewis, Joshua, Michael Rowntree, and Mike Bickle. "Billion Soul Harvest: Interview with Mike Bickle." YouTube video, 1:11:58. Uploaded by The Remnant Radio. May 21, 2022. Accessed July 17, 2022. https://www.youtube.com/watch?v=VxazUrMRjqo.

Lewis, Joshua, Michael Rowntree, Michael Brown, Craig Keener, Sam Storms, Ken Fish, Jack Deere, Michael Miller, Dawson Jarrell, Joel Richardson, and Mike Winger. "Testing the Prophets: Testing the Prophecies Given in 2020." YouTube video, 8:11:30. Uploaded by The Remnant Radio. December 30, 2020. Accessed August 9, 2021. https://www.youtube.com/watch?v=GgE85J1mF9s&t=27915s.

Lewis, Joshua, Michael Rowntree, and Randy Clark. "The NAR Debate! Randy Clark Responds to Dr. Doug Geivett and Holly Pivec." YouTube video, 1:42:00. Uploaded by The Remnant Radio. April 19, 2022. Accessed June 24, 2022. https://www.youtube.com/watch?v=Bz8yCZXjH7I&t=2110s.

Lewis, Joshua, Michael Rowntree, and Michael Miller. "Fired from NAR Church." YouTube video, 1:27:45. Uploaded by The Remnant Radio. May 10, 2021. Accessed August 9, 2021. https://www.youtube.com/watch?v=2Soxn8O2v0A&t=4505s.

Lewis, Joshua, Michael Rowntree, and Elijah Stephens. "The New Apostolic Reformation: Is Bethel NAR? Questions for Bethel Leadership (Part 2)." YouTube video, 1:02:01. Uploaded by The Remnant Radio. October 26, 2020. Accessed August 9, 2021. https://www.youtube.com/watch?v=mMkKILXkKWs.

Lewis, Joshua, Michael Rowntree, and Todd White. "Todd White: Was Jesus Fully God? (Does Todd White Believe the Kenosis Heresy?)" YouTube video, 14:42. Uploaded by The Remnant Radio. September 23, 2020. Accessed July 13, 2022. https://www.youtube.com/watch?v=Re-oH3JRnac&t=1s.

Loftus, Elizabeth F., and Deborah Davis. "Recovered Memories." *Annual Review of Clinical Psychology*, vol. 2 (April 27, 2006) 469–98.

Mack, Mark, and Steven Kozar. "Behind the Scenes with a Former Bethel Elder." YouTube video, 1:13:07. Uploaded by The Messed Up Church. May 10, 2022. Accessed July 28, 2022. https://www.youtube.com/watch?v=NRHSFmha2lk&t=2992s.

Mann, Randi. "California's 7th Worst Wildfire Destroyed 1,077 Homes and Spawned a Fire Tornado." Weather Network. July 29, 2021. Accessed August 3, 2021. https://www.theweathernetwork.com/en/news/weather/severe/this-day-in-weather-history-july-26-2018-carr-fire-in-california.

Manwaring, Paul. "Apostolic—Sunday PM." Bethel.TV. Video, 1:24:24. October 19, 2014. Accessed June 24, 2022. https://www.bethel.tv/home.

Markell, Jan. "Wolves Not Sparing the Flock: Interview with Dirk and Joan Miller (Part 1)." Audio, 57:00. Olive Tree Ministries. June 16, 2018. Accessed August 6, 2021. https://olivetreeviews.org/radio-archives/wolves-not-sparing-the-flock-part-1.

Mattera, Joseph. "The Need for Prophetic Standards in the Church." *JosephMattera.org*. May 4, 2021. Accessed February 18, 2022. https://josephmattera.org/need-prophetic-church.

———. "Ten Reasons the Apostolic Movement Is Essential to the Global Expansion." *JosephMattera.org*. June 21, 2022. Accessed June 24, 2022. https://josephmattera.org/apostolic-movement-essential.

Mattera, Joseph, John P. Kelly, and Buford Lipscomb. "Global Christianity Roundtable with J Mattera, J Kelly & B Lipscomb." YouTube video, 1:41:14. Uploaded by USCAL. January 18, 2018. Accessed June 11, 2022. https://www.youtube.com/watch?v=cxLSc1ibfe4&t=1417s.

McClure, Jim. "Sozo Prayer." Life Focus Ministries. *Connecting with You* (blog). Accessed August 6, 2021. https://connectingwithyou.net/2014/07/12/sozo-prayer.

Mehta, Hemant. "Here Are 12 Christian Preachers Who Wrongly Predicted Trump's Re-Election." *Patheos*. November 24, 2020. Accessed August 10, 2021. https://friendlyatheist.patheos.com/2020/11/24/here-are-12-christian-preachers-who-wrongly-predicted-trumps-re-election.

Moore, Richard P. *Divergent Theology: An Inquiry into the Theological Characteristics of the Word of Faith, Third Wave Movement and the New Apostolic Reformation.* N.p.: CreateSpace, 2017.

Moreland, J. P. *A Simple Guide to Experience Miracles: Instruction and Inspiration for Living Supernaturally in Christ.* Grand Rapids: Zondervan Reflective, 2021.

Morris, Leon. *The Gospel according to Matthew.* Pillar New Testament Commentary. Grand Rapids: Eerdmans, 1992.

"Movement Impact." Arise and Build. Accessed June 25, 2022. https://ariseandbuild.
net/impact.

"NAR and Christian Nationalism." Accessed February 13, 2023. https://
narandchristiannationalism.com.

NET Bible. Accessed July 12, 2022. https://netbible.org/bible/John+14.

Parke, Caleb. "Christian Pastor Shawn Bolz: 'Lord Showed Me the End of the
Coronavirus.'" *Fox News*. March 3, 2020. Accessed August 9, 2021. https://www.
foxnews.com/faith-values/coronavirus-christian-pastor-shawn-bolz.

————. "Worship Leader Runs for Congress in California: 'Morals Are Low, Taxes Are
High.'" *Fox News*. September 30, 2019. Accessed August 7, 2021. https://www.
foxnews.com/politics/california-congress-worship-leader-sean-feucht.

Patterson, Julie. "Salvation Army, Bethel Church Partner to Help Carr Fire Victims."
New Frontier Chronicle. August 10, 2018. Accessed August 3, 2021. https://www.
newfrontierchronicle.org/salvation-army-bethel-church-partner-to-help-carr-
fire-victims.

Pierce, Annelise. "The Really Big Business of Bethel Church, Part 1: Show Us the
Money!" A News Cafe. May 13, 2019. Accessed August 1, 2021. https://anewscafe.
com/2019/05/13/redding/the-really-big-business-of-bethel-church-part-1-show-
us-the-money.

————. "The Really Big Business of Bethel Church, Part 2: Who's in Charge?" A News
Cafe. July 11, 2019. Accessed August 9, 2021. https://anewscafe.com/2019/07/11/
redding/the-really-big-business-of-bethel-part-2-whos-in-charge.

Pivec, Holly. "The 'Christian' Tarot Card Controversy at Bethel Redding." *Holly Pivec*
(blog). December 15, 2017. Accessed August 1, 2021. https://www.hollypivec.
com/blog/2017/12/the-christian-tarot-card-controversy-at-bethel-church-in-
redding-california/7409?rq=destiny%20CARDS.

————. "Important Facts about the Passion Translation." *Holly Pivec* (blog). June 23,
2018. Accessed August 12, 2021. https://www.hollypivec.com/blog/2018/06/
important-facts-about-the-passion-translation/7962.

————. "Is It Too Late to Save This Church from NAR?" *Holly Pivec* (blog). September
24, 2019. Accessed August 6, 2021. https://www.hollypivec.com/blog/2019/09/is-
it-too-late-to-save-this-church-from-nar/8494.

————. "The NAR Antidote to Coronavirus." *Holly Pivec* (blog). March 21, 2020.
Accessed August 3, 2021. https://www.hollypivec.com/blog/2020/03/the-nar-
antidote-to-coronavirus/9000.

————. "The Problem with Bethel Redding's Firestarters 'Prophetic Activation' Class,
Part 1." *Holly Pivec* (blog). June 27, 2017. Accessed August 2, 2021. https://www.
hollypivec.com/blog/2017/06/the-problem-with-the-firestarters-prophetic-
activation-class-at-bethel-redding/6727?rq=bethel%20firestarters.

————. "What's Being Missed with the 'Waking' of Olive at Bethel Church, Redding."
Holly Pivec (blog). December 19, 2019. Accessed August 1, 2021. https://www.
hollypivec.com/blog/2019/12/whats-being-missed-with-the-waking-of-olive-at-
bethel-church-redding/8840.

Pivec, Holly, and R. Douglas Geivett. *Counterfeit Kingdom: The Dangers of New
Revelation, New Prophets, and New Age Practices in the Church*. Nashville: B&H,
2022.

Prince, Joseph. "Joseph Prince Prophesied the Coronavirus in 2018." YouTube video,
8:45. March 4, 2020. Accessed August 10, 2021. https://www.youtube.com/
watch?v=ZxILcSMO7Uc.

"Prophetic Standards." April 29, 2021. Accessed August 9, 2021. https://propheticstandards.com.

Qureshi, Nabeel. "Nabeel's Vlog 012: My Visit to Bethel Church." YouTube video, 25:51. Uploaded by Michelle Qureshi Wilson on December 22, 2016. Accessed August 3, 2021. https://www.youtube.com/watch?v=fwH8C69RWRU.

Rajah, Abraham S. *Apostolic and Prophetic Dictionary: Language of the End-time Church*. Bloomington, IN: WestBow, 2013.

Ridderbos, Herman. *The Gospel of John: A Theological Commentary*. Grand Rapids: Eerdmans, 1997.

Roth, Sid, and Bill Johnson. "Impact the World through Kingdom Culture! (Bill Johnson)." YouTube video, 28:20. Uploaded by Sid Roth's *It's Supernatural*. September 2, 2018. Accessed August 9, 2021. https://www.youtube.com/watch?v=yn-FnCkN9w4&t=563s.

Roth, Sid, and Brian Simmons. *It's Supernatural!* Video, 28:30. February 2, 2015. Accessed July 12, 2022. https://sidroth.org/television/tv-archives/brian-simmons.

Sandhu, Amber. "Bethel Comes Out Against LGBT Bills Pending in State Legislature." *Redding Record Searchlight*. March 27, 2018. Accessed August 3, 2021. https://www.redding.com/story/news/local/2018/03/27/bethel-comes-out-against-lgbt-bills-pending-state-legislature/462776002.

Saucy, Robert. "An Open but Cautious Response to C. Samuel Storms." In *Are Miraculous Gifts for Today? Four Views*, edited by Wayne A. Grudem, 229–32. Grand Rapids: Zondervan, 1996.

Scheide, R. V. "Losing His Religion: A Former Bethel Student Speaks Out." A News Cafe. December 12, 2018. Accessed August 6, 2021. https://anewscafe.com/2018/12/12/redding/losing-his-religion-a-former-bethel-student-speaks-out.

Schreiner, Thomas R. *Spiritual Gifts: What They Are and Why They Matter*. Nashville: B&H, 2018. Kindle.

Sells, Heather. "More Than 40 Bethel Members Lose Everything in Carr Fire." *Charisma News*. August 8, 2018. Accessed August 3, 2021. https://www.charismanews.com/us/72487-25-bethel-staffers-lose-everything-in-carr-fire.

Shead, Andrew G. "Burning Scripture with Passion: A Review of The Psalms (The Passion Translation)." *Themelios* 43.1 (2018) 58–71. Gospel Coalition. Accessed August 12, 2021. https://www.thegospelcoalition.org/themelios/article/burning-scripture-with-passion-a-review-of-the-psalms-passion-translation.

Silk, Danny. *Culture of Honor: Sustaining a Supernatural Environment*." Shippensburg, PA: Destiny Image, 2009. Kindle.

———. "Setting the Five-Fold on Fire—Sunday AM." Bethel.TV. July 30, 2017. Video, 58:07. Accessed June 24, 2022. https://www.bethel.tv/home.

Silvoso, Ed. *Ekklesia: Rediscovering God's Instrument for Global Transformation*. Bloomington, MN: Chosen, 2017. Kindle.

Silvoso, Ed, Bill Johnson, Ché Ahn, Kris Vallotton, and Shawn Bolz. "Acts 19: God's Response to COVID-19." Video, 1:01:23. Uploaded to Transform Our World's Facebook Page. March 20, 2020. Accessed August 11, 2021. https://www.facebook.com/transformourworld/videos/683699715769733.

Simpson University. "BSSM Student Housing at Simpson." Accessed August 6, 2021. https://www.simpsonu.edu/Pages/About/Conference/Bethel-Housing.htm.

———. "Scholarship Program." Accessed August 6, 2021. https://www.simpsonu.edu/Pages/About/Financial/Bethel-Revivalist-Scholarship.htm.

"South Africa's 'Doom Pastor' Found Guilty of Assault." *BBC News.* February 9, 2018. Accessed August 9, 2021. https://www.bbc.com/news/world-africa-43002701.

Stankorb, Sarah. "What Happens After Christian Prophets Admit They Were Wrong about Trump?" *Medium.* February 12, 2021. Accessed August 10, 2021. https://gen.medium.com/with-trumps-defeat-christian-prophets-admit-i-was-wrong-967a13abb8a7.

Storms, Sam. "A Defense of Singing Songs from Bethel and Hillsong." Enjoying God Ministries. August 6, 2021. Accessed July 21, 2022. https://www.samstorms.org/enjoying-god-blog/post/a-defense-of-singing-songs-from-bethel-and-hillsong.

———. *Understanding Spiritual Gifts: A Comprehensive Guide.* Grand Rapids: Zondervan, 2020. Kindle.

Strand, Paul. "'A Billion-Soul Harvest': The End Times Ushering in History's Greatest Revival?" CBN News. April 28, 2018. Accessed August 11, 2021. https://www1.cbn.com/cbnnews/cwn/2018/april/a-billion-soul-harvest-the-end-times-ushering-in-historys-greatest-revival.

Swan, Emily. "Trump, Evangelicals, and the Seven Mountain Mandate." Medium. December 12, 2019. Accessed August 6, 2021. https://medium.com/solus-jesus/trump-evangelicals-the-seven-mountain-mandate-af660291f537.

SwordoftheSpirit528. "Sozo Inner Healing Deception." *Narrow Path* (blog). November 30, 2018. Accessed August 6, 2021. https://narrow-path.net/2018/11/30/sozo-inner-healing-deception.

Synan, Vinson. "2000 Years of Prophecy." In *Understanding the Fivefold Ministry*, edited by Matthew D. Green, 49–56. Lake Mary, FL: Charisma House, 2005.

Tan, Stephen. "At What Price Awakening? Examining the Theology and Practice of the Bethel Movement." Gospel Coalition Australia. September 20, 2018. Accessed July 13, 2022. https://au.thegospelcoalition.org/article/price-awakening-examining-theology-practice-bethel-movement.

Titkemeyer, Suzanne. "Did Bethel and Bill Johnson Exploit the Death of Olive Heiligenthal?" *Patheos.* July 15, 2020. Accessed August 1, 2021. https://www.patheos.com/blogs/nolongerquivering/2020/07/did-bethel-and-bill-johnson-exploit-the-death-of-olive-heiligenthal.

Trask, Thomas E. "Defining Truths of the Assemblies of God: Divine Healing." PDF. Reprinted from *Enrichment Journal* Q3, 2007. Accessed August 13, 2021. https://ag.org/Search-Results?q=defining%20truths&d=.

Vallotton, Kris. "Common Misconceptions of Prophetic Ministry." YouTube video, 10:58. Uploaded by Kris Vallotton. October 2, 2010. Accessed July 17, 2022. https://www.youtube.com/watch?v=kkN5tTTooDs.

———. "Covenant Culture—Sunday PM." Video, 1:14:24. Bethel.TV. January 26, 2020. Accessed June 24, 2022. https://www.bethel.tv/home.

———. *Destined to Win: How to Embrace Your God-Given Identity and Realize Your Kingdom Purpose.* Nashville: Nelson, 2017.

———. *Developing a Supernatural Lifestyle: A Practical Guide to a Life of Signs, Wonders, and Miracles.* Shippensburg, PA: Destiny Image, 2007.

———. "God has called us to be in a covenant family . . ." Video, 8:25. Uploaded to Kris Vallotton's Facebook Page. August 10, 2017. Accessed August 3, 2021. https://www.facebook.com/watch/?v=10154992049933741.

———. "The Gospel without power is not the Gospel at all!" Facebook. July 26, 2019. Accessed August 7, 2021. https://www.facebook.com/kvministries/posts/10156632149348741.

———. *Heavy Rain: How to Flood Your World with God's Transforming Power.* Bloomington, MN: Chosen, 2016. Kindle.

———. "Life of a Disciple, Part Two: Prayer That Shapes History—Sunday AM." Video, 52:34. Bethel TV. July 21, 2019. Accessed August 21, 2019. https://www.bethel.tv/home.

———. "My Apology—U.S. Presidential Election Prophecy 2020." Video, 5:24. Uploaded to Kris Vallotton's Facebook Page. January 8, 2021. Accessed August 9, 2021. https://www.facebook.com/kvministries/posts/10158084221228741.

———. *Poverty, Riches and Wealth: Moving from a Life of Lack into True Kingdom Abundance.* Bloomington, MN: Chosen, 2018. Kindle.

———. "The Power of the Five-Fold Ministry—Sunday AM." Video, 43:22. Bethel.TV. February 9, 2020. Accessed June 24, 2022. https://www.bethel.tv/home.

———. "The Power of the Five-Fold Ministry—Sunday PM." Video, 1:09:51. Bethel. TV. February 23, 2020. Accessed June 24, 2022. https://www.bethel.tv/home.

———. "Prophetic Gifting vs. Calling: How to Know Which One You Carry." KV Ministries. June 4, 2021. Accessed August 9, 2021. https://www.krisvallotton.com/prophetic-gifting-vs-calling.

———. "Remembering One of Our Heroes" (Bethel.TV Moments). YouTube video, 13:16. Uploaded by Kris Vallotton. June 7, 2018. Accessed July 12, 2022. https://www.youtube.com/watch?v=SQfWJymxlwo.

———. "Sovereign Providence." Video, 50:59. Bethel.TV. December 8, 2019. Accessed July 9, 2022. https://www.bethel.tv/home.

———. "What Is an Apostle?—Sunday PM." Bethel.TV. May 7. 2017. Accessed July 9, 2022. https://www.bethel.tv/home.

———. "Why Miracles, Signs and Wonders Should Be Normal for Every Christian." KV Ministries. June 24, 2018. Accessed August 11, 2021. https://www.krisvallotton.com/miracles-signs-wonders-normal-every-christian.

Vallotton, Kris, and Dann Farrelly. "Bethel's Risk-Taking Culture." *Rediscover Bethel.* Youtube video, 6:50. Uploaded by Bethel. July 13, 2021. Accessed August 1, 2021. https://www.youtube.com/watch?v=oAoYlE31H2k.

———. "Church Denominations and Denominationalism." *Rediscover Bethel.* Youtube video, 13:53. Uploaded by Bethel. July 2, 2021. Accessed August 9, 2021. https://www.youtube.com/watch?v=mccuOXKu9_k.

———. "Does Bethel Church Belong to the New Apostolic Reformation (NAR)?" *Rediscover Bethel.* YouTube video, 8:18. Uploaded by Bethel. July 6, 2021. Accessed August 7, 2021. https://www.youtube.com/watch?v=6_2cFs32Rss&t=1s.

———. "Episode 4: The Church, Ministry, and the New Apostolic Reformation." *Rediscover Bethel.* YouTube video, 1:16:11. Uploaded by Bethel. June 30, 2021. Accessed August 1, 2021. https://www.youtube.com/watch?v=TVAVfD5OSkU&t=860s.

———. "Episode 5: Prophecy, Risk, and the Prosperity Gospel." *Rediscover Bethel.* YouTube video, 1:41:02. Uploaded by Bethel. July 7, 2021. Accessed August 1, 2021. https://www.youtube.com/watch?v=CuKoxpb43RU&t=3391s.

Vallotton, Kris, and Bill Johnson. *The Supernatural Ways of Royalty.* Shippensburg, PA: Destiny Image, 2017. Kindle.

Verbi, Samuel, and Ben Winkley. "The Story of BSSM Alumni." Eido Research. 2016. Accessed August 1, 2021. https://www.eidoresearch.com/reports/the-story-of-bethel-school-of-ministry-alumni.

"Victims of Johnson's Sozo Ministry Speak Out." *Closing Stages.* July 31, 2012. Accessed August 6, 2021. https://closingstages.net/2012/07/31/victims-of-johnsons-sozo-ministry-speak-out.

Virtue, Doreen, and Lindsay Davis. "Ex-Bethel Student Tells All: Lindsay Davis Testimony." YouTube video, 1:19:54. Uploaded by Doreen Virtue on June 2, 2019. Accessed August 6, 2021. https://www.youtube.com/watch?v=winCHM9yuY4&t=401s.

Virtue, Doreen, and Oscar Whatmore. "Former Bethel Prophecy Teacher Reveals Inside Information about BSSM." YouTube video, 58:00. Uploaded by Doreen Virtue. July 7, 2020. Accessed August 6, 2021. https://www.youtube.com/watch?v=_gwpYdAD-pY.

———. "Why Sozo Is Dangerous." YouTube video, 12:16. Uploaded by Doreen Virtue. July 9, 2020. Accessed January 1, 2022. https://www.youtube.com/watch?v=rS9KCAOmK7s&t=633s.

Wagner, C. Peter. *Changing Church.* Ventura, CA: Regal, 2004.

———. *Dominion! How Kingdom Action Can Change the World.* Grand Rapids: Chosen, 2008.

Wagner University. "Meet Our Residential Training Instructors." Archived at the Wayback Machine December 31, 2021. Accessed June 11, 2022. https://web.archive.org/web/20211231041517/https://wagner.university/faculty.

Wallnau, Lance, and Bill Johnson. *Invading Babylon: The 7 Mountain Mandate.* Shippensburg, PA: Destiny Image, 2013. Kindle.

Welch, Craig. "The Rise and Fall of Mars Hill Church." *Seattle Times.* September 13, 2014. Accessed August 9, 2021. https://www.seattletimes.com/seattle-news/the-rise-and-fall-of-mars-hill-church.

White, Paula, and Brad Knight. "We are streaming live! 10 AM Sunday Service." Video, 3:06:16. Uploaded to City of Destiny Church's Facebook Page. May 5, 2019. Accessed August 7, 2021. https://www.facebook.com/107953565893198/videos/2234211750167173.

Wiget, Andreas. "Interview with Jesse, a Former Charismatic and Bethel Grad." *Medium.* May 2, 2022. Accessed May 9, 2022. https://medium.com/@andreaswiget/interview-with-jesse-a-formercharismatic-and-bethel-grad-7a5418a23208.

Wilson, Andrew. "What's Wrong with the Passion 'Translation?'" *Think.* January 6, 2016. Accessed August 12, 2021. https://thinktheology.co.uk/blog/article/whats_wrong_with_the_passion_translation.

Winger, Mike. "Bill Johnson's Theology and Movement Examined Biblically." YouTube video, 1:19:15. February 13, 2018. Accessed August 7, 2021. https://www.youtube.com/watch?v=r3tEv26OMTU.

———. "The Passion Project: Scholars Review the Passion Translation." YouTube videos. Last updated May 19, 2021. Accessed August 12, 2021. https://www.youtube.com/playlist?list=PLZ3iRMLYFlHuv-ISp_iIw1WL8zaEm86L8.

Yoars, Marcus. "The Radical Revivalists." *Charisma Magazine.* June 9, 2011. Accessed August 9, 2021. https://charismamag.com/spiritled-living/church-ministry/the-radical-revivalists.

Subject Index

Introductory Note

We use "NAR" throughout this index as an abbreviation for "New Apostolic Reformation" (for example, "NAR networks," a main heading in the index, refers to networks within the New Apostolic Reformation). "NAR" appears in other main headings and in many sub-headings of this index. There is a main entry for "New Apostolic Reformation" that is not abbreviated.

Where an important concept is implicit without being named in the text, the concept appears as a heading or sub-heading in the index. For example, the phrase "healing in the atonement" is used in the index for a concept that is referred to in note 34 on pages 7–8, though the phrase does not appear at that location. The index entry for "kenotic Christology" provides another example; here the concept is referenced on page 10, though the label for this doctrine of Jesus's self-emptying does not appear on that page, while the label does appear on page 92. (It may also happen that a concept is explicit in one passage and implicit in another passage, and both locations are noted for that concept.)

Some footnotes span multiple pages. Terms or concepts that appear on the first page of the note are indexed to that page, and only to that page even if the discussion of that term or concept carries over to the next page. For example, the subject of "miracles: failure to work" is treated in footnote 15 of chapter 8, a footnote that begins on page 169 and carries over to page 170. The locator for this discussion is given as "169n15" in the index. However, if a term or concept appears only on the second page of a footnote, only that page is noted (along with the appropriate footnote number) in the index. For example, for "Agabus," the reader is referred to 118n45; although note 45 begins on page 117, the discussion of Agabus appears in the continuation of note 45 on page 118.

Occasionally, if an important mention of a person or topic appears on a page and also in a key footnote for that page, both reference locators will be given. For example, we include for "angels: apostolic authority over" both page 67 and note 41 on page 67.

References for individual NAR apostles and prophets are given under their respective names in the index. There is not a list of NAR figures under the main headings of "apostles" or "prophets."

Throughout the index, "Bethel Church" refers to Bethel Church of Redding, California.

Book titles, even when the books themselves have been discussed at some length, have not been indexed here. Also, we have not included author names for all citations in the footnotes, but when it has seemed to us that a name and its location does call for a listing in the index, we provide the name and the relevant page numbers.

Bold font for page numbers is used to identify major treatment of a subject at that location, a convention we use only sparingly.

obedience to, 99, 119, 126n3, 138,
179
obligated to answer prayer, 137
permission of suffering by, 8
power of, 1–2, 9n41, 14n65, 99,
132, 133n26, 134–35, 137,
140n53, 155–57
prayer addressed to, 136, 137–38
presence of, 2, 5, 33, 88
put in a box, 99
"reckless" conception of, 4
reconciliation with, 179
relationship with, 99
seeking more of, 1–2, 5, 28, 176–77
sovereignty of, 140n53, 157n60,
157n60, 178
trust in, 156n57
visions of, 1–2
will of, 8, 8n36, 129, 132, 136, 138,
139–40, 156n57
will to heal, 8–10, 91
worship of, 127 (*see also* worship)
See also Holy Spirit, the; Jesus
Christ: deity of; kingdom:
of God; revelations
GOD TV, 72n53
gold dust, x, 5
Goll, James, xin2, 91n42, 96, 108
gospel, the
Bill Johnson's teaching about, 151–
52, 155
dispute about, 151, 178
backed with signs and wonders,
151, 155
false versions of, 152, 178
of forgiveness, 152n31
of the kingdom, 151–52, 155
preaching of, 25, 151, 178
recovery of needed, 179
revisionist conception of, 178–79,
182
signs and wonders central to, 25,
151–52, 178
true nature of, 178–79
See also gospel of the kingdom;
Great Commission, the;
repentance; salvation
Gospel Light Publications, 163n5

gospel of the kingdom, 151–52, 155,
158. *See also* bringing
heaven to earth;
dominionism; evangelism;
evangelist(s); gospel, the;
Great Commission, the;
kingdom, the
government
and fivefold ministry, 35n12, 112
apostolic versus denominational, 39,
39n25, 40, 47n51, 84
as sphere of apostolic authority, 66
by God, 8n34, 69n45
of the church by apostles and
prophets, xi, xiii, 26n109,
30n136, 32–78, 80n7,
90n37, 112, 123, 127n4,
177–80
of churches by pastors, 39n25, 40,
68, 123, 179
revelation for national, 93
See also Christian Nationalism;
church: and state;
dominionism; politics;
theocracy
grace
akin to an anointing, 45n44, 98n2,
154n42
as God's operational power, 98n3,
133n26
gifts, 189
imparted through grave soaking,
14n65
NAR conception of, 14n65, 43,
45n44, 189
received through covering, 43n40,
70
salvation by, 89
stewarding, 154n42
grave soaking, x, 12–15, 192. *See also*
mantles
grave sucking. *See* grave soaking
Great Commission, the
as bringing heaven to earth, 92,
127–28, 145, 177, 189
dominionism and, 92, 127–28
Jesus's teaching about, 128

Scripture Index

Introductory Note

Some quotations, paraphrases, and mentions of specific verses in the Bible appear in this book without an accompanying citation for the passage. This is more often the case when we have quoted others who refer to specific passages without noting the Scripture reference for those passages. This index supplies the relevant Scripture reference and indicates that the reference does not appear on the indexed page using an asterisk (*). (A good example of this occurs for Galatians 4:19.) We adopt this practice even if there are multiple page references for the passage and on some pages the reference is actually given (for example, for Matthew 24:24, where the reference is cited on page 60 but not on page 59 where the teaching of this passage is alluded to).

Printed in Great Britain
by Amazon

40061281R00158